Chaucer and Boccaccio

Also by *Robert R. Edwards*

THE DREAM OF CHAUCER: REPRESENTATION AND REFLECTION IN CHAUCER'S EARLY NARRATIVE

RATIO AND INVENTION: A STUDY OF MEDIEVAL LYRIC AND NARRATIVE

THE POETRY OF GUIDO GUINIZELLI

THE MONTECASSINO PASSION AND THE POETICS OF MEDIEVAL DRAMA

JOHN LYDGATE, 'THE SIEGE OF THEBES' (editor)

JOHN LYDGATE, 'TROY BOOK: SELECTIONS' (editor)

ART AND CONTEXT IN LATE MEDIEVAL ENGLISH NARRATIVE: ESSAYS IN HONOR OF ROBERT WORTH FRANK, JR. (editor)

MATRONS AND MARGINAL WOMEN IN MEDIEVAL SOCIETY (co-editor with Vickie Ziegler)

THE OLDE DAUNCE: LOVE, FRIENDSHIP, SEX, AND MARRIAGE IN THE MEDIEVAL WORLD (co-editor with Stephen Spector)

Chaucer and Boccaccio
Antiquity and Modernity

Robert R. Edwards

First published 2002 by
PALGRAVE
Houndmills, Basingstoke, Hampshire RG21 6XS and
175 Fifth Avenue, New York, N. Y. 10010
Companies and representatives throughout the world

PALGRAVE is the new global academic imprint of
St. Martin's Press LLC Scholarly and Reference Division and
Palgrave Publishers Ltd (formerly Macmillan Press Ltd).

ISBN 0–333–97008–X

This book is printed on paper suitable for recycling and made from fully managed and sustained forest sources.

Library of Congress Cataloging-in-Publication Data
Edwards, Robert, 1947–
    Chaucer and Boccaccio: antiquity and modernity/by Robert R. Edwards.
      p. cm.
    Includes bibliographical references and index.
    ISBN 0–333–97008–X
      1. Chaucer, Geoffrey, d. 1400—Knowledge—Literature. 2. Boccaccio, Giovanni, 1313–1375—Appreciation—England. 3. Boccaccio, Giovanni, 1313-1375—Influence. 4. Chaucer, Geoffrey, d. 1400—Sources.
5. English poetry—Italian influences. 6. Aesthetics, Medieval.
7. Aesthetics, Ancient. 8. Intertextuality. I. Title.

    PR1912.B6 E39 2002
    821'.1—dc21

2001050084

10 9 8 7 6 5 4 3 2 1
11 10 09 08 07 06 05 04 03 02

Printed and bound in Great Britain by
Antony Rowe Ltd, Chippenham, Wiltshire

For Patrick Cheney

Scholar, critic, colleague, and friend

Contents

A Note on Texts and Abbreviations

Quotations from Chaucer will follow *The Riverside Chaucer*, 3rd edn, gen. ed. Larry D. Benson (Boston: Houghton Mifflin, 1987). Quotations from Boccaccio will cite the texts in *Tutte le opere di Giovanni Boccaccio*, gen. ed. Vittore Branca, 12 vols. (Milan: Mondadori, 1964–83). Translations from the *Decameron* are taken from G.H. McWilliam, trans., *The Decameron* (Harmondsworth: Penguin, 1972). Gower's *Confessio Amantis* will be quoted from the text in *The English Works of John Gower*, ed. G.C. Macaulay, 2 vols., EETS, e.s. 81–82 (London: Oxford University Press, 1900–1). John Lydgate's *Troy Book* is quoted from *Lydgate's Troy Book*, ed. Henry Bergen, 4 vols., EETS, e.s. 97, 103, 106, and 126 (London: Kegan Paul, Trench, Trübner & Co., 1906–35); and his *Siege of Thebes* from *Lydgate's Siege of Thebes*, ed. Axel Erdmann and Eilert Ekwall, 2 vols., EETS, e.s. 108 and 125 (London: Oxford University Press, 1911, 1930). The *Roman de la rose* is quoted from the edition by Daniel Poirion (Paris: Garnier-Flammarion, 1974); the translation cited is Charles Dahlberg, trans., *The Romance of the Rose* (Princeton: Princeton University Press, 1971). Classical authors will be quoted from the texts and translations in the Loeb Classical Library. The work of Patristic writers and medieval commentators will be quoted from the digitized texts in CETEDOC. Commonly cited works and series will use the following abbreviations:

Corpus Christianorum, Continuatio Mediaeualis	CCCM
Corpus Christianorum, Series Latina	CCSL
Corpus Scriptorum Ecclesiasticorum Latinorum	CSEL
Early English Text Society	EETS
Middle English Dictionary	*MED*
Oxford English Dictionary	*OED*
Société des anciens textes français	SATF

Preface

'So that what there was of Invention, in either of them, may be judg'd equal.'

Dryden

The continual project of Chaucer criticism is to discover a context for his writings – or, more precisely, to define some external framework that will ground and warrant our critical interpretation of his work. This is an always unrealized project, and one might object that it tacitly abandons poetry and reflects a latter-day skepticism about the capacity of imaginative writing to create meaning on its own terms or to inspire its readers to adopt new perspectives and ways of understanding. But from the late Middle Ages onwards, finding a context has been tied inextricably to reading Chaucer. Chaucer's contemporaries and self-professed disciples variously locate him in the traditions of the *Roman de la rose* (Deschamps), love poetry (Gower), philosophy (Usk), rhetorical poetics (Lydgate), and learning (Hoccleve). The history of Chaucer's reception is the story of interpretive frames and of the literary values and other investments that lie behind them.

My governing premise in this book is that the most illuminating context for reading Chaucer is his relation to other writers, to the imagined literary realm that he identifies, in his longest extant piece of revision, as 'the world of autours' (*Legend of Good Women* G 308). Throughout his career, Chaucer conspicuously inserts himself into this textual world as a reader, reviser, and compiler.[1] His earliest poems grow out of encounters with Ovid and the great French poets of the fourteenth century – Machaut, Deschamps, and Froissart – and, behind them, with the *Roman de la rose*, itself a world of pagan and Christian, courtly and satiric authors. His greatest works reflect a continuing and profound engagement with authors, antecedent texts, and the poetic tradition of Latin and the two most accomplished European vernaculars of his day, French and Italian. Indeed, to judge by Chaucer's practice, classical authors are radically mediated by the vernacular. Dante shows how a vernacular poet can gain a place among the *auctores*. Other writers produce the redactions, compilations, and translations that serve as intermediaries in late medieval culture. We thus possess a direct record of his relations – historical and imaginative – with all the authors

'Cristene and hethene,' and we can distinguish his references and allusions to them from his sustained textual engagement with their works.[2] Chaucer's writing is, in practice, a poetry of intertextuality.

The most commanding feature of Chaucer's intertextuality is the complex relation of his works to those of Giovanni Boccaccio. Scholars have pointed to the impact of Dante as a model of vernacular literary authority, and they have recognized the abiding influence of French poets in Chaucer's lexicon, themes, and sources after he discovered the great Trecento writers. Yet Boccaccio is the writer from whom Chaucer takes the most. He is a direct source in ways that we can plot with relative precision for some works, and his writings offer analogues and models for others. Boccaccio's textual presence and the scope of his literary projects prove equally important. The encounter with Boccaccio's experiments in vernacular classicism marks the point at which Chaucer leaves the path of the courtly amateur poet and engages the world of authors in its full poetic and cultural depth. Later, it is Boccaccio's validation of contemporary civic life in the middle strata that furnishes an example of ways to recount the narratives of 'sondry folk' and dynamic changes in the social sphere. Boccaccio, then, is a primary influence for Chaucer not just for his textual sources but also because of what those texts open up in relation to literary culture. In particular, his work offers ways of approaching two domains of great concern in late medieval England – antiquity and modernity. Through Boccaccio, Chaucer invents antiquity and modernity as areas for poetic imagination and cultural understanding. There are other domains that figure prominently in Chaucer's mature writing – religion and gender, for example – and these likewise have a place in Boccaccio's writing. But antiquity and modernity are the areas where Boccaccio holds open the prospect of new possibilities of expression and understanding for Chaucer.

My second premise is that Chaucer's intertextuality is historical as well as poetic. Taken in a narrow sense, Chaucer's writings are notoriously hard to locate as a record of his age. The documents of Chaucer's public life say nothing of his writing. His audience is aristocratic and professional rather than marginalized or dispossessed.[3] Chaucer's subversions of orthodoxy do not betoken social or religious resistance (as do Langland and Lollardy). His only clear reference to contemporary historical events – an allusion to the Rising of 1381 – is already textualized in the language of Gower's visionary poem *Vox clamantis*.[4] The one area of documented influences and links, of history in a narrow sense, is the world of authors. Equally important, these literary relations furnish a

ground on which a broader historical understanding of the work becomes intelligible and persuasive. The turn toward history in recent
literary studies situates Chaucer's textuality within larger social developments and forces, such as the rise of the self-conscious subject, the
transformation of late feudal structures, the articulation of power relations, and the emergence of marginalized groups into new social roles
and cultural authority. Meanwhile, the theorization of textual scholarship has permitted new approaches to questions of audience, patterns of
transmission, and the politics of representation. The study of gender,
sexualities, and emergent social formations finds a vitally contested site
both in Chaucer's imaginative world and in historical responses to it,
including our own readings.

To make a claim for textuality and literary relations as historical
context is to follow the lead of Chaucer's first readers, his fourteenth-
century poetic contemporaries and the fifteenth-century writers who
established his place in English literary history. But I wish to invoke
more than the authority of early poetic witnesses and the presiding
figure of father Chaucer. Chaucer's gestures toward the world of authors
are by turns performative, allusive, deferential, subversive, and appro-
priative. In other words, Chaucer acts toward literary tradition precisely
as we would expect him to act in response to other large historical
forces. What the turn to history has done for Chaucer scholarship is to
make available an interpretive framework for his continual practice of
borrowing, citation, and active revision: Chaucer engages classical and
vernacular writers under the rubric of cultural analysis and criticism.
The narratives he rewrites arrive already charged with ethical, social,
political, psychological, and artistic significance. He encounters them
simultaneously as expressions of poetic imagination and stories that
serve social and political purposes.

Chaucer's intertextuality, then, is at once poetic and historical – a
gesture toward an imaginary world of authors and a practice of writing
within a particular moment. In framing Chaucer's poetry within literary
tradition and culture rather than directly in politics, I am conscious of
diverging from a dominant, though perhaps not a majority, view. Recent
scholarship has taught us much about the social resonances in Chaucer's poetry, notably the shifting terms of power relations and individual
agency within established social arrangements. On this view, politics
and history are foundational; they stand as the reality against which
other forms of expression – discursive as well as imaginative writing,
pageant, spectacle, and the performance of daily life – can be defined
and interpreted. I shall be arguing for a different formulation. Chaucer's

poetry is profoundly skeptical of such foundations; at every step, it defers and disables the interpretive reduction sustained by foundational claims. Yet its aim is not to escape history by claiming a sovereign realm of individual imagination or a space of aesthetic withdrawal. Rather, the poetry seeks to understand cultural production, including politics and other historical forces, through representation, as it is implicated in language and discourse. Chaucer's writing treats narratives of human action and desire as objects of reflection, knowledge, debate, and on-going contestation. In this respect, his poetry obviously bears close affinities with the full range of Boccaccio's work.

In reading Chaucer through Boccaccio, I am not interested in making the latter a foil for the former. Much Anglo-American criticism has been dedicated to showing how Chaucer achieves a sophistication and refine-ment of his sources in Boccaccio. The aim of comparison in this book is not evaluation but interpretation. I want to examine how Boccaccio's representations of antiquity and modernity furnish powerful models for Chaucer to extend, resist, and reconceive. I hope to show how Chaucer's reading of Boccaccio generated poetic invention and positioned Chau-cer's work to engage major concerns in late medieval culture.

Every work of critical interpretation grows out of the solitude of reflection and the spirit of conversation. I have been particularly fortu-nate in the latter. My dedication records my debt to Patrick Cheney for a decade of intense, generous discussion about medieval and Renaissance poetry and for reading my work with care and commitment to the twin enterprise of scholarship and criticism. No one has had a better col-league to help him in thinking through texts, literary tradition, and the shifting dimensions of our own critical practice. I also owe thanks to Winthrop Wetherbee, R.A. Shoaf, Derek Pearsall, and Giuseppe Maz-zotta, who read parts of this book as it emerged. Piero Boitani generously provided an invitation to test some of my ideas at the Bennett Sympo-sium in Perugia. Carole Newlands, Joseph Kockelmans, Alfred Triolo, Santa Casciani, Mark Vessey, Anthony Cutler, and Cosimo Perrotta kindly shared the specialist's knowledge of their fields. Whatever errors of understanding that remain in this book are mine; in the end, we say what we always meant to say.

I want to thank the individuals and institutions that have supported this project. Don Bialostosky and the English Department at Penn State have assigned me talented graduate students as research assistants: the good work of Colin Fewer, Patricia Nickinson, and Danielle Smith has made mine easier. The College of the Liberal Arts granted me a sabbat-ical leave to finish the draft of the book, and the Institute for the Arts and Humanistic Studies provided funds to support research and a standard of faculty achievement that I hope to honor. I am grateful to Clare Hall at the University of Cambridge for appointing me a Visiting Fellow during my research leave and for creating an ideal environment for study and thoughtful exchange. The Cambridge University Library and Pattee Library at Penn State have made the enterprise of scholarship both possible and pleasurable. I thank Larry D. Benson and Joseph Wittig for making available the Glossorial Database of Middle English, with digital texts for Chaucer, Gower, and the Chaucer Apocrypha.

I have also had a splendid teaching environment in which to develop the ideas of this book. My students are my first audience, and their questions have shown me what I needed to clarify, rethink, and amend. Participants in a summer seminar on 'Chaucer Ancient and Modern' sponsored by the National Endowment for the Humanities taught me much about my topic from their own research and classroom experience, and I thank them for their suggestions and valuable commentary. Our collective project was enhanced by visits from Barbara Hanawalt, Benjamin Hudson, Rita Copeland, and David Wallace, who offered us exciting formulations of what antiquity and modernity meant in the later fourteenth century. For two summers, Patrick Cheney and I directed a seminar for dissertation-level graduate students on 'Tradition, Revision, and Continuity in Renaissance and Medieval Literary Studies' sponsored by the Andrew W. Mellon Foundation. The contributions of these students and of faculty visitors who joined us have done much to help me understand the nature of my project as an effort in critical and historical understanding.

Material for this book has been taken in part from several earlier studies: 'Faithful Translations: Love and the Question of Poetry in Chaucer,' in *The Olde Daunce: Love, Friendship, Sex and Marriage in the Medieval World*, ed. Robert R. Edwards and Stephen Spector (Albany: State University of New York Press, 1991), pp. 138–53; and 'Pandarus's "Unthrift" and the Problem of Desire in *Troilus and Criseyde*,' in *Chaucer's Troilus and Criseyde: 'Subgit to alle Poesye' – Essays in Criticism*, ed. R.A. Shoaf (Binghamton: Medieval & Renaissance Texts & Studies, 1992), pp. 74–87. Chapter 5 appeared in *Mediaevalitas*, ed. Piero Boitani and Anna Torti, J.A.W. Bennett Memorial Symposium (Woodbridge, Suffolk: D.S. Brewer. 1996), pp. 15–41; and Chapter 6 in *The 'Decameron' and the 'Canterbury Tales': New Essays on an Old Question*, ed. Leonard Michael Koff and Brenda Deen Schildgen (Madison, NJ: Fairleigh Dickinson University Press, 2000), pp. 226–46. I am grateful to the editors, journals, and presses for permission to reprint material.

My greatest debt, as always, is to my wife, Emily Rolfe Grosholz, whose gifts as a poet and achievements as a philosopher remain an inspiration to the heart and the mind; and to our children, Benjamin, Robert, William, and Mary-Frances, who bring joy and richness to our lives.

Introduction

The critical focus of this book is on Chaucer's invention of antiquity and
modernity through his engagement with Boccaccio. By way of introduction, I want to gloss the key terms that define this project. The first term
is conventional; the others require more extensive discussion. By invention, I mean that Chaucer follows the protocol for rewriting in medieval
poetic theory and reads antecedent texts for what remains latent,
potential, as yet unexpressed in their representation of fictional worlds.
He negotiates both the language and the silences left by previous
authors to see what else might be explored or reimagined from their
work or situated in a different imaginative context.[1] Chaucer's poems
thus emerge from a critical engagement with source texts and literary
precursors. Invention furnishes a technique of composition at the same
time that it presupposes a theory and practice of intertextuality. As
modern readers, we can turn to Chaucer's sources and, where needed,
to the analogues and genres that provided his fictions of antiquity and
modernity, and we can read them with attention to both poetic revision
and the larger cultural work that revision performs.[2] What emerges from
our comparisons is not simply a catalogue of revision but a dialectical
understanding of poetry and history.

'Dayes olde': the shape of antiquity

Sometime in the early 1380s Chaucer began a series of poems devoted to
antiquity. This project of composition marked both an extension and
drastic refocusing of his earlier narrative writing. Chaucer had already
dealt with classical authors and narratives as sources of 'wonder' in his
dream visions. The poems of the 1380s have an altogether different
character. The Knight's Tale, *Anelida and Arcite*, *Troilus and Criseyde*,

and the *Legend of Good Women* portray antiquity directly, as a topic in its own right. Drawing on the classical *auctores* and especially on Boccaccio's experiments with classicizing narratives in the vernacular, Chaucer depicts in these poems a separate and integral world.

Chaucer's project of writing antiquity is a focused and selective appropriation of the past. One notable feature is the suppression of British antiquity – the story, as told by chroniclers and antiquaries, of Brute's arrival and the dynasties following him through King Arthur and the coming of the Saxons. Chaucer mentions Geoffrey of Monmouth, the source for British antiquity, among the epic poets and historians of Thebes and Troy (*House of Fame* 1470), and contemporaries such as John Trevisa accepted Geoffrey's chronology from the *Historia regum Britanniae*.[3] But Chaucer's treatment of the topic is either topical or ironic. Northumbria and King Alla figure in the Man of Law's Tale of Custance, while the Franklin situates his tale in the pseudo-antique of '[t]hise olde gentil Britouns in hir dayes' (V.709). The Wife of Bath's Tale, Chaucer's only substantial narrative of British antiquity, is an anti-romance designed to invert the Arthurian world that follows from the supposed Trojan origins of Britain.

The antiquity that fascinated Chaucer was the one contained in the stories of Thebes, Troy, and Rome. These topics comprise a master narrative of the classical past. They begin with the mythological founding of the city and civil society through internecine conflict, and they end with the historical struggles of oligarchy and empire. In Chaucer's poetry, these topics stand by themselves. Chaucerian antiquity is removed from the medieval universal histories that correlated events from pagan history with incidents in Jewish history from the Old Testament. It is Lydgate, not Chaucer, who dates the building of Thebes 'Vpon the tyme of worthy Josuè' (*Siege of Thebes* 188) and calculates its destruction four hundred years before Rome (4622–5). Though Chaucer evokes a time before culture in his Boethian balade 'The Former Age,' he offers no scheme of periodization comparable to Ranulph Higden's *Polychronicon* (also translated by Trevisa) or the succession of Chaldeans, Egyptians, Greeks, Jews, and Christians in Book 5 of Gower's *Confessio Amantis*.[4]

Modern criticism has emphasized the thematic consistency of Chaucerian antiquity. According to most readings, Chaucer tries to see classical antiquity on its own terms, at least as the late Middle Ages understood those terms. Morton W. Bloomfield established the salient features of this understanding over half a century ago. While acknowledging some measure of anachronism in Chaucer, he argued that the poetry incorporates a distinct sense of history, based on an appreciation of accurate chronology, cultural difference, and the succession of past, present, and future.[5] On this view, pagan antiquity is located in time, within a framework of successive periods and ages. Though cut off from the promise of Christian salvation, it remains a discrete and coherent cosmos, a historical and cultural space open to imagination and invention. Implicitly, Chaucer is the counter-example to the claim that historical consciousness arises with the Renaissance and that no one in the Middle Ages could see the classical past as a conceptual whole.[6]

Bloomfield's argument about Chaucer's sense of history has been framed specifically by later scholars within late medieval historiography and the classicizing of pagan antiquity. Alastair J. Minnis contends that Chaucer depicts himself 'as a Christian historian who approaches pagan antiquity with detachment, and with respect for the historical identity of the pagans.' Chaucer's main interest, explains Minnis, lies in pagan theology, such as cultic belief in the gods and idols, and in pagan philosophy, with its themes of fate, fortune, predestination, and free will.[7] Antiquity represents the limit of human reason to operate on its own, unaided by grace or divine revelation. In a later formulation, Minnis sees differences within this general model of antiquity: 'The past our poet made varies from poem to poem. *Troilus* and *The Knight's Tale* present, with different interests and emphases, pagan worlds which are surprisingly autonomous, self-contained and internally consistent, though of course ultimately limited in comparison with Christianity,' while a work like the Franklin's Tale is 'a rather anxious and sometimes unsympathetic imitation of aristocratic antiquarianism' which follows Boethian ideas of nobility.[8] The language that describes these different visions of antiquity throughout Chaucer's poetry is frequently archeological or ethnographic, describing the 'gyse' and 'usance' observed 'at thilke tyme.'

Our prevailing view of Chaucer's antiquity, then, situates Chaucer's writings inside the logic of medieval historiography. At the same time, it leaves open the question of poetic and cultural function. As Janet Coleman has remarked, 'there is little doubt that during both the Renaissance and the middle ages, the past was only significant with regards to its interpretation, its present intelligibility.'[9] What function does an historically imagined antiquity serve in Chaucer's poetry? In what discursive forms does the past become intelligible in Chaucer? These questions rather than Chaucer's fidelity to medieval historiography are the ones I want to address in the first half of this book.

Perhaps the most powerful attraction of antiquity for Chaucer is that it simultaneously presents difference and similarity. Separated from

Christian revelation, the classical world is contained in a secular history it cannot escape and a salvation history it can never significantly enter.[10] It thus holds open an alternative realm of philosophical speculation and exploration about selfhood, experience, behavior, community, and institutions. In the moral sphere, antiquity is a means for interrogating the nature of secular virtue, for examining desire, choice, and predicaments under the constraints of history. A.C. Spearing argues that the combination of ancient settings derived from Boccaccio with Boethian philosophy represents Chaucer's distinct innovation, unexampled in earlier medieval romances.[11] The very pastness of antiquity makes it an object of aesthetic representation and poetic scrutiny: because it is completed, it can be seen whole but reimagined partially. Antiquity is a source for narratives to engage the imagination and for an educational curriculum founded on such texts.[12] The narrators who serve as surrogates for the poet and for his aristocratic and professional audience furnish models of readerly experience reaching across time. Their apostrophes and commentary go beyond moralization to register a complex empathy.

But if antiquity represents difference and holds out the prospect of imaginative freedom, it also serves as a source of identity. Its narratives are 'olde appreved stories / Of holynesse, of regnes, of victories, / Of love, of hate, of other sondry thynges' (LGW F 21–3) – that is, stories of the classical past grouped under medieval poetic *topoi*. At a cultural and political level, the narratives of antiquity are dramatically overdetermined. They provide a point of mythological origin for nations, an exemplary history about medieval institutions and statecraft, and a mirror for medieval aristocratic values, conduct, and deliberation. The Trojan story, as the opening of *Sir Gawain and the Green Knight* makes clear, is a foundation myth for medieval vernacular cultures, towns, and states which emerge through the *translatio imperii* from Troy to Rome, Lombardy, France, and finally Britain. The story shows the complex workings of fate, fortune, and human choice in dynasties and kingdoms. Conversely, as Thomas Walsingham demonstrated by claiming that Nicholas Brembre planned to seize London and rename it 'New Troy,' it can signify rebellion.[13] The Troy story also serves as a handbook for chivalry, for public and personal governance, and for lessons about erotic desire. Henry V's overt intention in commissioning Lydgate to write his *Troy Book* is to preserve the memory of '[t]he worthynes ... / And the prowesse of olde chiualrie' so that their example of virtue can be pursued and sloth avoided (Prologue 77–8). In medieval chronologies, the story of Thebes is the immediate precursor of the Trojan catastrophe, and it reveals the dark underside of the ideology and ideals associated with Troy – contested origins, fraternal conflict, the will to power, the threat of social disintegration.[14] In the matter of Rome, the Trojan story becomes an imperial epic, while other narratives tell the stories of aristocratic families in the face of tyranny.

The genres that Chaucer brings to antiquity are tragedy and complaint. Both genres highlight moments of cultural stasis and aesthetic arrest within an imagined world – chivalry in mourning over Arcite's sudden death, the interim of pleasure for Troilus and Criseyde before history overtakes them, the Ovidian retrospect of complaint by noble women who have been 'falsed' by their men. In those moments, the complex significance of late medieval investments in the past emerges. Because antiquity serves as the legitimating source and authorizing pattern for identity and social relations, inventing antiquity is where the craft of vernacular writing becomes cultural analysis. To explore antiquity is to probe what medieval high culture wishes to claim for itself. And if the classical past is a surrogate for chivalric social forms and established institutions, it is also a domain where representation puts contemporary forms of ideology into question by making them act, speak, and reveal themselves.

'Now-a-dayes': Chaucerian modernity

In the Prologue to the Miller's Tale, Chaucer carefully portrays a moment when antiquity gives way unexpectedly to modernity. The Knight has told his 'noble storie . . . worthy for to drawen to memorie' (I.3111–12), and the Host proposes that the Monk follow, 'Somwhat to quite with the Knyghtes tale' (3119). At this point, the drunken Miller breaks the decorum of the pilgrimage with his counter-claim: 'I kan a noble tale for the nones, / With which I wol now quite the Knyghtes tale' (3126–7). We are accustomed to reading this passage as a dramatic frame that casts the Miller's Tale as an inversion of the Knight's Tale and later sets up the Knight's intervention to end the Monk's tedious recitation of ancient and modern tragedies. But the Miller's transgressive entrance also conveys much about Chaucerian modernity. If his 'noble tale' matches ('quits') the Knight's 'noble storie,' it delineates two forms of temporality: one form is directed to the exemplary work of 'memorie,' while the other is urgent and improvisational, 'for the nones.' As the Miller demonstrates through his story, modernity can operate through the same language and structures as antiquity but to different ends – self-authorization, assertion, and misrule within a brokered social compact.

The Miller's Prologue makes it clear that modernity in Chaucer is more difficult to define than antiquity as an historical period or a bounded sphere of poetic and cultural imagination. For modernity is not merely a time period with clear demarcations of chronology or sequence; it is driven, rather, by the Miller's imperative 'for the nones.' Mapped onto a variety of narrative settings, including some with the trappings of antiquity, modernity depicts the mobility of social worlds. Much as antiquity is foreshortened in time, determined, and closed, modernity remains open to some measure of experiment, improvisation, and human autonomy. In English, the term 'modern' seems to appear first in the late fifteenth or early sixteenth century, and it signifies the 'present.'[15] In earlier medieval usage, modern usually means 'contemporary.' Chaucerian modernity, I shall argue, incorporates these conventional meanings, while expressing the present as a specific form of historical consciousness.

Historically, the difference between *moderni* and *antiqui* covers several oppositions: Christian versus classical writers, medieval versus early Christian writers, late medieval versus high medieval philosophers.[16] By the fourth century, Christian writers developed a historical view of their institutions and practices.[17] In his *De nugis curialium*, written for the court of Henry II and Eleanor of Aquitaine, Walter Map gives voice to the paradoxical interweaving of past and present in social institutions. The court, he says, is temporal, 'changeable and various, space-bound and wandering, never continuing in one state,' yet 'the court is not changed; it remains always the same' (dist. 1, c. 1).[18] For Map, the qualities of his own continually mutable age lie in the stories of men localized by their occupations, communities, and social identities. In a later passage, where he contemplates a writer's reception both in his own age and over time, Map rhetorically inserts the disaffection of modernity into his own age, as if it literally were a permanent structural feature: 'Omnibus seculis sua displicuit modernitas' ('Every century has disliked its own modernity' [dist. 4, c. 5; pp. 312–13]). This dominant medieval sense of 'modern' typically serves to contrast contemporary conditions to an idealized past, as in Gower's lament over the disintegration of the state and the church (*Confessio Amantis* Prologue 93–498); or it furthers satiric ends, as in Alceste's reproof of Cupid's court in the *Legend of Good Women* (F 352–6) for its spite and envy.

The most important feature of modernity in Chaucer's poetry, I believe, is not just contemporaneity but the experience of change. It is an historical commonplace that Chaucer wrote in an age of crisis, with vast shifts in demography, population, commerce, and social structures.

Among his contemporaries, Gower simultaneously expresses a belief in providence and a sense of human confusion in the face of changing fortune: 'The hevene wot what is to done, / But we that duelle under the mone / Stonde in this world upon a weer' (*Confessio Amantis* Prologue 141–3). Religious and political dissent, contained if not entirely dispelled, appear alongside a new social mobility for women and for other subordinated and marginalized groups. Jean Froissart recognizes that the citizens of London have become a dominant force, the 'chiefs du royaume d'Angleterre et puissans que ils sont' ('real leaders of the kingdom').[19] Law struggles throughout the period to contend with new social forces and ambitions. Those cultural and ethical values that seemingly hold their place against change, such as the concept of *trouthe*, acquire new meanings.[20] Still, the decisive element, as Charles Muscatine points out, is perception – the late medieval social consensus of crisis – rather than any historical reality that we might reconstruct for the poet's age.[21]

The most influential readings of Chaucer's modernity divide between two versions that have largely served to reinforce one another. On the one hand, Chaucer creates characters who exhibit self-consciousness, interiority, will, agency, and alienation – characters, in short, with the features that we recognize as defining qualities of the modern subject. On the other, he situates these characters within large-scale, determining historical forces that impose social and cultural identity, constrain action and gratification, and shape political consciousness in the service of a dominant order, even if all the motives of that order are obscure or hidden to itself. Taken alone, each version of modernity produces an incomplete, distorted, and ahistorical reading of the poetry. The former merely shifts the creation of an autonomous, fully realized individual chronologically from the Renaissance back to the late Middle Ages; the latter holds out an ahistorical 'medieval world view.' Both require amnesia, as David Aers notes, to formulate their grand schemes.[22]

Some of the best critical thinking recognizes that these two focal points of modernity are related dialectically. The portrayal of selfhood and subjectivity in Chaucer depends fundamentally on the pressures of historical forces. This dialectic generates in turn an array of narratives that stage resistance as a defining mechanism of psychological and political identity. Thus Lee Patterson sees the Canon's Yeoman's Tale as modern because it is an example of the 'emancipatory practice' of self-fashioning and of 'social disruption' that challenges underlying assumptions of medieval intellectual life.[23] In other ways, the Miller displays an emerging class consciousness by pitting natural law against social hierarchy, and the Wife of Bath triumphs, at least momentarily, by subverting and appropriating antifeminist rhetoric.[24] If the aim of Petrarchan humanism, as David Wallace suggests, is to embellish the 'will of the state as embodied in the person of a single masculine ruler,' the Clerk's tale of Griselde relocates Petrarch's story in terms of language, politics, gender, knowledge, and meaning; and it brings back into view, as Carolyn Dinshaw argues, what is not said and left out.[25]

These accounts of Chaucerian modernity operate, however, within the model of challenge and containment familiar from historicist approaches to early modern culture. The Canon's Yeoman recedes before the authority of the Parson at the end of the *Canterbury Tales*; the Miller's rebellion is short-lived; the Wife still speaks a masculine language; Griselde is finally absorbed into patriarchy, hierarchy, and lineage. The modernity I want to propose for Chaucer has a different configuration, one in which forms of subjectivity are already present but escaping history and dominant cultural forms is not an option. Only in the rhetorical commonplaces that the poetry challenges but subverts is there a suggestion of some imaginary position outside will and desire and before history. Chaucer is 'modern,' then, when he portrays characters within social and cultural institutions transforming from traditional medieval structures into new arrangements and relations.

What we might call the matrix of modernism – its embeddedness in earlier, antithetical cultural formations – is visible to late medieval culture as well as to later critics and scholars. Brunetto Latini, who provides a framework of ethical and political theory for Gower, stresses the sociability of humankind: 'Naturele chose est a l'home k'il soit citeins e k'il se converse entre les homes et entre les artiers; et contre nature seroit habiter es desers ou n'a point de gent, por ce ke l'ome se delite naturelement en compaignie' (*Trésor* II.5.2).[26] Following Aristotle's *Ethics*, he divides civil government into three *signories*: monarchy, oligarchy, and commune (the last being 'la trés millour entre ces autres' [II.44.1]). All forms of civic governance, Brunetto says, fashion identity by compelling work, establishing laws, and penalizing those who do not observe those two mandates. But his argument here is very different from the expected claim that culture and positive law are the consequences of man's fall from grace. Rather, life within society provides a chosen means to support the subject as both a fully realized self and a social being with links to social affinities and friends: 'Li plus covenable governemens ki soit en la vie de l'ome, et a mains de paine et de travail, est celui ke l'om consire de maintainer soi et sa mesnie et ses amis.'

Brunetto's stress on the commune is consistent with our own sense that modernity finds a particular expression in the city as a social, political, and cultural formation. John M. Ganim has argued that the two most famous descriptions of medieval London, William Fitz Stephen's twelfth-century *Descriptio* and John Stow's late sixteenth-century *Survey of London*, reflect 'anxieties surrounding the identification of the city with modernity and national identity.'[27] These cartographic descriptions, he points out, are rhetorical and symbolic; and they look back nostalgically to an idealized order (as in Stow's absorption of Fitz Stephen), while registering profound ambivalence toward changes, especially those affecting social relations (the eclipse of charity and the 'common commoditie'). The anxieties and ambivalence that emerge in these accounts are, by contrast, the constituent elements of the absent London that Wallace finds in the *Canterbury Tales*. In urban figures like the Cook and the Canon, the politics of association turn into bad faith, contention, and betrayal. 'There is,' says Wallace, 'no idea of a city for all the inhabitants of a space called London to pay allegiance to; there are only conflicts of associational, hierarchical, and antiassociational discourses, acted out within and across the boundaries of a city wall or the fragments of a text called *The Canterbury Tales*.'[28]

The modernity that Chaucer examines shares the dynamism of civic life captured in these accounts, but it exists on a more various landscape of locales. As Ganim and Wallace recognize, the city exists as a discursive formation, a means for explaining how selves and subjects function within institutions constructed through human invention. Chaucer's modernity shows these institutions repeatedly under pressure, at points where accepted explanations (natural law, tradition, convention) no longer cohere convincingly yet no alternative is feasible. It stages narratives of agency by which characters negotiate desire and intention within already transforming structures. Modernity in this sense is the project of the *Canterbury Tales*, though certainly not the only poetic interest of Chaucer's great unfinished poem. The most important literary structure of Chaucer's modernity, I believe, is the fabliau. Chaucer revives the fabliau in English through the Miller's Tale and the Reeve's Tale as a counterpart to Boccaccio's *novelle*. He adapts the genre as a means for representing the experience of change in the Shipman's Tale and the Pardoner's Tale. Fabliau is also the form submerged beneath the narratives usually associated with the Marriage Group. The Merchant's Tale is Chaucer's longest fabliau. The Wife of Bath's Prologue coyly invites us to see her bad husbands and possibly part of her life through the fabliau. In the tales of married love recounted by the Clerk and

Franklin, fabliau is the alternate story that always threatens to be told if their narrative resolutions falter.

Chaucer and Boccaccio

Giovanni Boccaccio is the shadow author behind Chaucer's invention of antiquity and modernity. Nowhere acknowledged but demonstrably present in the last two decades of Chaucer's career, Boccaccio is the direct source for the Knight's Tale, *Troilus and Criseyde*, and the Franklin's Tale, and for the form and some of the narratives in the Monk's Tale; he is the originary but remote source for the Clerk's Tale; moreover, his writings provide analogues for the *Legend of Good Women*, Miller's Tale, Reeve's Tale, Shipman's Tale, and Merchant's Tale. Chaucer's silence stands over and against the depth of his engagement with Boccaccio's work, and our explanations for it are only partial. Minnis explains the silence over the close rewriting of the *Filostrato* by arguing that Chaucer seeks to represent himself as a historian and so must invent a fictive Latin source ('myn auctour called Lollius') with the appearance of authority.[29] Wallace suggests that Chaucer thereby repeats Boccaccio's own strategy in the *Filocolo* of disguising vernacular sources with an invented Latin author.[30]

What may apply to the *Troilus*, however, does not necessarily explain other cases. The Knight's Tale gives the impression of Latin *auctoritas* by quoting Statius and claiming a source in 'olde stories' (I.859); earlier, *Anelida and Arcite* had made the lie overt: 'First folowe I Stace, and after him Corynne' (21). The Franklin's Tale obscures its origins in Menedon's story (*Filocolo* 4.31–4) by staging the fictional recovery of a lost vernacular tradition, the Breton lay (IV.709–13). The Monk's Tale may offer oblique acknowledgment of its Boccaccian source by its manuscript subtitle: 'De Casibus Virorum Illustrium.' The other tales claim no authorial warrant. For the stories of pagan antiquity, Spearing speaks what every reader suspects about Boccaccio's influence on Chaucerian antiquity and modernity: Chaucer 'recognized the special value of this crucial model . . . and wanted to keep it to himself.'[31]

Chaucer's silence over Boccaccio appears somewhat less anomalous when seen against his links to the French poets who proved equally decisive earlier in his career. Though Chaucer acknowledges Oton de Granson as the source for the balades he translates in the 'Complaint of Venus' (82), he marks his borrowings from Machaut and Froissart – earlier and far more extensive narrative refashionings – only by internal allusion and citation within his poetry.[32] This suggests that the issue is not vernacular writing or the shadow cast by accomplished contemporary writers; rather, Chaucer's engagement is with the works themselves and the possibilities they bring to English poetry.[33] Reading Chaucer against Boccaccio thus has much to tell us about what Chaucer does as a fundamentally revisionist poet, how he shapes his borrowed stories, and where he seeks to locate them in English and European literary tradition. In addition, Chaucer's narratives about the antique and modern worlds are part of a cultural poetics at work in late medieval England. They represent a project, already formulated in Dante and carried out across the range of Boccaccio's writings, in which literary tradition is used to describe, analyze, and challenge the structures and arrangements within which human agency, understanding, will, and desire play out. From Boccaccio's works, Chaucer constructs imaginative worlds, both remote and contemporaneous, to examine how characters inhabit fictional moments and contingencies with artistic, philosophical, and cultural resonance.

The material means by which Chaucer discovered Boccaccio's writings are notoriously hard to identify. He may have known Boccaccio's work through manuscripts and translations that do not identify Boccaccio as the author.[34] Though Chaucer traveled to Italy in 1373, as proposals circulated for the lectures on Dante's *Commedia* that Boccaccio subsequently delivered, the most likely occasion for his acquiring manuscripts and returning with them to England was his second trip to Italy in 1378.[35] The *Filostrato* and *Teseida* are works that clearly had to have been consulted repeatedly in manuscript as Chaucer rewrote them. For Menedon's story, the source of the Franklin's Tale, he may have read cursorily in the *Filocolo* (as Petrarch earlier describes reading the *Decameron*), or he may have read an independent manuscript of the 'Quesitoni d'amore,' the sequence of thirteen love stories in Book 4 of the *Filocolo* which contains Menedon's tale.[36]

The influence of the *Decameron* on Chaucer is even more problematic than that of Boccaccio's earlier writings. In his Preface to *The Fables* (1700), John Dryden treats both writers as the authors of 'novels'; and he suggests parallels in form, style, subject matter, and the use of the vernacular.[37] While the *Decameron* offers analogues to some stories in the *Canterbury Tales*, the stronger influence has been seen in it as a model for a collection of short narratives contained within a frametale and animated by a literary *felaweshipe* that generates shifting thematic overlays and concentrations. No external evidence demonstrates that Chaucer knew the *Decameron* first hand, nor did he rework any of its stories as closely as he did the *Teseida*, *Filostrato*, and Menedon's story.

Modern scholars reconcile their conviction that Chaucer must have known the collection with the absence of direct evidence that he did so by proposing that Chaucer could have read or heard parts of it during his Italian journey.[38] The *Decameron* would thus be a memorial text rather than a textual source. Implicitly, it is a paradigm and influence too powerful to need (or perhaps allow) the documentation we ask of sources rather than intertexts. Indeed, much of the scholarship has shifted ground from showing the influence of the *Decameron* to arguing for ways we might assume its influence.[39] As we shall see later, its importance, whether direct or oblique, extends beyond that of a formal model or narrative source, for the *Decameron* raises questions about writing, ethics, and history, about agency and action in the social sphere that Chaucer addresses in the *Canterbury Tales*.

However Chaucer came to know Boccaccio's writings, they represent an important example of poetic ambition within vernacular high culture.[40] Boccaccio consciously undertakes the cultural projects of writing antiquity and modernity and thereby linking the serviceable past and the dynamic present. His early compositions in the milieu of the Angevin court at Naples might be characterized broadly as an effort to connect classical culture with vernacular forms and themes, hence with the medieval progeny of an imagined antiquity. The *Teseida* (1340–41), the culminating work of his formative period in Naples, is an amplification and extension of the *Thebaid* that seeks to contain Statius's savage critique of classical heroism within medieval courtly conventions and to fuse epic with romance. The *Filostrato* (*ca.* 1335) isolates the interior, erotic world of Troiolo and Criseida from the large pattern of Trojan history and then uses their story as a partial analogue to the poet's narrative frame – in particular, the meta-fiction of the poet's envoi to his imagined mistress. The *Filocolo* (1336) presents the tale of Florio and Biancifiore as a romance of lovers' separation and recovery that leads simultaneously to familial restoration and the transformation of pagan into Christian culture.

The court of Robert the Wise, like the Edwardian and Ricardian courts Chaucer knew, directly patronized Latin and French rather than its own vernacular, but its support of learning sustained an environment for Boccaccio's studies of classical sources and his experiments with their subject matter. The works from which Chaucer most clearly borrows are the products of Boccaccio's formative period. Boccaccio's writings on antiquity show the full encounter of a vernacular tradition with classical materials, with a cultural past at once different and similar. As A.C. Spearing suggests, Boccaccio's textuality nuances and enriches the historiographical conventions that affected Chaucer: 'Chaucer, guided by his reading of Boccaccio, attempted with extraordinary success to reimagine a classical pagan culture in its own terms, as possessing its own integrity, its own world-view – a culture imaginable because it had much in common with that of medieval Christianity, but interesting because it was also crucially different.'[41] Boccaccio's project, like Dante's, was literary and cultural. In his poems on antiquity, Chaucer found a poetics of emulation rather than absorption; their concern was not merely to imitate the ancients but to resituate their cultural authority. Scholars have traditionally seen topical meanings in these writings, but recent critics argue for a coherent program of writing.[42]

In the *Decameron*, Boccaccio invents a form of modernity focused on contemporary society. Vittore Branca has famously described the collection as a mercantile epic in which the underlying values of Italian civic life are tested.[43] In his Proem, Boccaccio insists that the tales are a mixture of love stories and other events ('piacevoli e aspri casi d'amore e altri fortunati avvenimenti') taken from modernity and antiquity ('ne' moderni tempi avvenuti come negli antichi'). His phrasing ('casi d'amore') promises a kind of exemplary discourse that he promptly cancels out by reversing the expected sequence of ancient and modern. The figures portrayed in his tales are rooted in the particularity of families, towns, and regions, and their exemplarity depends on action rather than character or type. In the 'Questioni d'amore,' Boccaccio had experimented with a narrative frametale and unifying theme for stories by young, aristocratic characters, but the sequence of tales is premised on voluntary withdrawal and leisure (*otium*), not the enforced sequestration of feminine readers, as in the *Decameron*. The stories recounted in the 'Questioni' are set either in an indistinct present or in a past without a sense of historical distance. By contrast, the frame of the *Decameron* is precisely the moment of crisis when pestilence threatens social order and institutional structures. The plague is, of course, the immediate cause and metaphorical effect of family and social disintegration, alienation, economic collapse, and immorality: 'la reverenda auttorità delle leggi, così divine come umane, quasi caduta e dissoluta' ('all respect for the laws of God and man had virtually broken down and been extinguished in our city'). For Boccaccio as for Chaucer, modernity emerges when nature and divinity are interrupted as categories of understanding and the socially embedded world of experience reveals itself as made up.[44]

The mercantile civic culture portrayed in the *Decameron* is already fully realized for Boccaccio. His stories of contemporaries and near-contemporaries are set inside social forms mature enough to be textualized as anecdote, example, and illustration. N.S. Thompson credits Boccaccio with creating the authenticating fiction that the stories occurred in known locations with known or named characters.[45] The *brigata*, withdrawn from Florence to Fiesole, tell these tales retrospectively, looking back rhetorically to a unity and coherence – a social logic – that they may not find on their return to Florence (the three young men, we recall, go off to seek 'altri piaceri,' and the young women eventually return home). The opening phrase – 'Umana cosa' – signals Boccaccio's topic and opens the prospect of writing about a human world held together by empathy, rivalry, and the conventions of social life. In this way, Boccaccio goes beyond the exemplarity of moral lessons in hagiography or the lives of famous men and women. He adapts the middle style of classical and Christian rhetoric to stories of contemporary life where praise and blame still operate while the larger moral framework beneath them stands in doubt.[46] At one level, Boccaccio's modernity severs literary discourse from ethics; at another, it returns representation to history. The *Decameron* is directed to urban oligarchic readers whose class has replaced feudal aristocrats as a social and historical force. As David Wallace points out, Chaucer discovered not just the texts of the Trecento authors, but also 'the cultural and political contexts that they were designed to affirm or critique; he was thus able to imagine them *at work*, as cultural forces, before translating them to England as written or remembered texts.'[47]

Chaucer's literary modernity takes a different form from Boccaccio's predominantly urban and mercantile ethos. If the *Decameron* registers the trauma of the plague and social dislocation, the *Canterbury Tales* are situated elsewhere in its aftermath, ostensibly within natural and spiritual renewal. The Parson's Tale, which ends an incomplete work, abjures fiction and offers a penitential discipline for salvation. But the world that unfolds between the General Prologue and the final tale is not realized like Boccaccio's, and the poet's retrospective storytelling is a device for narration. Within the *Tales*, modernity represents social and historical reality as an emergent structure, tentative and provisional, still located within established feudal structures yet transforming the possibilities of choice and agency, identity and understanding. Chaucer's poems capture moments hovering uncertainly between the imperatives of aristocratic and mercantile culture and between the interpretive frames these arrangements bring to experience. History has not shown all its hand in Chaucer's modernity, just as his *Tales* do not give us a final design.

The chapters that follow examine the various ways in which Chaucer creates antiquity and modernity from and through Boccaccio. My focus is necessarily selective. I have not dealt extensively with the Monk's Tale and Boccaccio's *De casibus virorum illustrium* or with Boccaccio's other compendia, the *De mulieribus claris* and *Genealogie deorum gentilium*, because their stories are points of reference – entries in a catalogue raisonné of the past – rather than narratives to be explored. Nor do I examine the *Ameto* and the Merchant's Tale or remote analogues from the *Decameron* for other Canterbury tales. The first half of the book follows Chaucer's master narrative of antiquity, which begins with the story of Thebes, moves to the Trojan war, and ends with the tales of Greek and Roman heroines.

Chapter 1 explores the differing strategies adopted by Chaucer and Boccaccio in response to Statius's *Thebaid*. Statius's poem offers a devastating critique of classical heroism and political power. Boccaccio uses the Dantesque topics of arms, love, and virtue to contain the profound menace of Theban history within medieval chivalric conventions. Chaucer, I shall argue, not only imposes a different formal order on Boccaccio's materials but also probes the indwelling contradictions of Boccaccio's poetic strategy and the limited sphere finally allowed for human action. Chapter 2 examines the double necessity of history and eros in *Troilus and Criseyde*. Chaucer's rewriting of the *Filostrato* employs the perspective of historians like Guido delle Colonne who insist that choice and misperception shape the tragic destiny of Troy. A similar perspective develops in the poem's treatment of love, where consent, artfulness, and the unforeseen power of desire allow a measure of choice for escaping the pattern of destiny.

In his Theban and Trojan poems, Chaucer engages Boccaccio's work to portray the ancient world from a dominant aristocratic position where agency and choice operate for male heroic characters. Chapter 3 reads the *Legend of Good Women* as a poem that interrogates this aristocratic world. Using the conventions of Ovidian complaint, the *Legend* views the politics of desire from the short side of history. Its heroines reveal the alternatives lost in narratives of empire, the internal fragility of courtly culture, and the tensions bearing on aristocratic, patriarchal families. In most critical readings, the *Legend* stands anomalously as a poem that Chaucer abandoned. It is more likely, I propose, that Chaucer essentially abandoned antiquity because he had mapped its significance and explored its most compelling predicaments. What he left open was the possibility of a Christian antiquity, explored more fully in his religious tales.

The second half of the book concentrates on poems in which Chaucer represents a modernity based on contract and negotiation. Chapter 4 analyzes the fabliau as a paradigm for constructing a literary realm of contingency and improvisation. A form Chaucer revived in the English tradition and a counterpart to Boccaccio's *novelle* and other exemplary anecdotes, the fabliau stages the negotiations of appetite and will in a newly emerging personal and social sphere. The final two chapters, on poems traditionally associated with the Marriage Group, trace the emergence of a social matrix of exchange within a courtly world with fixed and traditional values. Relying on Boccaccio and other authors, Chaucer imaginatively captures a point of transition when the external forms of social life seem intact while the sphere of personal relations changes from hierarchy to negotiation. Chapter 5 examines the story of Griselda's patience and suffering as a hermeneutic problem that takes on changing historical significance as it evolves from Boccaccio's original tale in the *Decameron* through French versions, Petrarch's Latin translation, Chaucer's Clerk's Tale and even Chaucer's fifteenth-century readers. The final chapter, on the Franklin's Tale, demonstrates how both Chaucer and Boccaccio rewrite Menedon's story from the sequence of Love Questions in the *Filocolo*, shifting the narrative from an aristocratic cultural context into a domain where traditional arrangements are transformed into hybrid social practices and new relations of subjectivity and agency.

Antiquity and modernity are not the only topics in Chaucer's poetic engagement with Boccaccio. Misogyny and female virtue, religious faith, and the place of fiction are major, perhaps unresolved, concerns for both writers. What antiquity and modernity furnish, as against other topics, is a richly imagined cultural sphere. As Boccaccio understood and Chaucer came to realize after his initial experiments with dream visions, the stories that late medieval culture tells about its defining past and negotiable present are doubly inscribed in history. They come to poets as structures of imagination to extend and revise – to invent poetically – and they register, at the same time, the historical contexts of their own translation into new forms of expression.

1
'The strif of Thebes': Statius, Boccaccio, and Chaucer

The story of Thebes is the remote origin of Chaucerian antiquity. In medieval literary tradition, it encompassed not only the deadly rivalry of Eteocles and Polynices over the kingship of Thebes but also the story of Oedipus and even the dual founding of the city by Cadmus and Amphion. Often, it formed part of a universal history of cultures and kingdoms.[1] Chaucer's treatment of the matter of Thebes takes a different focus from this tradition, leaving behind the narrative additions of the *romans antiques* and other vernacular forms, which amplified the backgrounds of the story. In the Knight's Tale and *Anelida and Arcite*, Chaucer invents Theban antiquity in the aftermath of Creon's usurpation of kingship and Theseus's intervention to re-establish justice. In so doing, he places his work within a complex set of intertextual relations. In this chapter, I want, first of all, to distinguish the ways in which Chaucer exploits Statius's *Thebaid* and Boccaccio's *Teseida* as sources for his story. Chaucer uses Statius, I shall argue, as a hermeneutic emblem, a device to signal classical authority and thereby condition interpretation. His major poetic effort, however, is to rewrite the topics, story, and themes of Boccaccio's vernacular epic, which answers the program of Dante's vernacular poetics. My second concern will be to explore the opening narrative sequence of the *Teseida* and the Knight's Tale. The action of both these poems grows out of a narrative full of resonance for the main story. Suppressed in different ways by Boccaccio and Chaucer, this part of the story suggests what is at stake for their imagination of classical antiquity. Finally, I want to reassess the story Chaucer invents from Boccaccio. Read in isolation as 'al the love of Palamon and Arcite' (LGW F420) or in the context of the *Canterbury Tales*, the Knight's Tale is generally characterized as a celebration of aristocratic ideology. Read against the *Teseida*, as it was originally composed, Chaucer's poem refashions and interrogates the medieval aristocratic context that Boccaccio had used to contain the turmoil of Statius's poem.

The Statian emblem and Dante's three poetic subjects

At the beginning of the Knight's Tale and the opening of the story in *Anelida and Arcite*, Chaucer signals his ambitions of imitating and extending Statius's epic by conspicuously citing a passage from the *Thebaid*. His citation identifies the initial setting of his two poems with the moment in the *Thebaid* when Theseus returns in triumph from the Amazonian wars: 'Iamque domos patrias, Scithice post aspera gentis / Prelia, laurigero, &c.' But the ensuing action – the supplication of the Argive widows and Theseus's subsequent campaign against Creon – is held in suspense. The passage from Statius also represents an effort to appropriate the layout and bibliographical code of a classical text to Chaucer's poems. It gives them the look of a classical text preserved in a medieval manuscript, hence the appearance of works belonging to the world of authors.[2] In this way, Chaucer's poems imitate not just the subject matter but the presentation of classical poetry. This overt gesture toward the *Thebaid* contrasts, however, with what Chaucer does otherwise with Statius's poem. In the Knight's Tale, the text he directly engages is Boccaccio's *Teseida*, not the *Thebaid*. In *Anelida*, he leaves Theseus in his triumph and Creon ascendant on the throne of Thebes, in order to invent his own story of the 'slye wey' (line 48) by which Theban Arcite betrays Anelida and to devise the dramatic situation of her formal complaint. It might be argued that Statius is the source from which both these extrapolations emanate and that, in this sense, he is their 'author.'[3] But a close look at the texts reveals sharply differentiated uses of Statius and Boccaccio.

The argument for Statius's direct influence on Chaucer has grown more subtle and interesting as the evidence of textual engagement has moved from source study to interpretation. The animal imagery that pervades the *Thebaid* and signals the devolution from heroism to brutishness recurs in Chaucer, but it is transmitted as well through the *Teseida*. Some apparent details enter Chaucer's poem significantly dislodged from their original contexts in Statius. For example, Chaucer applies the simile of expectant hunters waiting to encounter savage prey to Palamon and Arcite as they begin their clandestine combat in the forest (I.1638–46). Boccaccio uses it as they enter the theatre for the formal tournament (7.106). Statius originally devised it to describe Eteocles's fear and uncertainty as he witnesses Tireas's summoning the spirits of the underworld to prophesy the outcome of the war (4.494–9). Chaucer's subsequent description of Palamon and Arcite – '[a]s wilde bores gonne they to smyte' (I.1658) – has no counterpart in Boccaccio, while the source proposed in Statius's description of the climactic combat between Eteocles and Polynices (11.530–6) is a highly wrought, extended simile here reduced to a cliché. A somewhat closer fit can be found in the similarity between Arcite's fall at his moment of triumph in the Knight's Tale and Polynices's fall from his chariot during the funeral games for Opheltes, the infant son of Lycurgus (6.495–512); as Statius points out, this incident shows the possibility of a different history for Thebes, which Fate averts (6.513–17).

Of the parallels with the *Thebaid* commonly cited, only the prefatory lines taken from Theseus's triumphal return constitute a direct borrowing. Boyd Ashby Wise shows how Chaucer recombines parts of the passage, and he suggests that the briefly sketched war against Thebes (I.893–1000) is a composite of sources, including Statius.[4] Elsewhere in the Knight's Tale, as Paul M. Clogan points out, glosses appended to manuscripts of the *Thebaid* offer individual details and references.[5] In *Anelida*, the Statian opening is itself prefaced by an invocation taken from Boccaccio. Statius thus functions as an authorizing presence, a figure who evokes a narrative world without directly supplying its language or its details in a pattern of borrowing. In his valuable study of Boccaccio's restructuring of the *Thebaid* within the *Teseida*, David Anderson proposes that Chaucer adopts Boccaccio's strategy of writing an 'allusive narrative' based on Statius: 'Chaucer's open imitation of the *Thebaid* in his main action suggests that, in many of its aspects, his "transforming art" was not a transformation *of* Boccaccio's work but *like* Boccaccio's work' in rewriting Statius within his own poem.[6] Yet as Anderson points out, Chaucer reduces the echoes of Statius that Boccaccio had woven into his poem, and the most important feature of Statius's influence for the Knight's Tale remains the outline of the story. The function of the *Thebaid*, in other words, is hermeneutic rather than narrative. Statius's poem provides a field of meaning against which to read the poem Chaucer invented from the *Teseida*.

We can find some indication of the hermeneutic meaning of the *Thebaid* by turning to medieval academic introductions to the poem. Conrad of Hirsau describes the Thebans as 'infelicissimi.' Statius, he says, wrote of their 'misfortune or unhappiness' to give the emperors Titus and Vespasian an example of virtue in Adrastus, the only figure to survive the expedition against Thebes.[7] The account of the *Thebaid* that Cassandra gives in *Troilus and Criseyde* (5.1485–1510) is drawn from

Latin summaries for the whole poem and for each of the individual books except the opening one; it rehearses a story of usurpation, deceit, divine malice, death, and sorrow. The shaping force of Statius's poem is rage. Rage accepts no limits or boundaries (*modus*), so it may wane, as in the momentary glut of heroic furor or even Tisiphone's failing powers at the last battle (11.92–6), but it is never transformed. Consequently, rage breaks the bonds of family, sworn oaths, and custom; or, alternatively, it creates a perverse affinity, as in the friendship of Tydeus and Polynices after their furious encounter as suppliants and exiles before Adrastus's palace. It also produces grotesque horrors like Tydeus's gnawing on the head of his killer or the battlefield strewn with severed body parts. At the political as well as personal level, rage is an uninflected will to power. Statius expresses its nature clearly in the phrases 'regendi saevus amor' (1.127–8) and 'nuda potestas' (1.150). He renders it tragic and bitterly ironic by noting how little Thebes really has worth fighting over.

In Statius's poem, rage is encoded historically across generations. Oedipus, Jocasta, even Laius summoned from the dead play direct roles in the poem. The chief characters are figures of excess nuanced by defect. Though impelled by anger, Eteocles and Polynices are diminished in their heroic stature by treachery and fearfulness in the first case and by intermittent courage in the second. The heroes who move against Thebes are either beyond limits in their fury (Tydeus and Capaneus), blindly caught up in struggle (Hippomedon) or woefully unprepared for the grim business of war (Parthenopaeus). Those who see some shape to events (Amphiarus and Adrastus) grasp them only dimly, and they falsify prophecy and prudence as needed. Despite the spectacle of military order, battles are joined impromptu, and they quickly dissolve into tactical as well as social chaos: 'nullo venit ordine bellum, / confusique duces volgo' (7.616–17). The most successful military foray in Statius's poem is Thiodamas's divinely inspired slaughter of the Thebans in their sleep. If the gods are constrained by Fate operating through Tisiphone, fortune and chance work freely in the meantime, while the gods settle their scores with men and each other. At the climactic combat between Eteocles and Polynices, Jupiter can only order the gods to turn away and to have the crime hidden from him (11.126–7). Peace and reconciliation come obliquely – in the embrace of Argia and Antigone over Polynices's body and then finally, perhaps, in the treaty (*foedera*) that Theseus imposes after defeating Creon.

Seen as an emblem, the *Thebaid* represents irrational conflict and transgression. It signifies the breakdown of those elements that ostensibly support classical heroism and its associated cultural, social, and

political forms.[8] As Frederick Ahl observes, 'The chronicle of Thebes is
that of fathers and mothers killing their children, of chaos within
groups that should be the stable structures of human life.'[9] For later
writers to cite the poem is thus to locate their stories against a background of bleak, exemplary meaning. The story Boccaccio and Chaucer
build on to this emblem is already identified as strange, powerful, and
turbulent. For his part, Boccaccio describes his story as something that
lies beyond ordinary literary discourse. It is an ancient, hence venerable,
story hitherto unknown by the Latin authors: 'una istoria antica, / tanto
negli anni riposta e nascosa / che latino autor non par ne dica' (1.2.2–4).
In his gloss to this passage, Boccaccio says that the story is remote
because it has not been translated before from the Greek. His image of
a hidden narrative (*istoria nascosa*) also suggests a story suppressed and
rendered inaccessible to traditional literary discourse. At its heart lies
materia pellegrina (gloss to 1.10), a subject strange and therefore delightful. The full meaning of this 'antichissima istoria,' as he says in the
dedicatory epistle to Fiammetta, will remain partially hidden to all but
him and his lady – 'alle più delle genti non manifesta.'

To judge from the testimony of the *Legend of Good Women*, the story
would have been strange for Chaucer's aristocratic audience, too. Alceste
calls it 'al the love of Palamon and Arcite / Of Thebes, thogh the storye
ys knowen lyte' (LGW F 420–1). In her formulation, the two chivalric
protagonists foreground the tension between love as a topic and Thebes
as the symbol of internecine conflict. Desire and history are joined as
the controlling themes, while the story here is unknown not to previous
authors, as in Boccaccio, but to readers and auditors who depend on
literary tradition to locate a set of readerly expectations. In *Anelida*,
Chaucer presents the story as already brought into convention. His
narrator's intention is to translate and compose '[t]his olde storie, in
Latyn which I fynde' (line 10) so as to preserve it in memory against
devouring age.

In amplifying the *Thebaid*, Boccaccio and Chaucer represent antiquity
differently, but they share a common thematic matrix. Since the Renaissance, critics have recognized that Boccaccio inserts his poem into
the framework Dante constructs in *De vulgari eloquentia* 2.2.7–8. There
Dante identifies arms, love, and virtue as the most worthy subjects
(*magnalia*) for the highest ('tragic') vernacular style.[10] Dante premises
his discussion on man's vegetative, animal, and rational souls. Each of
them, he says, has an object which it pursues – the useful, the pleasurable, and the good, respectively. To these objects correspond well-being,
love, and virtue. He concludes: 'Quare hec tria, salus videlicet, venus et

virtus, apparent esse illa magnalia que sint maxime pertractanda, hoc est ea que maxime sunt ad ista, ut armorum probitas, amoris accensio et directio voluntatis' ('So these three things, well-being, love, and virtue, appear to be those most important subjects that are to be treated in the loftiest style; or at least this is true of the themes most closely associated with them, prowess in arms, ardour in love, and control of one's own will').[11]

Boccaccio's immediate interest is in filling the omission that Dante notes at the end of this passage: 'Arma vero nullum latium adhuc invenio poetasse' ('As for arms, I find that no Italian has yet treated them in poetry'). The *Teseida* adds a narrative poem to Dante's lyric examples, and it thereby associates its author with Cino da Pistoia, the poet of love, and Dante himself, the poet who writes of virtue. But Boccaccio does not passively accept Dante's framework. He recombines the themes that Dante had separated analytically. The *Teseida* is about love, arms, and virtue. Chaucer, who did not know Dante's treatise, works, as we shall see, implicitly and intuitively within Boccaccio's restructuring.

At the start of the *Teseida*, Boccaccio overtly claims two of Dante's topics rather than one. He invokes not just Mars but also Venus and Cupid (1.3) as his presiding deities. At the beginning of Book 3, he makes the Ovidian gesture of signalling the departure of Mars and the turn to Cupid and his battles (3.1.4–7). In one sense, the subsequent history of Palemone and Arcita is an ironic reliteralization of Ovid's metaphor of erotic warfare and his authorial turn from epic to elegiac topics as a new form of poetic endeavor.[12] At the end of the *Teseida*, Boccaccio announces the completion of his poetic aim of writing a vernacular epic (12.84.6–8). The title chosen for the poem by its addressee, the fictional Fiammetta, connects the topics of arms and love – *Teseida delle nozze di Emilia*. In a broader sense, however, arms and love are subsumed under the third topic – virtue. The poem that Dante mentions as an illustration of virtue, 'Doglia mi reca,' is the fourth and last of a group of *canzoni* discussing ethical topics, by which Dante means Aristotelian moral virtue – habits of choice which keep one in the mean and produce happiness in their action.[13] The persistent question in Boccaccio's and Chaucer's poems is how the chivalric subject responds to arms and love against the background of Statian history and fatalism. Earlier romances, notably Chrétien de Troyes's *Erec et Enide*, had formulated the question as a dispute over balancing heroic obligations and erotic indulgence, and Boccaccio briefly evokes that earlier formation. But Boccaccio carries the question further by suggesting that arms and love are facets of an aristocratic subject who is to be judged finally by his moral agency, by how he exercises 'directio voluntatis' ('control of one's will'), as Dante thematizes the topic of virtue. His poetic concern is to explore the kinds of choices characters make in the exercise of arms and love. In practice, his focus is on how characters act within courtly ideology, which is the context, referent, and rationalization for arms and love.

Boccaccio and Chaucer develop their themes in a narrative located, like Statius's, in the aftermath of a larger, oppressive history. Statius begins by wondering where to begin in the violent story of Thebes: 'unde iubetis / ire, deae' ('Whence, O goddesses, do ye bid me begin' [1.3–4]). In the introductory sonnets and commentaries of the *Teseida*, Boccaccio is at pains to explain why his first two books digress from his main topic, which is the *istoria antica* of Teseo, Arcita, Palemone, and Emilia. His intention, he says, is to explain how Emilia and then Palemone and Arcita come into the story. Chaucer in turn begins the Knight's Tale and the narrative of *Anelida* by holding the moment of Theseus's triumphal return in abeyance. The Knight uses the device of *occupatio* to summarize Book 1 of the *Teseida* without recounting it. The narrator of *Anelida* turns to the domestic story of Arcite's betrayal. Piero Boitani rightly observes that the background story is not strictly necessary to Boccaccio's story. He suggests that Boccaccio adds Books 1 and 2 to his main tale because 'he wishes to write a learned work and is fascinated by his own exotic fantasy.'[14] I would propose that the suppressed background of the story, though framed differently in each poem, significantly shapes the main narrative action and the treatment of arms, love, and virtue. Boccaccio explores his main topics in perhaps their most radical form in Books 1 and 2 of the *Teseida*. Chaucer writes the lessons but not the story of those explorations into the Knight's Tale.

Boccaccio's Prelude

The opening books of the *Teseida* portray warfare that crosses the lines of gender and family. As background to the main action recounted in Boccaccio's poem, Teseo campaigns first against the Amazons and then against Creon, who has assumed mastery of Thebes at the end of its destructive internal rivalry. In both instances, Boccaccio portrays an ideal of chivalric heroism that extends across the apparent differences ✓ of the combatants. Teseo is the model of heroic action. He undertakes war for ostensibly high purposes – to remedy the excesses of the Amazons – and he is a figure of considered judgment. Valor, leadership, and deliberation are the recurring elements of Boccaccio's portrayal. Barbara Nolan has argued that Boccaccio uses Aristotelian and scholastic ethics as well as the literary tradition of princely advice to display his virtues.[15] In Book 1, Teseo is overwhelmingly a warrior and military leader. As he sails toward the kingdom of the Amazons, Boccaccio describes him through the epic simile of a lion hunting its prey:

> E come leoncel cui fame punge,
> il qual fier diventa e piú ardito
> come la preda conosce da lunge,
> vibrando i crin, con ardente appetito
> ẹ l'unghie e' denti aguzza infin l'agiunge;
> cotal Teseo, rimirando espedito
> il regno di color, divenne fiero,
> volonteroso a fare il suo pensiero.
>
> (*Teseida* 1.42)

Just as a lion driven by hunger grows bolder when it sees its prey from far, shaking its mane and stretching its claws and sharp teeth toward it with burning appetite, so Teseo, seeing their kingdom, became fierce and determined to do his will.

When the Amazons repel the Greeks' effort to land, Teseo at length jumps off his ship alone, determined to pursue glory by himself if his men will not follow him. He tells them, partly in scorn and partly by way of exhortation, that he would gain more honor alone than accompanied by men who want to live dishonored without prowess: 'ch'io sarò troppo più, solo, onorato / ch'essendo da cotali accompagnato' (*Teseida* 1.64.7–8). These qualities of personal bravery and martial command reappear in the battle against Creon. Teseo moves through the battlefield, cutting down whomever he encounters, and at the same time encouraging his troops, giving arms to those who have lost them, and helping the fallen regain their mounts (1.56).

The Amazons show the same chivalric heroism as embodied by Teseo. Described as 'crude e dispietate' (1.6.2) for the wholesale murder of their husbands, they nonetheless reproduce the essential features of epic heroism. The means for this martial character is transformation: they have become fully masculinized as heroic characters. Ipolita exhorts them to wield arms and banish femininity: 'nell'arme sempre esercitate poi, / cacciando ogni atto feminil da voi' (1.25.7–8). They possess a masculine soul ('virile animo' [1.26.1]). Elected their queen, Ipolita is simultaneously 'mastra di guerra' (1.8.8). Even as she remains beautiful, she banishes fearfulness and fashions herself a chivalric figure: 'sì rimosse / da sé ciascuna feminil paura' (1.9.3–4). As a prudent governor, Ipolita consolidates power and brings order to her land. When the women turn to her at Teseo's approach, she reacts with a heroic furor to match his: 'di mal talento e di furore accesa' (1.21.8). In council (1.23–35), she speaks with the same deliberative seriousness shown by Hector, Priam, and Agamemnon in chronicle histories of antiquity like Guido delle Colonne's *Historia destructionis Troiae* or, later, John Lydgate's *Troy Book*.[16] She subsequently prepares the defenses of their port to tactical advantage. The Amazons, who offer particularly fierce resistance to Teseo's landing, use fire and arrows with deadly effect: 'perciò ch'ell'eran di cotal mestiere, / più ch'altre, somme e vigorose e fiere' (1.56.7–8). When the Greeks eventually secure their landing and force them to retreat, the Amazons fall back to their fortified castle, prepared to endure a siege. It is a measure of how far the Amazons have absorbed an idealized heroism that Ipolita chastises Teseo for acting not as a knight ('come cavaliere') but as a brigand: 'come disleale uom barattiere / subitamente assalisti mia terra' (1.104.3–4).

If the Amazons show masculine valor relocated in women, Creon demonstrates that, within the cultural world of the *Teseida*, the underlying conventions of *armorum probitas* remain stable in the face of profound moral ambiguity. Boccaccio explains in a gloss (2.10) that Creon acts out of vengeance in not allowing burial of the Greeks fallen before Thebes because his own son had fallen in combat outside the walls and remained unburied. He thus writes out the episode in Statius where Creon's son Menoeceus is persuaded to commit suicide by Tiresias in order to preserve Thebes, and Creon is seen sympathetically, at least for a moment, as a grief-stricken father. Boccaccio's Teseo seizes Creon's prohibition as an occasion to secure further glory and fame, and rightly accuses Creon of committing evil beyond the killing of the kings: 'ma or Creon fa nuovo a' morti torto' (2.46.8). Still, Creon remains a figure of heroic stature. Boccaccio's gloss describes him as 'uomo nobilissimo e possente.' Teseo says he is 'fiero Creonte' (2.47.1). As Teseo rages through the battlefield and exhorts his men, Creon is his exact counterpart: 'Da l'altra parte il simile facea / Creonte, come ardito conduttore' (2.58.1–2). Their equivalence recalls Aeneas and Turnus rather than the debased fraternal rivalry of the *Thebaid*.[17] After Teseo wounds him mortally, Creon continues to resist subjection. Boccaccio adds a speech in which Creon escapes Teseo's victory through death and disputes even Teseo's claim to memory and fame:

> 'Fanne tuo piacere,
> pur che io muoia avanti che vittoria
> io veggia a te e a tua gente avere;
> ché l'alma mia almeno alcuna gloria
> ne porterà con seco nel parere,
> e segnato terrà nella memoria
> che 'n dubbio i tuoi o' miei lascio d'onore;
> e credo che li miei hanno il migliore.'
>
> (*Teseida* 2.64)

'Do as you please, so long as I die before seeing you and your people have victory; for my soul will carry with it at least some glory and will remember that victory was uncertain between your men and mine; and I believe mine will have the better of it.'

Creon's defiance echoes the high disdain of Farinata in Dante's *Inferno*, and it reappears in Palemone and Arcita. Their haughty bearing ('lo sdegno / real' [2.89.1–2]) identifies them immediately as nobles. After their capture, they insist they have discharged the obligation of loyalty by taking arms, yet they clearly recognize Creon's misdeeds: 'quando / Creon contra di te l'empie arme prese, / fummo con lui, co' nostri, a sue difese' (2.88.6–8). Statius had been careful to show the uncertain loyalty that illegitimate rule commands. In his poem, the Thebans make reluctant plans to fight for Eteocles when news of the Argive advance reaches them (4.345–53); and Creon, distraught at his son's sacrifice, bluntly declares the limits of civic tolerance when Eteocles hesitates to confront Polynices (11.269–75). Boccaccio removes these qualifications. Standing with their own kind ('co' nostri'), Palemone and Arcita perform an act of fealty both to Thebes and to their troubled lineage.

The portrayal of love in Books 1 and 2 of the *Teseida* develops in connection with the theme of war, not in opposition to it. Ipolita tells the Amazons that they have taken arms against love: 'contro a Cupido avete presa guerra' (1.24.6). But their seeking refuge in the besieged castle inevitably recalls the ending of the *Roman de la rose*, where the lover finally overcomes resistance. Teseo, in fact, writes Ipolita to say that he undermines the citadel to bring down her pride (1.110.5–8), as if she were a disdainful mistress. When Ipolita dispatches emissaries to treat with Teseo, instructing them not to return without peace, Boccaccio interrupts the action to insert a stanza describing Ipolita according to the poetic conventions of the Dolce Stilnuovo. She is the 'matutina stella / o fresca rosa del mese di maggio' (1.125.3–4). She possesses the attributes of beauty, *valore*, wealth, and lineage conventionally ascribed to the love object in lyric poetry. In a way that Chaucer adopts in *Troilus and Criseyde*, Boccaccio consciously describes her as she is seen and experienced within the erotic gaze of the male speaker in lyric. Teseo literally enacts the rhetoric of lyric, falling in love with his foe when he sees her. His experience in the public moment of his entry into Thebes is a matter of interior, lyric subjectivity: 'e seco nella mente si diletta / d'aver per cotal donna tanta amara / fatica sostenuta' (1.131.3–5).

As Teseo is transformed from warrior to lover, the Amazons undergo, in turn, a reverse metamorphosis, changing from masculine warriors back into women. Anderson points out that Hypsipyle's story of the Lemnian women in Book 5 of the *Thebaid* affords some parallels with the Amazons. In that story, the sight of Jason and the other heroes prompts the return of desire in the Lemnian women (5.431–54). Statius's Amazons, though, remain obdurate (12.529–31). By contrast, Boccaccio emphasizes that the captured Amazons return to what – and such – as they were earlier: 'tornate eran quali eran davanti' (1.132.3). The qualities they reassume are the features of feminine identity established by courtly discourse: they are 'belle, leggiadre, fresche e graziose' (1.132.4). Equally important, the resumption of these qualities brings with it a model of female subjectivity. Shame, banished when they murdered their husbands, returns as they look on the Greek victors whom they are to marry. Arms thus lead to love, and love to the restoration of institutions and social structures. As the women resume the social identities they had violently rejected, the courtly world returns to its accustomed place: 'sì era del tutto transmutata / la real corte, a quel che prima' (1.133.5–6).

Boccaccio carefully elaborates arms and love in the background narrative of the *Teseida*, and those topics are closely linked to Dante's third topic, virtue (*virtus*). The immediate cause of Teseo's war with the Amazons is the transgression of gender roles and the continuing menace to men that the Amazons present. Teseo moves against Creon not, as he says, to usurp the throne and install his own son, but to restore reason and order: 'a ragion rilevare in sua gloria' (2.47.7). In each instance, Teseo endows arms with the further purposes of gaining honor, fame, and glory. He also appropriates the claims of justice to his heroic ambitions. His attack on the Amazons corrects their supposed *difetto* (1.8.3) – their sin and their loss of sexual and social identity. He wages war against Creon at the urging of the Argive widows who ask him to remedy evil ('a tale ingiuria vendicare' [2.14.8]). In his gloss to the opening of Book 2 Boccaccio allies Teseo's fame with his role as avenger: 'il quale [Teseo] in quegli tempi era famosissimo vendicatore d'ogni ingiuria' (gloss to 2.10). He thus follows Statius's dubious suggestion that Theseus recuperates the possibility of righteous fury without renewing a wholesale taste for war: 'iustas belli flammatur in iras' (*Thebaid* 12.714). The spectacle of his triumphal return to Athens, first with Ipolita and Emilia standing beside him in his chariot and later with Palemone and Arcita before him, is a theatrical display of his magnificence and righteous anger.

What lies behind the wrongs that Teseo avenges goes much deeper, however, than the immediate causes of his actions. The transgressions of gender and custom signify a threat spoken only obliquely at the beginning of the *Teseida*, yet this threat underwrites the ethics and ideology of the story for Boccaccio and Chaucer, and it explains Teseo's centrality in both poems. The Amazons rebel against subjugation to their husbands: 'alle qua' forse parea cosa fiera / esser da' maschi lor signoreggiate' (1.6.3–4). They resolve to seize *signoria*, the authority to rule (1.6.7). Ipolita names the threat they represent when she exhorts the Amazons to defend the *libertà* they have gained (1.27.8, 1.35.3, 5. 1.88.1). Indeed, her complaint against Teseo is that he comes to reimpose masculine will on their freedom (1.26). In this way, Boccaccio redeploys a concept that comes only at the cost of death in Statius. Maeon defies Eteocles's power with his suicide and earns Statius's praise as one who challenged a king openly and cleared the path for freedom: 'qui comminus ausus / vadere contemptum reges, quaque ampla veniret / libertas, sancire viam' ('thou who daredst scorn a monarch to his face, and thus hallow the path of ample freedom' [3.100–2]). Oedipus, Antigone, explains as she pleads to Eteocles for his life, has nursed a wretched freedom and wish for death: 'pridem indomito sub pectore vivit / libertas misera et saevae spes aspera mortis' ('in his untameable heart there long hath dwelt a stifled freedom and a savage longing for pitiless death' [11.714–15]). In the *Teseida*, by contrast, liberty is not a final act of defiance, but an impulse to be subjugated and reintegrated within social arrangements.

Creon represents a different but equally turbulent extreme of liberty. He enters Boccaccio's poem as the fully developed figure whose evolution from grieving father to implacable tyrant Statius so astutely sketches. In the *Thebaid*, Eteocles unwittingly foretells his rise when he claims that Creon hides ambition beneath his tears (11.300–2). Oedipus later challenges Creon as a usurper working by treachery (11. 677–9). Yet it is Fortune who installs him on the throne, and once he takes power, his transformation is immediate. Statius marks the change by applying to him the terms that earlier describe the empty motives of fraternal rivalry: 'pro blanda potestas / et sceptri malesuadus amor' (11.655–6). Creon is thus destined to re-enact the abuses of earlier rulers. To claim a measure of legitimacy, he equates his suffering with Oedipus's and thereby asserts the dubious right to continue the dynasty of Cadmus. In Boccaccio's revision, Creon's abuse consists precisely in his order not to bury the dead. Creon thereby carries personal vengeance into the public sphere. Capaneus's widow calls it 'l'aspra tirannia' (2.30.7). In Dante's moral-poetic scheme, Creon's prohibition against burial is a distortion of individual freedom and a misdirection of will.

Boccaccio resolves the Amazonian and Theban threats by reincorporating them within a corrigible authority. Teseo's conquest of the Amazons returns them to established roles and responses. Unlike Statius's captives, they are paired off with the victors willingly ('volontieri' [1.135.3]), and they resume a subordinate position and experience the emotions that go along with it. As Boccaccio portrays them, their subjectivity proceeds from the social and political structures impinging on them. Teseo's plan to marry Emilia to his cousin Acates (1.137) would complete the program of subjugation, and it promises to bring the Amazons under full dynastic control. At the same time, the terms of their subjugation allow the women a new sphere of authority within the old order. Teseo has offered the alternatives of force or negotiation all along – 'per forza o per patti' (1.91.7) – and the agreement he reaches with the Amazons exchanges his marriage with Ipolita and their feudal dependence on him for his granting them the right to live under laws administered by Ipolita (1.124). Similarly, Teseo abandons his initial impulse to kill Palemone and Arcita because he recognizes they are not guilty of betrayal – 'nullo di loro essendo traditore' (2.98.2). Condemning them to eternal imprisonment, he constrains them within a realm of aristocratic honor, service, and privilege (2.99). At the end of Book 2 of the *Teseida*, nothing stands outside his adaptive authority. There is no authentic cultural other, only authorized and defective images of a single model.

As a moral agent, Teseo is thus the mean between Amazonian liberty and Theban excess. Boccaccio portrays him as a figure of both force and deliberation.[18] Arms and negotiation are the mechanisms of his policy. Robert W. Hanning aptly describes him as 'the active principle throughout the poem,' and he is both an authorial and thematic 'emblem of controlled variousness' in a shifting world with diverse subjects.[19] On the battlefield, Teseo's bravery shades imperceptibly into the capacity to inspire and mobilize his troops, the *commilitioni*, glossed by Boccaccio as knights (*cavalieri*), whom he exhorts to undertake wars and to persevere in the face of setbacks. His own motives are glory, fame, and virtue. When he strays from those motives toward erotic pleasure ('diletto' [2.3.8]), his friend Peritoo appears, like Mercury exhorting Aeneas in *Aeneid* 4, to remind him of the priority of honor and fame over love and sexual *otium*. But arms are a necessary, not a sufficient, condition. It is through the ethical dimension of Teseo's character – his powers of moral reflection, social judgment, and political deliberation – that Boccaccio fully inscribes a medieval aristocratic ideology in his classical world. In Statius, Theseus appeals to natural and positive law to exhort his men to war against Thebes: 'terrarum leges et mundi foedera mecum / defensura cohors, dignas insumite mentes / coeptibus' ('Soldiers, who will defend with me the laws of nations and the convenants of heaven, take courage worthy of our emprise!' [12.642–4]). Boccaccio rewrites his moral attributes under the rubric of Vergilian *pietas*.[20] This quality is the one to which the squalid, distraught Argive widows appeal: 'sie pietoso' (2.33.2), they ask him. Teseo is able to penetrate through their 'abito doglioso' (2.25.4), which contrasts so dissonantly with the sumptuous display of his triumphal entry, and to recognize the social authority hidden in their grief ('la maestà nascosa' [2.36.5]). With Palemone and Arcita, too, he recognizes the status signified by their arrogance and holds contained within himself any sense of offense.

As he develops the themes of arms, love, and virtue, Boccaccio sets out a unified cultural world under Teseo's authority. Scythia, Thebes, and Athens are joined not merely through domination but by sharing a common set of conventions to regulate personal experience, social relations, and political action. As Capaneus's widow says in the *Thebaid*, the Argives are not a foreign race – 'non externa genus' (12.548). Nor are the Thebans. Teseo acts, in effect, to forestall the possibility of a cultural other, to cancel Thebanness as a form of difference as well as disorder. Yet if the two initial threats are brought inside Teseo's authority, it follows that the ones emerging later on will be internal to his totalizing control. The example of Etiocle and Polinice hovers over the end of Book 2 as a threat now located within. Meanwhile the gods, as Ipolita remarks to the Amazons (1.116–17), can withdraw their favor. In the pagan world sketched out at the beginning of the *Teseida*, human action and cultural structures occupy the foreground, while the gods and destiny remain at a distance and human passions are absorbed internally to an aristocratic code.

Chaucer elects not to follow Boccaccio's example of recounting these two long prefatory episodes to his story. Nonetheless, the background accounts that open the Knight's Tale bear the trace of his critical reading of Books 1 and 2 of the *Teseida*, and they reflect his understanding of antiquity through Boccaccio's poem. He grasps the social and political threat posed by the Amazons, remarking twice that Theseus conquers 'the regne of Femenye' (I.866, 877). He recognizes the *Rose* as the literary subtext of Teseo's encirclement of the Amazons, referring to 'how asseged was Ypolita' (I.881). Capaneus's widow accurately identifies the qualities that define Creon – 'Fulfild of ire and of iniquitee' (I.940). Her reference to his 'tirannye' (I.941) echoes Boccaccio's phrase 'l'aspra tirannia' (2.30.7). Chaucer also follows Boccaccio's lead in expressing Theseus's attributes through aristocratic terms. As in the *Teseida*, Theseus is initially described as a warrior, and Chaucer credits his achievements to wisdom and chivalry (I.865). Fame, too, remains a determining motive in Theseus's decision to aid the Argive women; he acts to avenge them so that 'al the peple of Grece sholde speke / How Creon was of Theseus yserved' (I.962–3). Chaucer carries Boccaccio's inscription of Teseo within Vergilian *pietas* in a new direction, though, transforming a classical virtue of fidelity to custom into a medieval personal and aristocratic attribute. Evadne entreats him to let '[s]om drope of pitee, thurgh thy gentillesse' (I.920) fall on the supplicant women, and Theseus responds to their plea with 'herte pitous' (I.953). Chaucer also suggests an indwelling tension in Theseus's character by describing the figure of the Minotaur on his banner. There is no corresponding passage in Boccaccio. The apparent source in Statius (12.665–71) is the figure on the boss of Theseus's shield, which depicts his earlier conquests to the Thebans. In Chaucer, the symbol points to the darker history that Theseus himself carries, the story of Ariadne recounted in the *Legend of Good Women*. Chaucer thus takes from the opening books of the *Teseida* a sense of the 'hidden story' and adds his own suggestion that Boccaccio's resolution of Statius produces its own problems and contradictions.

Chaucerian revision

The changes Chaucer makes to the *Teseida* in writing the Knight's Tale have long been seen as evidence of his artistic superiority to Boccaccio. The guiding principles for his changes seem to be aesthetic symmetry and narrative economy. While following Boccaccio's narrative outline, Chaucer arranges the story to create a formal pattern in which episodes balance one another structurally.[21] Arcita is the main protagonist of Boccaccio's story, but Palamon and Arcite are equally prominent in the Knight's Tale. Their rivalry occurs early on in the story, and it juxtaposes idealistic and naturalistic conceptions of love. Chaucer adds a description of Diana's temple to balance the descriptions of Mars's and Venus's temples in Boccaccio and to give a rare space for feminine subjectivity.[22] In the climactic tournament, he pairs Emetreus with Arcite as a counter to Lygurge's support for Palamon. Correspondences between the gods and the human characters are drawn out in parallel hierarchies.[23] At the same time that he balances structure and characterization, Chaucer rearranges other important narrative details. Saturn resolves the conflicting promises made to Palamon and Arcite, which Venus and Mars negotiate between themselves in Boccaccio.[24] The flight of Arcita's soul and his dismissal of worldly glory are suppressed. The Boethian elements already present in Boccaccio assume heightened prominence and furnish the conceptual frame of the tale. But in reconceiving Boccaccio's topics, Chaucer introduces differences that suggest more than an aesthetic reformulation. Boccaccio uses arms, love, and virtue to contain the turbulent and radically unstable world of Statian heroism within a medieval aristocratic code. As Winthrop Wetherbee argues, the chivalric program expressed through romance suppresses or marginalizes the dark side of classical subject matter.[25] Chaucer employs the same topics to point up the tensions that persist within and despite Boccaccio's strategy of control and ideological domestication. In the end, he creates a poem with greater order and still more questions.

In the Knight's Tale war remains a distinct, if muted, threat until the very end of the poem. Though the Theban dynasty, like the city, is devastated in the background narrative, Palamon and Arcite represent the possibility of a genealogical bridging that would restore Theban eminence and potentially ally Thebes with Scythia. After Perotheus secures Arcite's release from prison, Palamon speculates that Arcite may gather a Theban force to 'make a werre so sharp on this citee / That by som aventure or some tretee / Thow mayst have hire to lady and to wyf' (I.1287–9). He envisions the same two means – arms or negotiation – that Teseo uses as his instruments of policy in the *Teseida*. Escaping Theseus's prison, he intends to act precisely as he feared Arcite might: 'thanne wolde he take his way / To Thebes-ward, his freendes for to preye / On Theseus to helpe him to werreye' (I.1482–4). When Theseus halts the combat in the grove, he forestalls this political threat by making Palamon and Arcite his friends (I.1823–4), but he stops short of Teseo's strategy of restoring their castles and possessions and thereby making Palamon and Arcite in effect his vassals (*Teseida* 5.105). Indeed, one of the issues for the parliament called at the end of the poem is to establish political alliances and 'have fully of Thebans obeisaunce'

(I.2974), just as Palamon 'wolde have fully possessioun / Of Emelye' (I.2242–3).

Within this political framework, arms are represented by either savage struggle or ceremonial spectacle. Arcite wants to observe chivalric etiquette in his duel with Palamon, but their strife devolves to the brutishness that Statius originally made the defining quality of heroic fury. Read against the Theban intertext, the clichés of chivalric combat acquire a particular and unsettling resonance:

> Thou myghtest wene that this Palamon
> In his fightyng were a wood leon,
> And as a crueel tigre was Arcite;
> As wilde bores gonne they to smyte,
> That frothen whit as foom for ire wood.
> Up to the ancle foghte they in hir blood.
>
> (I.1655–60)

Wetherbee observes, 'The setting in which they fight, up to their ankles in gore, is a version of the archetypal Theban landscape, the Cadmaean field saturated with the blood of the dragon who had destroyed Cadmus's original colonists, and that of the warriors who had sprung again from Cadmus's sowing of the dragon's teeth, only to all but destroy themselves in civil conflict.'[26] Theseus encounters Arcite and Palamon fighting 'as it were bores two' (I.1699) and chastises them for fighting without a supervising authority: 'Withouten juge or oother officere, / As it were in a lystes roially' (I.1712–13). John Lydgate reveals the significance of this encounter when he echoes Chaucer's phrase in the *Siege of Thebes*: 'with-oute Iuge' (line 1366). There the phrase describes the battle of Tydeus and Polynices at Adrastus's palace, the *nuda pugna* (*Thebaid* 1.413) of two wretched exiles – one already a fratricide, the other about to become one – who quickly join in friendship and the brotherhood of military adventure.

The Theban references in these scenes point toward what is immediately at stake, but the full meaning of arms as a poetic topic becomes apparent in the description of Mars's barren, cold temple. In the gloss to his description (7.30–8), Boccaccio identifies Mars with the irascible appetite that is aroused by losing or not having delightful things, and he makes anger the dominant passion. Chaucer revises Boccaccio's description by giving concrete detail to the allegorical attributes and insisting on the murderousness and civil discord that attend war. A history of violence, he suggests, is written in the stars for not only common men but also emperors and lovers. Elizabeth Salter remarks that the inclusion of 'so many images of casual horror' with conventional martial images 'curiously webs the heroic with the pathetic.'[27]

Theseus tries to redirect these elements by giving them a purpose and ideological function. The tournament he establishes ostensibly modifies violence in the service of love, as Palamon and Arcite settle their judicial claims for possession of Emily aided by a hundred knights, each 'redy to darreyne hire by bataille' (I.1853). These knights are drawn, like Teseo and his men in Books 1 and 2 of the *Teseida*, by the promise of fame: 'For every wight that lovede chivalrye / And wolde, his thankes, han a passant name, / Hath preyed that he myghte been of that game' (I.2106–8). The combatants stand in for every knight who loves 'paramours' (I.2112). In the verbal portraits of Lygurge and Emetreus and the visual display of chivalry before the tournament, Chaucer presents arms allied with desire as an aesthetic spectacle: 'It were a lusty sighte for to see' (I.2116). Amplifying Boccaccio's suggestion, he has Theseus try to transform battle into game and ludic contest. The rivalry of Palamon and Arcite, which Boccaccio had earlier styled an 'amorosa battaglia' (*Teseida* 7.8), is acted out in Theseus's theatre for the benefit of the chivalric world; Emily is the accident and pretext. And despite Arcite's misadventure, Theseus returns to Athens from the tourney '[w]ith alle blisse and greet solempnitee' (I.2702) and treats 'eyther syde ylik as ootheres brother' (I.2734); their differences in allegiance fade before their common identity. The funeral and games subsequently held for Arcite are a continuing part of the social pageant of arms enacted by 'the Grekes' and not the close of a discrete episode.

The most significant feature of Chaucer's treatment of arms is the displacement of war and violence into symbolic action. Whatever threat Palamon or Arcite might pose as Thebans is contained within Athenian aristocratic ceremony. A figure like Lygurge may be a subtle reminder of the unstable Theban history that lies behind the celebration of chivalric display. But Chaucer largely diverts the lessons of his literary predecessors. In Boccaccio, for instance, Arcita reminds Palemone of Thebes's internecine conflicts (*Teseida* 5.55–9) and seeks to make peace with him before their duel so as to avoid a renewal of the fraternal strife between Eteocle and Polinice (5.63). Before the tournament, they in fact reestablish 'buona pace / e l'amistà antica' (6.6.1–2). In Chaucer, Arcite complains, 'ybroght is to confusioun / The blood roial of Cadme and Amphioun' (I.1545–6). Though Palamon overhears him, the allusion utterly passes him by and has no force. The full critique of Dante's *armorum probitas* is to be found in the temple of Mars, whose lessons are hidden from the characters in Chaucer's poem but made explicit to his readers.

Much as Chaucer displaces arms to slaughter and ceremony, he deconstructs the aristocratic conventions of love. Boccaccio offers an ambivalent mix of lyric idealization and misogyny, but Chaucer goes to the foundations of aristocratic desire, which are the power of the erotic gaze and the dynamic of masculine rivalry. The key episode is the first sight of Emily, a scene significantly rewritten from the *Teseida*. Up to this point in the Knight's Tale, Palamon and Arcite have been two versions of a single figure. Discovered in a pile of bodies on the battlefield, lying side by side under the same heraldic device, they are cousins born of royal mothers. Their shared identity endures until they find the same object of desire – that is, find someone different from themselves as each is mirrored in the other and identified by the same sign ('Bothe in oon armes' [I.1012]).

Chaucer plots the exact moment at which this common identity splits into adversarial opposition. When Palamon sees Emily, the sigh he utters captures the last syllable of her name (Emelya / A, [I.1077–8]) in a small imitation of his desire to possess her fully. Palamon enacts, like Teseo, the rhetoric of the love lyric, for the sight of Emily leaves him '[a]s though he stongen were unto the herte' (I.1079). As Boccaccio makes clear in his explanation of love (gloss to 7.50–66), desire is appropriately expressed in the imagery of penetration. Arcite mistakenly consoles Palamon, thinking he bemoans their imprisonment, and he offers a proleptic version of the Boethian wisdom that Theseus will announce after the poem's tragic reversal. But when Arcite suffers the same effect from beholding Emily, Palamon regards him 'dispitously' and asks whether he speaks of her 'in ernest or in pley' (I.1125). This sharp differentiation revises Boccaccio's account in several important respects. Chaucer has Palamon see Emily before Arcite and intensifies the reversal of feeling in the two princes by marking it as a sudden shift from friendship to enmity. By contrast, Boccaccio protracts the scene and has the two lovers comfort one another with words: 'Così ragionan li due nuovi amanti, / e l'un l'altro conforta nel parlare' (3.26.1–2). It is not until after Arcita returns disguised as Penteo and is overheard by Palemone's servant complaining of his love that Palemone gives in to jealousy. Even then Boccaccio makes Tisiphone the cause for repeating and protracting the fraternal strife of Thebes (5.13).

Chaucer's difference from Boccaccio might be described as a preference for immediate effect and dramatic economy over psychological process and mythographic amplitude. By condensing Boccaccio's richly

nuanced account, Chaucer has placed 'al the love of Arcite and Pale-
mon' in the foreground of the tale. Consequently, the terms designating
their relationship – 'the seurete and the bond' (I.1604), 'trouthe'
(I.1610), and 'felaweshipe' (I.1626) – cannot contain the desire they
are supposed to regulate. Among recent critics, Anderson has stressed
the correspondence between the will to power in Statius and the lovers'
rivalry in the Knight's Tale.[28] The relationship is framed, however, as a
proportion rather than a simple equation, for a middle term brings arms
and love into significant relation. The desire to rule impoverished
Thebes is equivalent to fighting to recover the bodies of Tydeus, Polynices, and the Argive dead; possession of the corpses is equivalent, in
turn, to possession of the unobtainable beloved, for those fallen heroes
are denied entry to the underworld and condemned to wander un-
accommodated. Arcite conveys both the fury and hopelessness of such
struggle in another telling comparison:

> 'We stryve as dide the houndes for the boon;
> They foughte al day, and yet hir part was noon.
> Ther cam a kyte, whil that they were so wrothe,
> And baar awey the boon bitwixe hem bothe.'
>
> (I.1177–80)

For the lovers, the pressure of desire intensifies beyond the personal
relations secured by fellowship, the most sociable of Chaucer's terms.
Arcite, pressing his claim to love Emily despite Palamon's seeing her first,
associates love with natural law and asserts its power to supersede human
conventions: 'And therfore positif lawe and swich decree / Is broken al
day for love in ech degree' (I.1167–8). Love thus puts at risk the social and
cultural forms built on nature. As Boitani observes, Chaucer's characters
are profoundly isolated from each other.[29] Arcite may profess that love is
a form of natural law that supervenes convention, but it produces narrow
determinism at the personal level and disruption of the social covenants
that allow societies to escape their history: 'Ech man for hymself, ther is
noon oother' (I.1182). At the same time, love transforms Palamon and
Arcite into mediators of each other's desire. Exiled, Arcite imagines that
the prison is a 'paradys' (I.1237) that may eventually allow Palamon to
win Emily. Palamon meanwhile concedes the advantage to Arcite, whom
he thinks may be able to take Emily by arms or force a settlement that
leads to marriage. Though they proclaim the spontaneity of their love,
each operates through the agency of the other. They dwell not on the
ostensible object of desire but on their rivalry.[30]

In his portrayal of Emily, Chaucer makes a second and equally important revision. Boccaccio's Emilia is a figure of erotic ambivalence, both in
her actions and the motives ascribed to her by the narrator. She initially
goes to the garden out of her own inclinations ('di propria natura'), but
the narrator hastens to assure us that she is not impelled by love: 'non
che d'amore alcun fosse constretta' (3.8.3). She hears Palemone's sigh,
knows what it means, and delights in being desired; the narrator asserts,
however, that she is unready for complete love (3.19). Taking pains to
adorn herself, she returns to the garden time and again alone or in
company, and so becomes a conscious actor in a pageant of display,
surveillance, and seduction. Boccaccio ascribes her motive not to love
but feminine vanity (3.30).

By contrast, Chaucer is careful to suppress the erotic texture of Boccaccio's portrayal and the limited, though still real, autonomy it confers.[31] He omits, for instance, any trace of Boccaccio's later portrait of
the fifteen-year-old Emilia, with its hints of sexual pleasure and its
overstated reticence about describing her private parts (12.59–63).[32]
Chaucer also reduces and defers Boccaccio's misogynistic critique.
Emily is unaware of the Theban knights who watch her in the garden
from their adjacent prison.[33] When Theseus discovers Arcite and Pale-
mon battling in the grove, he makes this point an ironic reproof of their
love, while professing love's irresistible power:

> But this is yet the beste game of alle,
> That she for whom they han this jolitee
> Kan hem therfore as muche thank as me.
> She woot namoore of al this hoote fare,
> By God, than woot a cokkow or an hare!
> (I.1806–10)

In the first half of the Knight's Tale, then, Emily exists chiefly as an
object of desire, captured first by Theseus as part of the Amazonian
booty and now awaiting her final disposition according to the outcome
of a tournament whose major cultural anxiety is to avoid 'destruccioun /
To gentil blood' (I.2538–9), that is, the interruption of male genealogy.
At issue is not the intrinsic quality of love but the mechanism of exchange.

Other features of the Knight's Tale reveal Chaucer's focus on the
troubled effects of love. The Knight describes Arcite's desire as *amor
hereos*, a mania caused by melancholy 'in his celle fantastik' (I.1376).
Palamon undergoes a comparable 'martirdom' (I.1460) in prison. The

scenes depicted in Venus's temple deal not so much with desire as a concupiscible appetite (Boccaccio's definition in his gloss to *Teseida* 7.50–66) as with the somatic effects of love:

> First in the temple of Venus maystow se
> Wroght on the wal, ful pitous to biholde,
> The broken slepes, and the sikes colde,
> The sacred teeris, and the waymentynge,
> The firy strokes of the desirynge
> That loves servantz in this lyf enduren. . . .
> (I.1918–23)

Like Boccaccio, Chaucer fills this description with allegorical personages who represent facets of erotic indulgence, but he replaces Boccaccio's mythological examples with a short roster of biblical and classical figures undone by the power of Venus. The lesson conveyed by the *ekphrasis* is that love operates as a form of necessity.

The resolution to Palamon and Arcite's rivalry goes still further toward questioning love in the aristocratic contexts that Boccaccio imposed on his classical materials. Palamon's prayer to Venus explicitly rejects fame and glory. In the *Teseida*, this amounts to a cancellation of Teseo's heroism and acceptance of the sexual *otium* against which Peritoo warns Teseo. In Chaucer, it is a repudiation of a larger social structure, the chivalry gathered for the tournament. Palamon envisions an Ovidian heroism and prays Venus, 'I wolde have fully possessioun / Of Emelye, and dye in thy servyse' (I.2242–3). The first request is taken from Boccaccio: 'tanto ti priego, ciò è che io sia / in possession di Emilia, donna mia' (7.45.7–8; cf. 7.46.7). What such possession really means, beyond the fantasy of desire fully sated, is never explained, and it remains problematic in both the Knight's Tale and *Troilus and Criseyde*. The second item, death in Venus's service, has no precedent in Boccaccio, and it obliquely forecasts Arcite's downfall.[34]

Emily's response to the lovers' desire, deferred throughout Chaucer's poem, is registered only at the moment of Arcite's apparent victory when she casts a 'freendlich ye' on him. Chaucer mentions her version of the erotic gaze in order to inject a misogynistic aside: 'For wommen, as to speken in comune, / Thei folwen alle the favour of Fortune' (I.2681–2).[35] His source is a longer passage in the *Teseida* (8.124–8) which describes Emilia's sudden desire and prepares for the warning to readers of Arcita's epitaph not to squander heroic prowess for love: 'Qual se', io fui; / e per Emilia usando il mio valore / mori': dunque ti guarda da amore' (11.91.6–8). Boccaccio's ambivalence about love may explain, too, Arcite's final words to Emily. Chaucer changes them from Boccaccio's 'A Dio, Emilia' (10.113.7) to a more enigmatic 'Mercy, Emelye' (I.2808), a cry for pity and perhaps a bitter word of thanks.[36] Success in love, like prowess in arms, confers only uncertain victory.

The full significance of arms and love emerges in the broader metaphysical and moral framework of the Knight's Tale, which at once focuses and deepens the topic of virtue. As we have seen, Chaucer draws out the tacit contradictions of Boccaccio's appropriation of Dante's topics. He shows how Boccaccio's effort to repair Statius's world by bringing it within medieval aristocratic conventions is only partially successful. Boccaccio installs Teseo as the moral center of his poem, endowing him with the qualities of martial valor, erotic restraint, political judgment, and personal piety. Chaucer imagines, however, a more complex sphere of moral action, at least for male aristocratic subjects.[37] He challenges not Theseus's centrality but the supposition that virtue, thematized by Dante as the direction of the will, is the decisive element. The Knight's Tale locates Theseus and the other characters within a framework of necessity that calls into question the extent to which they can authentically give a direction to the will. Equally important, however, it shows how choice can reflect a real, if limited, heroism.

Chaucer places the topic of *virtus* far more insistently within a metaphysics than does Boccaccio. Fate, Fortune, and the gods play major roles in the *Teseida*, to be sure. But as Salter notes, they are not developed as thematic interests.[38] Boitani contends that Boccaccio never decides which of these forces is pre-eminent: 'in Book IV it seems to be Fate (or divine Providence) that takes the lead, in Book VI, it is Fortune's turn; in Books VII and IX it falls to the gods.'[39] The Boethian principles that Chaucer found inconsistently applied in the *Teseida* provide a means for establishing a provisional framework of understanding in the Knight's Tale. Chaucer does not impose a Boethian resolution so much as rearrange the various perspectives on choice and action that Boccaccio had already offered into a coherent perspective. Moreover, the view he finally sets out in Theseus's First Mover speech comes at the end of a process that reproduces the partial understandings characters achieve in the story.

The efforts to grasp events throughout the Knight's Tale are, like Troilus's famous speech on predestination (*Troilus and Criseyde* 4.953–1078), incomplete, misdirected, or confused. Arcite's consolation of Palamon when he utters his sigh at first seeing Emily invokes Fortune,

Saturn, and the stars (I.1081–91). Arcite urges him to bear their imprisonment patiently because there is no other choice:

> Fortune hath yeven us this adversitee.
> Som wikke aspect or disposicioun
> Of Saturne, by som constellacioun,
> Hath yeven us this, although we hadde it sworn;
> So stood the hevene whan that we were born.
>
> (I.1086–90)

When Arcite is freed, he bewails the turning of Fortune that takes him away from the sight of Emily and voices a wisdom he only partially absorbs: 'We seken faste after felicitee, / But we goon wrong ful often, trewely' (I.1266–7). In a parallel speech, Palamon chastises the 'crueel goddes' (I.1303) for releasing Arcite. Like Boethius at the beginning of the *Consolation*, he questions justice and providence: 'What governance is in this prescience, / That giltelees tormenteth innocence?' (I.1313–14).[40] He sees himself concretely at the mercy of two deterministic forces among the gods – the implacable anger of Saturn and Juno and the power of Venus, which leaves him victim to jealousy.

The lovers' confusions about the forces impinging on them are paralleled by the uncertainty with which the Knight surrounds decisive moments in his story. Mercury appears to Arcite with a message whose exquisite ambiguity can be appreciated only after his tragic death: 'To Atthenes shaltou wende, / Ther is thee shapen of thy wo an ende' (I.1391–2). His victory in the tournament ends his woe as a lover, while his unforeseen death conveys the irony that desire has both its object and release in death; each is the 'ende' or final cause of love's woe. The point is made again as Arcite lies dying: 'Now with his love, now in his colde grave, / Allone, withouten any compaignye' (I.2778–9). By suppressing the scene of Arcita's apotheosis and his dismissal of worldly goods, Chaucer has preserved the ambiguity, just as he preserves the ambiguity of Arcite's final 'Mercy, Emelye.' Palamon breaks out of prison for uncertain causes – '[w]ere it by aventure or destynee' (I.1465). Arcite is led to confront him in the grove by the power of Fortune, which he in no way grasps (I.1488–90). Theseus discovers them, guided by providence, '[t]he destinee, ministre general, / That executeth in the world over al / The purveiaunce that God hath seyn biforn' (I.1663–5). The original passage in Boccaccio refers to Fortune (*Teseida* 6.1.1), and Boccaccio's phrasing recalls, in turn, Dante's Fortune (*Inferno* 7.73–96) rather than destiny.[41] As he plans the tournament to resolve their dispute, Theseus places the outcome under necessity: 'ech of yow shal have his destynee / As hym is shape' (I.1842–3). Egeus's words of consolation after Arcite's death, directed in the *Teseida* to Palemone, who cannot hear them for his grief, echo Mercury's dark message and offer cold comfort: 'This world nys but a thurghfare ful of wo, / And we been pilgrymes, passynge to and fro. / Deeth is an ende of every worldly soore' (I.2847–9).[42] By the end of the tale, then, the moral dimension of choice has been rendered deeply problematic by necessity, chance, and human misperception.

Against this background, Theseus's First Mover speech addresses not just the significance of arms and love as literary topics but also the framework in which choice can be authentic and meaningful. Here as elsewhere, Chaucer revises the *Teseida* to create a different formulation. Teseo follows the rhetoric of consolation by beginning with the commonplace that all men must die (12.6.1–3). Chaucer's opening substitutes a broader view of metaphysical harmony for Boccaccio's narrow determinism and chivalric orientation: 'The Firste Moevere of the cause above, / Whan he first made the faire cheyne of love, / Greet was th'effect, and heigh was his entente' (I.2987–89). The passage is based largely on Boethius's extraordinary meter extolling the power of divine love to forge unity out of diverse elements at various levels of reality – the heavens, the earth, social life, and the individual (*Boece* 2.m8). Within this central theme of beneficent creation, Chaucer elaborates the notion that Providence has set limits on creaturely existence (*Boece* 4.pr6) and that every part derives from a divine whole as it moves from being to becoming (*Boece* 3.pr10) – 'of a thyng that parfit is and stable, / Descendynge so til it be corrumpable' (I.3009–10). The important stipulation, which he adds from Book 4, prose 6, is that 'speces of thynges and progressiouns / Shullen enduren by successiouns' (I.3013–14). Providence operates, that is, at the level of the species, setting limits within which individual choice and action are possible. There remains a margin of liberty and free will within these limits, but it operates in one temporal direction: 'mowe they yet tho dayes wel abregge' (I.2999).

The second change Chaucer introduces is to reframe the meaning of Theseus's famous admonition, 'Thanne is it wysdom, as it thynketh me, / To maken vertu of necessitee, / And take it weel that we may nat eschue' (I.3041–3). In Boccaccio, Teseo proposes that fame can redeem honor regardless of how one dies. With this in mind, he counsels, 'E però far della necessitate / virtù, quando bisogna, è sapienza, / e il contrario è chiara vanitate' (12.11.1–3). Seeking to approximate classical values, he argues that fame is the only remedy against the brute necessity of death, and he recommends this wisdom to Arcita's mourners, because they face the same predicament as the dead lover. We live sorrowfully, he asserts, within contingency ('viviam di cose sempre contingenti' [12.11.8]), a term by which Boccaccio specifically means human mortality (gloss to 12.11.8). Chaucer makes decisive changes to the sequence of Teseo's argument. He defers Teseo's appeal to fame and inserts in its place a passage (I.3035–40) that treats the necessity of death as an aspect of providence rather than a limit to be bypassed through worldly renown. In this way, Theseus's admonition is not only practical advice in the face of necessity, but a call to piety – 'whoso gruccheth ought, he dooth folye, / And rebel is to hym that al may gye' (I.3045–6). Taken by itself, the admonition has the force of proverb, but Chaucer's motif of piety returns it to some of its traditional contexts in Patristic and medieval religious thought.[43] Augustine, for example, says that God made man with free will, constraining him to neither virtue nor necessity.[44] Bernard of Clairvaux emphasizes the connection between virtue and will when he says, 'fac de necessitate virtutem, quia nulla est virtus sine convenientia voluntatis.'[45] Though Theseus, like Teseo, inhabits a pagan universe and identifies Jupiter as 'prince and cause of alle thyng' (I.3036), he envisions a metaphysical framework that nonetheless reaches beyond the classical topics that Teseo deploys in his consolation speech.

In criticism of the Knight's Tale, Theseus's speech has long been a key to interpretation. Its assertion of providential order in the face of tragedy and unforeseen reversals expresses a central theme that Charles Muscatine has made the dominant reading of the poem.[46] Recent critics have challenged the view that the tale celebrates order and serves not only a thematic but also an elevated ideological purpose. David Aers, for example, emphasizes the role of violence in creating and maintaining order. The tale, he contends, 'is a critical, often highly ironic, exploration of secular rule, its forms of power and its uses of language.'[47] V.A. Kolve observes that Theseus 'does not stand outside the suffering and confusion he attempts to declare rational and purposive.'[48] Lee Patterson argues that Chaucer's critique is directed not against order but against chivalry itself, which he sees as a form of public selfhood and false consciousness that 'forecloses self-reflection and critical distance'; it is 'a failure of self-understanding' that leaves its subjects oscillating between helplessness and unconstrained desire.[49]

Set against the doctrine it proclaims, Theseus's speech clearly does not escape the contradictions that Chaucer develops throughout the poem.[50] The paradoxical determinism claimed for love is never explained, so love remains an irresistible force, while lovers are held responsible for their actions and bear the consequences of their choices. Jupiter is identified as the First Mover, but he, like Venus, must accept that Saturn will impose a solution through violence.[51] A First Mover, in any case, does not explain the reason behind Arcite's death.[52] The culmination of Thesus's speech is the marriage of Palamon and Emily, which Chaucer greatly elaborates from Boccaccio's scene in which the various kings return home and leave Palemone 'in gioia e in diporto' (12.83.4) to make love with Emilia seven times on their wedding night. Theseus's own admonition to 'make of sorwes two / O parfit joye, lastynge everemo' (I.3071–2) is punctuated by an appeal to pragmatic social reality, for he reminds Emily that Palamon is 'a kynges brother sone, pardee' (I.3084). The problems of such accommodation remained visible enough for Lydgate to echo the scene in his own answering *Canterbury Tale*, where the Theban nobles prevail on Jocasta to marry Oedipus '[t]he worthy Cyté to kepen and gouerne' (*Siege of Thebes* 772).[53]

The speech disappoints if we expect it to serve as a summation rather than a frame for moral understanding. Chaucer inherited the subject of virtue from Boccaccio, introduced some hard-won philosophical clarification to the surrounding framework, and created a sense of narrative closure that remains contingent and provisional. H. Marshall Leicester, Jr., has rightly called this 'conventional or social closure, in which the audience agrees, often tacitly, to act as if a resolution has taken place when in fact it has not.'[54] Theseus's speech aims at no more than claiming a territory in which the direction of the will can be a meaningful human act, even in the face of providence, destiny, and Fortune. Constrained by desire and acting out a tragic pattern visible only from retrospect, Palamon and Arcite nevertheless exercise control over the will by choosing to act within the limits that contain them. Their virtue, and indeed their heroism, consists in acting in good faith with limited knowledge before unimaginable forces. In this way, Chaucer presents an alternative to the boundless passions and repetitions of Statian history and to the totalizing aristocratic codes of the *Teseida*. He recovers the margin of liberty that comes at the cost of death in Statius and that Boccaccio recognizes but suppresses at the start of his poem. The classical world that Chaucer invents under the sign of Statius and through Boccaccio stands beyond grace and redemption. It is a world finished but unresolved, with silences and occlusions that challenge its heroic claims, yet it remains full of human and moral significance.

2
The Twin Necessity of *Troilus and Criseyde*

Troilus and Criseyde is the poem in which Chaucer makes his most profound exploration of classical antiquity, and it is the one in which he works most closely with Boccaccio's text. The connection is scarcely accidental. As A.C. Spearing and John Burrow point out, Boccaccio showed the means to represent private behavior and inner lives – in short, inwardness and subjectivity – within the ancient world.[1] Scholars like Sanford Meech and more recently Barry Windeatt have mapped the multiple levels of Chaucer's invention of Boccaccio's *Filostrato* in the *Troilus* – from word-by-word translation to shifts in emphasis to the addition, suppression, and resituating of material.[2] The wider significance of Chaucer's rewriting of Boccaccio has been debated intensely since C.S. Lewis's famous formulation that Chaucer 'medievalized' the *Filostrato*.[3] It is one indication of how much medievalization can imply that the term covers not only Lewis's sense that Chaucer wrote a rhetorical, didactic story of courtly love but also later views that he did quite the opposite, that his classical sources had already done the same, and that Chaucer's contemporaries would have condemned or countenanced his love theme.[4]

The debate on whether *Troilus and Criseyde* is a poem of courtly love has largely obscured the first point of Lewis's influential essay, on which the others depend. Chaucer, says Lewis, approached the *Filostrato* 'as an "Historial" poet contributing to the story of Troy' (p. 19). By this he means that Chaucer's invention of antiquity is directed to an audience fascinated with 'that whole world of story which makes this drama's context' (p. 20), especially its historico-mythic texture. In the *Filostrato*, Boccaccio portrays antiquity as a background, a tapestry of war, parliaments, human sociability, family, and aristocratic pleasures. Antique lovers serve, in turn, as a partial allegory for the poet and his fictive mistress. Chaucer, I shall argue, shows antiquity not just as an analogue for courtly life, but as a cultural world buckling under pressure. As in the Knight's Tale, he reconceives Boccaccio's text to examine the central problems of destiny and choice in a world where history has already taken shape. At the same time, he takes up a parallel problem that the Knight's Tale raises but does not interrogate closely, while the *Teseida* negotiates it through the rhetoric of love lyric – namely, the deterministic character of love. Like Palamon and Arcite, Troilus is seemingly constrained by love's power. Like Emily, Criseyde is the object of unsought attachment that nonetheless transforms her resistance and complicates her sense of self. Chaucer's poem places its ancient characters in their most significant predicaments when they confront the twin necessity of historical and erotic determinism.

Historical determinism and historical alternatives

One of the most striking features of Chaucer's reconception of the *Filostrato* is the inscription of Troilus's rise and fall within the larger arc of Trojan history. Boccaccio presents the course of the war as a backdrop to the love affair between Troiolo and Criseida. As Giulia Natali points out, Calcas's escape and Troiolo's death provide a brief opening and rapid conclusion to the poem; the only battle described in any detail is marked off grammatically and stylistically from the main love topic.[5] Boccaccio focuses on an interior realm that remains separate and largely cut off from the public sphere of history, even as exterior events bear on it. In a scene that Chaucer omits, Troiolo faints when he hears the parliament's decision to exchange Criseida for Antenore, and Priamo, Ettore, and his brothers try to revive and comfort him (*Filostrato* 4.18–21). Here the kingdom is transparently dynastic, and dynasty translates directly to family and intimacy.

The private and social space inhabited by Boccaccio's fictional characters is identical to that occupied by the 'gentili uomini e le vaghe donne' of his 'Proemio' – those young aristocrats at leisure, also fictional, who debate the initial love question of the *Filostrato*'s frame tale and ostensibly provide a context for Boccaccio's composing the poem and sending it to Filomena. Their literary counterparts, in turn, are the company of young nobles withdrawing from the midday heat to debate Love Questions in Book 4 of the *Filocolo* and the *brigata* escaping Florence to Fiesole in the *Decameron*. The space reserved for their wit and eroticized banter stands apart and distinct from the larger forces around them. It is simultaneously the space of art and imagination, which play out in a poetic interim bracketed by the outside historical events of the narrative.

Though Chaucer creates a private, interior realm for eros and art, he allows no comparable sense of withdrawal in his poem. To be sure, private locales abound in Troy.[6] Mark Lambert stresses 'the life of peace' within the besieged city and Leonard Michael Koff the 'portable places' that the lovers re-create for themselves.[7] Despite these locales and the alternating lyric and narrative moments staged in them, there is no escape from the overall historical pattern that overshadows the course of Troilus and Criseyde's love. The cycle of Troilus's 'double sorwe... [f]ro wo to wele, and after out of joie' (1.1–4) mirrors the epicycles of Trojan and Greek advantage on the battlefield and spans the decisive period in which Hector and Troilus die, leaving the city at the Greeks' mercy, without its chief defenders, and thereby vulnerable to the treason of Aeneas and Antenor, which causes its downfall. As critics since George Lyman Kittredge have argued, civic destiny parallels individual fate.[8] This identification of the town and its prince, as Stephen Barney and Martin Stevens note, extends to common poetic images for each.[9]

By aligning political and personal destiny, Chaucer returns to the predicament that ends the Knight's Tale. His Trojan characters, like their Theban precursors, must act in the face of a necessity which they only partially apprehend.[10] The aesthetic and philosophical problem is complicated, however, by the narrative structure of *Troilus and Criseyde*. In the Knight's Tale, the narrator enters his story only as he makes structural transitions.[11] But in *Troilus and Criseyde*, Chaucer's narrator comes to assume a prominence equal to his characters. He writes his poem from the vantage point of an historian who already knows the outcome yet empathizes with the characters caught in the web of events. The effect of this narrative structure is most clearly described in Morton W. Bloomfield's account of the narrator's position: 'As a faithful historian, he cannot evade the rigidity of decisive events – the given.' Because events occurred in the past, the narrator 'cannot change the elements of his story.' He consequently operates at a distance from his tale, and this narrative distance is the 'artistic correlative' of predestination.[12]

Modern readings of the poem have developed two further points Bloomfield makes – the narrator's countervailing sympathy for his characters and the parallels between the narrator and the reader. Winthrop Wetherbee has given the most nuanced recent account of the narrator's attachment to the characters and his eventual separation from them, while Donald R. Howard rightly observes that the narrator models what his readers think of the pagan world.[13] Yet the strong sense of determinism invested in the poem's narrative structure remains a fundamental problem for Chaucer's representation of the private world of antiquity. At first glance, the poem seems to allow the slimmest of margins for autonomy and human choice, hence for the moral complexity of its story. Scholarship has portrayed the poem as deeply fatalistic, both in its view of pagan history and in the philosophical terms it brings to the story for medieval and modern readers. Walter Clyde Curry long ago announced that 'an absolutely inescapable necessity governs the progress of the story.'[14] But it is clear that Chaucer does not propose a univocal determinism as the thematic counterpart of Troilus and Criseyde's love. Determinism is the shape of history in Chaucer's poem, and multiple forces bear on it. The literary tradition of Trojan history accepts alternatives to the final pattern of necessity. The philosophical system that Chaucer elaborates from Boccaccio preserves free will within providence and destiny. The poem itself presents its defining historical frame in a way that preserves a place for intention in public and personal destiny.

The chronicle history of Troy claims its origins and authority in Dares and Dictys but finds its most influential expression in Benoît de Sainte-Maure and Guido delle Colonne. Within its overall pattern of tragic destiny, the story may be, as Lee Patterson has argued strongly, an unreadable history, one whose lessons remain undecipherable to its principal actors and either banal or romantic to its later redactors.[15] Nonetheless, Trojan historiography contains numerous reminders of historical alternatives to the final shape of events. This history plays the same role in *Troilus and Criseyde* as Theban history in the Knight's Tale. Like the *Thebaid*, it is the story within which Chaucer's poem claims its own subject matter to invent, and it is the hermeneutic figure that offers a means for reading the new poem and its hero, the *infelix puer* of Vergil (*Aeneid* 1.474–8) and the grammarians, who writes the example of his heroism in the dust with his downturned spear.[16]

Chaucer's narrator is at pains to separate what he recounts in his poem from the encompassing story of Troy. His avowed purpose is not to tell 'how this town com to destruccion' (1.141): 'But the Troian gestes, as they felle, / In Omer, or in Dares, or in Dite, / Whoso that kan may rede hem as they write' (1.145–7). Barry Windeatt observes, 'The very rehearsal of the names of these "authorities" on the Trojan War acknowledges the keener sense in *Troilus* of how the action exists in significant relation to a sequence of historical events.'[17] Patterson rightly contends that the narrator provides these ostensibly banished histories with 'a rich texture of private motivation and psychological depth without ignoring their significance as history.'[18] Equally important, the passage legitimizes Homer, representative of the poetic tradition, within the historiography represented by Dares and Dictys, the supposed eyewitnesses to the war privileged by medieval writers over the poets.[19] The narrator goes on to fabricate a counter-authority to official historiography for Troilus's private story, creating the fictitious writer Lollius to occupy the place of Boccaccio. Yet as Barbara Nolan points out, the 'Lollian' history thus invented is the internal record of mutability and deceit that operates on a large scale in Trojan history.[20] In Benoît and Guido, the necessary pattern of history unfolds as a series of choices that could have been different. In John Lydgate, who conspicuously brings *Troilus and Criseyde* back to chronicle history, the role of choice is even more apparent because of the importance Lydgate invests in prudence as a moral and political value.[21]

The tension between tragic destiny and alternatives in history is already present in accounts of the origins of the Trojan war, as Chaucer's audience would have known them. Lamedon wrongly suspects that Jason and Hercules threaten his kingdom when they put into Trojan territory to rest during their journey to Colchis to capture the Golden Fleece. He thus sets in motion a series of avoidable conflicts that leads twice to Troy's destruction. Guido moralizes the catastrophes suffered as well as those about to follow: 'quales sunt in hoc mundo ceci rerum euentus' ('in this world the results of things are blind' [Book 5, p. 43]).[22] Lydgate aptly expresses Guido's sense of the disparity throughout between cause and effect: 'of sparkys þat ben of syȝte smale / Is fire engendered þat devoureth al' (1.785–6). Medea's father unthinkingly sits her beside Jason at the banquet in Colchis, and so takes the first step toward destroying his dynasty; as Lydgate remarks, 'þin honour, þi worschip, & þin hele / Was lost in haste, and sche to meschef brouȝt / In straunge londe, with sorwe and myche þouȝt' (*Troy Book* 1.1912–14). When Priam is inflamed by rage at the Greeks' refusal to return Hesione after the destruction of Lamedon's Troy, Guido chastises him for his anger and for not exercising 'matura consilia' to avoid bad advice (Book 6, p. 56). At the council Priam calls, Hector rationally argues against war and Helenus prophesies doom if war is begun. Ironically, it is Troilus who delivers the final, decisive speech for war. The Trojans subsequently ignore Cassandra's prophecies both after the parliament and after Paris returns with Helen, the prize captured to repair the loss of Hesione in Troy's first fall.[23]

In the politics and battlefield tactics of the war, the chronicle tradition offers further examples of other outcomes that could have followed from deliberation and action. Agamemnon, somewhat disingenuously, sends Ulysses and Diomede to Priam with a proposal to avert war if Helen is returned and damages paid for Paris's destruction of Venus's temple at Cytherea (Book 12, p. 106). The Trojans could have achieved complete victory in the first set-piece battle, had Hector not been persuaded to desist by his cousin Ajax Telamon (Book 15, p. 146). The pattern is repeated later when only Ajax Telamon prevents Paris and Troilus from burning the Greeks' ships (Book 25, p. 191) and then when Diomede alone keeps Penthesilea from annihilating the Greeks (Book 28, p. 213). After Thoas's capture, Priam is prepared to put him to death; but Aeneas advises saving him for a prisoner exchange, which eventually sends Thoas and Criseyde to the Greeks in return for Antenor, Aeneas's collaborator in betraying Troy (Book 18, p. 155). In Vergil (*Aeneid* 2.262), Thoas is among the warriors concealed in the wooden horse. The opportunity to forestall treachery occurs again when Hector opposes the truce in which the exchange is actually proposed (Book 19, p. 160). During the truce, Achilles and Hector offer to settle the war by single combat (Book 19, p. 162), but no one else on either side will accept the risk of losing. After Hector and Deiphebus are dead, the Greeks debate ending the war because Achilles has fallen in love with Polyxena and withdrawn from the fighting (Book 25, p. 196). He re-enters only as Troilus is about to destroy the Greek camp (Book 26, p. 202).

Historical necessity unfolds, then, in the Troy story as a combination of fate and human choice working together not just to force an outcome but also to preclude alternatives. Guido prefaces the story by remarking on the play between destiny and unforseen consequences: 'Sed inuida fatorum series, que semper quiete uiuentibus est molesta, ab inopinatis insidiis sine causa inimicitiarum et scandali causas traxit' ('But the envious connections of the fates, which are always troubled by peace for the living, draw together the causes of enmity and error without reason by unexpected traps' (Book 2, p. 11). His chief terms are *series* and *inopinatis insidiis* – the linkages effected by necessity and the snares not seen by purposive, intending human agents. In explaining Hector's decision not to pursue advantage in the first major battle, Lydgate amplifies Guido to blame the Trojans' 'pitous slouthe, / Of pride only, and of foly routhe' (3.1967–8), and he connects Hector's choice to the larger patterns of necessity. The Trojans would have had decisive victory, he says, 'saue cruel Fate / Is redy ay with Fortune, to debate / Ageyn þinges þat gynne in welfulnes' (3.1975–7). His language echoes the vocabulary of medieval tragedy, juxtaposing 'welfulnes' at the outset and 'wrechidnes' at the end, with Fortune spinning the 'vnwar tournyng of hir false whele' (3.1981). Lydgate goes on, however, to make a point that Pandarus also makes to Troilus in Chaucer's poem: Fortune's favor must be answered by a willingness to accept Fortune in her beneficent aspect and to act on her favors when they are offered.

Like the chronicle histories, the philosophical system that Chaucer elaborates in *Troilus and Criseyde* leaves open a realm of significant choice between the necessary shape of events and the sphere of human action. The narrator as historian must respect and reproduce, in Bloomfield's phrase, 'the rigidity of decisive events.' Indeed, he is constrained by those events, as are his characters. How the events come to take a determinate shape is another matter, and it is here that alternatives emerge within Boethian philosophy. Jill Mann points out that chance and perspective are key elements in the poem's philosophical system.[24] Chance events intrude into both human schemes and the large pattern of necessity. As Lady Philosophy explains in Chaucer's translation of the *Consolation*, 'hap is an unwar betydinge of causes assembled in thingis that ben doon for som oothir thing' (*Boece* 5.pr.1.90–2). Chance is an unforeseen effect ('unwar betydinge') operating apart from one's original intention ('thingis that ben doon for som oothir thing'). In Chaucer's poem, Pandarus's fabrications, which in many respects imitate the poet's own creative acts, depend on chance at key points in the progress of the love affair – Troilus's sudden appearance on horseback in Book 2 and the rainstorm in Book 3. The protagonists, who think they know their intentions, are transformed by unforeseen occurrences – their sudden sight of the other and then the deepening force of their attachment. The fate of Troy is sealed in part by the unanticipated reappearance of Calkas, who disappears from the story after his defection to the Greeks and returns to seek Criseyde's exchange with Thoas for Antenor.

Chaucer's poem artfully exploits the differences in perspective that lie at the heart of Boethius's reconciliation of divine providence with free will. Because it stands outside time, divine providence necessarily foresees what will occur. Human will, which proceeds from reason (*Boece* 5.pr.2), exercises its choices within time, hence in temporal succession and forward movement. Boethius illustrates the difference by distinguishing between the providential necessity for the sun to rise and a man's deciding to walk: 'oon of hem, or it was idoon, it byhovide by necessite that it was idoon, but nat that oothir' (5.pr.6.225–6). Furthermore, a chosen act, once done, cannot be undone. In consequence, one can look back to see that a succession of choices made in time takes on the shape of necessity. This retrospect is properly called destiny; it differs from providence by being time-bound, associated as it is with 'moevable thinges' and human perception rather than divine knowledge (4.pr.6.42–78). Mann remarks, 'Only after they have happened are portions of the destinal pattern realized in time and made perceptible to human observers. "Necessite", then, does not represent the intrusion of divine control into human affairs; it is the pattern achieved by the totality of temporal events, working according to their own causes and effects.'[25] Guido depends on these differences in perspective to voice a profound ambivalence when enumerating the great cities and kingdoms that follow from Troy's destruction: 'Sed si tante proditionis causa fuerit subsequentis boni causa finalis humana mens habet in dubio' ('The human mind doubts whether the cause of such treachery was the final cause of the goods following from it' [Book 2, p. 12]).

Chaucer famously dramatizes these differences in perspective through Troilus's fatalistic speech in the temple when he learns that Criseyde will be exchanged for Antenor (4.958–1078). Troilus makes a flawed and incomplete argument: 'For al that comth, comth by necessitee: / Thus to ben lorn, it is my destinee' (4.958–9). It is the argument that Lady Philosophy corrects in the *Consolation* by distinguishing simple from conditional necessity: the atemporal perspective of divine providence differs from the viewpoint of man in time.[26] These philosophical differences show in the disparities between human intentions in the poem. Less remarked than Troilus's speech but equally illustrative of the difference is Criseyde's effort to read the signs of peace that occasionally punctuate the larger Troy narrative. She tries to ease Troilus's fears of their separation by telling him, 'Ye sen that every day ek, more and more, / Men trete of pees' (4.1345–6). Troilus protests that Calkas will never recant his prophecy of the city's doom (4.1478–82), and Diomede later confirms to her the Greeks' resolve to seek a full measure of vengeance against Troy (5.883–910). As history closes against her, Criseyde futilely but authentically injects the alternative of reconciling the conflict and ending the repeated cycle of violence over lost women.

Troilus's martial heroism provides another, quite different, instance of human perspective and intention operating within a destinal pattern. After he falls in love, Troilus in effect privatizes his position in the war: 'But for non hate he to the Grekes hadde, / Ne also for the rescous of the town, / Ne made hym thus in armes for to madde' (1.477–9). As he plays the lion in the field (1.1074) and spends his days 'in Martes heigh servyse' (3.437), he cultivates a reputation whose aim is to secure his

standing with Criseyde. The narrator remarks, 'this encrees of hardy-
nesse and myght / Com hym of love, his ladies thank to wynne, / That
altered his spirit so withinne' (3.1776–8). Yet Troilus's perspective as a
lover and his intention of offering Criseyde valorous service unwittingly
contribute to his death. As Troilus makes himself, in Pandarus's words,
'worthi Ector the secounde' (2.158), he prepares himself for Hector's
fate. Chaucer follows the chronicle histories in reporting that Hector is
killed without warning by Achilles as he despoils a fallen Greek: 'Unwar
of this, Achilles thorugh the maille / And thorugh the body gan hym for
to ryve' (5.1559–60). 'Unwar of this' translates Guido's phrase 'non
aduertente Hectore' (Book 22, p. 175), just as the oddly perfunctory
sentence 'Despitously hym slough the fierse Achille' (5.1806) accurately
renders Boccaccio: 'miseramente un dí l'uccise Achille' (8.27.8). Chaucer's medieval readers would know that Achilles plots an ambush to
murder Hector and then arranges another ambush to dispatch Troilus.
In *Troy Book*, Lydgate emphasizes the repetition by mixing Chaucer's
phrasing for Hector's death with his description of Achilles's cowardly
assault on Troilus: 'þis Achilles wonder cruelly, / Be-hynde vnwarly, or
þat he toke hed, / With his swerd smyteþ of his hed' (4.2760–1).

Troilus's service is enmeshed in a pattern of necessity that not only lies
beyond his understanding but is, in fact, realized by his acting on his
intentions. The fatalism expressed in his speech on predestination mystifies and obscures a more subtle process. Boethius describes it as an
'inprovisus inopinatusque concursus' and Chaucer translates Boethius
in the phrase 'the cours unforseyn and unwar' (5.pr1.75–6) – a convergence of unforeseen motives. While destiny in some sense hovers over
the poem, choice and action move events whose larger shape must
unfold in time. It is worth noting that these differences in perspective
operate as well in the dynamics of literary response, which comple-
ments our interpretation of the poem's structure and its theme of determinism. Reading forward with knowledge of the poem's outcome, we
think we enjoy the perspective of providence. But reading is a temporal
process, with provisional closures and occasional missteps. The position
we actually occupy as readers caught in the succession of events lets us
see only destiny, not providence.

As in the Knight's Tale, Fortune is a mechanism for explaining the
poem's reversals and setbacks; it rationalizes mutability, endowing
change with a personified agency, if not always an apparent purpose.
It also functions, as Larry Scanlon points out, to effect political shifts
without transforming political structures.[27] Chaucer modifies the *Filostrato* by giving the name of Fortune to the oscillating pattern of Greek

and Trojan advantage in the war: 'thus Fortune on lofte / And under eft gan hem to whielen bothe / Aftir hir course, ay whil that thei were wrothe' (1.138–40). For Chaucer, Fortune has the Dantesque cast that Boccaccio applies to it in the *Teseida* (6.1.1) when, as the 'executrice of wierdes' (3.617), it blocks Criseyde's departure from Pandarus's house and leads to the lovers' consummation. Fortune wills their subsequent meeting (3.1667). It oversees their season of contentment in the same way that it stands above the epicycles of military advantage: 'And thus Fortune a tyme ledde in joie / Criseyde and ek this kynges sone of Troie' (3.1714–15).

In the second half of the poem, Fortune, the 'traitour comune' (4.5), hovers above the impending catastrophe. After the exchange is announced, Troilus complains to Fortune and Love (3.260–336). Pandarus argues that Fortune can help Troilus if he is enterprising enough to carry off Criseyde (4.600–2). On her last night with Troilus, Criseyde affirms that Fortune cannot efface the virtues she found in him (4.1681–2). As the final events unfold, however, Fortune's turnings outstrip human intentions. Fortune deceives both Troilus and Pandarus when Criseyde fails to return on the tenth day (5.1134). Cassandra expounds Troilus's dream in the framework of ancient noble lords overthrown by Fortune (5.1457–63). Immediately thereafter Fortune shifts from the Trojans with Hector's death (5.1541–61) and from Troilus with Criseyde's unequivocal love for Diomede (5.1744–7). Chaucer portrays a much more complex view of Fortune than the Man in Black articulates in his complaint in the *Book of the Duchess* (617–78) or Pleintif and Fortune set out in the triple ballade on 'Fortune,' yet the structure remains constant: Fortune is known from retrospect, from the effects of change.

Chaucer's historical and philosophical models, then, afford a surprisingly rich view of necessity and choice in antiquity. Chaucer exploits this view for rewriting the *Filostrato* as a philosophical poem with a scope well beyond Boccaccio's elegant love-plea and his monitory example of female perfidy. Some of the most important additions and changes in *Troilus and Criseyde* assert the role left open to will and action. Calkas foresees the destruction of Troy at the very start of the poem, yet there is a hint of overdetermination in his prophecy: 'this Calkas knew by calkulynge, / And ek by answer of this Appollo' (1.71–2; reiterated at 4.114–16). Chaucer adds the motif of astral determinism to underwrite divination, responding perhaps to the claim Briseida makes in Guido (Book 19, pp. 165–6) that the voice Calchas heard at Delphi was not Apollo's but that of an infernal fury. When Chaucer's narrator invokes the Furies and Mars at the start of Book 4 to show 'the losse of lyf and love yfeere / Of Troilus' (4.27–8), the downward turn of Fortune's wheel sets in motion a chain of effects that begins with Antenor's capture. Chaucer subsequently adds, however, the scene in which Hector speaks against the exchange of Thoas and Criseyde for Antenor. Hector objects that Criseyde, unlike Thoas, is not a prisoner, and he goes on to announce a principle – 'We usen here no wommen for to selle' (4.182) – that obliquely calls up the precipitating event of the war in the capture of Hesione and later Helen. The narrator invokes Juvenal to chide the people for their outcry at 'wys' (4.190) Hector's opposition to the trade, but an equally important context for viewing Chaucer's addition is the scene in Benoît (3772–840) and Guido (Book 6, pp. 59–60) where Hector prudently opposes the war.[28] Troilus's silence at the Trojan parliament in Chaucer's poem, motivated as it is by the need to conceal his 'affeccioun' (4.153), is a pointed contrast to his decisive argument at Priam's council in the chronicle histories in favor of the war. Against the 'substaunce of the parlement' (4.217), Pandarus holds out the alternative of ravishing Criseyde. As Martin Stevens remarks, he 'gives expression to the independent self; he is the voice of human free will.'[29]

The mythography Chaucer develops in *Troilus and Criseyde* embodies a comparable tension between destiny and historical alternatives. Chaucer uses classical myths for topical references, structural analogues, and ironic effect. The most significant mythological frame is the one Cassandra expounds in Book 5 to interpret Troilus's dream of the boar (5.1457–1519). Chaucer substitutes this passage for the episode in the *Filostrato* where Cassandra reproves Troiolo's love for Criseida. The 'olde stories' Cassandra recounts in Chaucer's poem are a narrative of destructive conflict between rivals and within Tydeus's family, followed by the equally destructive Theban war. Cassandra reads this narrative as an example of Fortune's overthrowing 'lordes olde,' thus as a tragedy; and she announces its direct application to Troilus, 'This Diomede is inne, and thow art oute' (5.1519). The genealogical movement across generations from Meleager to Tydeus to Diomede imparts a sense of inevitability to this story. The narrator remarks in this wholesale addition to Boccaccio that Cassandra 'descendeth down from gestes olde / To Diomede' (5.1511–12), sketching the long reach of fate over time.

Seen in these destinal and dynastic terms, Troilus is an actor in the most recent episode of a continuing story of deadly rivalry. Yet Chaucer preserves Boccaccio's suggestion earlier in the *Filostrato* (7.24) that even this myth contains historical alternatives. Commending himself to Criseyde as a lover, Diomede asserts, 'I am, al be it yow no joie, / As gentil man as any wight in Troie' (5.930–1). Nobility, like Fortune, works across nations but within culture and social hierarchy. He then suggests that events might well have taken a different course in the Theban history that precedes the Troy story:

> 'For if my fader Tideus,' he seyde,
> 'Ilyved hadde, ich hadde ben er this
> Of Calydoyne and Arge a kyng, Criseyde!
> And so hope I that I shal yet, iwis.
> But he was slayn – allas, the more harm is! –
> Unhappily at Thebes al to rathe,
> Polymyte and many a man to scathe.
>
> (5.932–8)

Chaucer omits Diomede's further complaint that strangers have displaced an ancient, venerable lineage on the throne, and he ignores Diomede's claim of divine descent (*Filostrato* 7.24.5–7). Knowledgeable medieval readers would connect Diomede's displacement with his exile after the war, his unlikely role as protector of Troy in partnership with Aeneas, and his eventual return to Argia (Guido, *Historia*, Book 22, pp. 249–52). Here the force of Diomede's will lends another perspective to the determining shape of mythological descent. Whereas Chaucer's Cassandra sees the inexorable descent of events over time, Diomede looks to a future in which his actions can prevail over circumstances. He envisions and claims possibilities wholly different from fatalistic acceptance or despair.

Erotic determinism

The pattern of historical destiny that stands behind yet finally overtakes events in *Troilus and Criseyde* has its thematic counterpart in erotic determinism. Chaucer explores this latter theme schematically in 'The Complaint of Mars,' but the more telling comparison is with the Knight's Tale. Like Palamon and Arcite, Troilus is suddenly overcome by the power of Love. At the spring ritual honoring Pallas, the visual image of Criseyde penetrates his consciousness in much the same way as Palamon and Arcite, imprisoned in Theseus's tower, are wounded by the sight of Emily.[30] An important difference, of course, is that Troilus's love is ostensibly retribution for his 'surquidrie' (1.213), his arrogant dismissal of other lovers in the temple. The God of Love does not merely capture another disciple but acts '[r]ight for despit, and shop for to ben wroken' (1.207).

Love's vengeance, though proverbial, is a motif that Chaucer deliberately accents. In the *Filostrato*, Boccaccio mentions it in a comment preceding Troiolo's first glimpse of Criseida; he intends merely to remark the irony of Troiolo's falling in love after reproving other lovers (1.25.6–8). Chaucer makes vengeance a cause and thereby prepares for a much more problematic meditation on the nature of love. Love is repeatedly addressed and invoked throughout *Troilus and Criseyde*. Like the philosophical passages he adds, it is a topic on which Chaucer lavishes revision. At various times, love encompasses courtly service, sexual appetite, friendship, charity, and divine power. Within these shifting senses, the constant issue is how characters position themselves in response to love – how they confront its power, assent to it, and act within the constraints they feel it exerts over them. We shall see later that Chaucer holds out several ways of escaping erotic determinism, but for the moment I want to focus on love as a form of determinism running parallel to historical necessity in the poem.

The coercive power of love is the subject of Chaucer's first long addition to the *Filostrato*. Immediately after introducing Love's vengeance, Chaucer expands Boccaccio's image of the 'blind world' to express Love's overwhelming power. The narrator explains Troilus's sudden fall from prideful disdain as a case of will encountering superior might: he 'wende nothing hadde had swich myght / Ayeyns his wille that shuld his herte stere' (1.227–8). The imagery of rising and falling surrounds Troilus's subjugation to Love's power and thereby links the course of his love affair with the larger pattern of tragic reversal.[31] In expanding Boccaccio's text, Chaucer gives the narrator's voice an expository and hortatory prominence. Combining the figure of Love's power from the *Roman de la rose* with Boethius's diction and an echo of Arcite's speech in the Knight's Tale (1.1163–68), the narrator declares, 'Love is he that alle thing may bynde, / For may no man fordon the lawe of kynde' (1.237–8).[32] The application he subsequently draws, presumably for his audience of young lovers, is a further echo of Theseus's admission of Love's power (I.1785–78) and his admonition to make virtue of necessity:

> Now sith it may nat goodly ben withstonde,
> And is a thing so vertuous in kynde,
> Refuseth nat to Love for to ben bonde,
> Syn, as hymselven liste, he may yow bynde....
> (1.253–6)

Besides its fusion of courtly with philosophical discourse, this passage is remarkable for the themes it puts immediately in play within the poem. It envisions a complementarity of constraint and volition. Love's power to compel is correlated with virtue, and the free choice of accepting it means recognizing a power that is already part of human inclination. At the same time, the narrator constructs a false syllogism in which the meaning of love shifts, in scholastic terms, between natural and rational love.[33] The first half of the poem navigates among these points both in its psychological portraiture and its moral speculation about the relation of passion to will.

Troilus makes the strongest case for Love's determinism, following the lead of his predecessor in the *Filostrato*, though Chaucer pointedly omits Troiolo's concession that love may diminish in time for various reasons (*Filostrato* 4.59). Troilus is, as F. Anne Payne describes him, a hopeful but unsuccessful determinist.[34] Alone in his chamber, before Pandarus comes on the scene, he repeats the narrator's proposition: 'Sith thow most loven thorugh thi destine' (1.520). When Pandarus arrives, he begins his disclosure by saying, 'Love, ayeins the which whoso defendeth / Hymselven most, hym alderlest avaylleth' (1.603–4). In its reminiscence of Dante's Francesca (*Inferno* 5.100–5), the phrasing simultaneously conveys necessity and doom. Pandarus praises Love's power to 'convert' (1.999, 1004) a reluctant lover, but other destinal powers exercise their influences, too. Troilus's fortuitous appearance under Criseyde's window as Pandarus presents his suit occurs 'of necessitee' (2.623). Venus's astrological position aids his case when Criseyde debates within herself the alternatives of love or rejection (2.680–3). As Troilus waits in the stew at Pandarus's house, he invokes all the planetary gods as well as the three Fates and destiny (3.705–35). But as he futilely awaits her return from the Greek camp, Cupid's influence turns from beneficent to potentially malign. Praying Cupid to compel her to return, Troilus asks the god not to become for him the same implacable foe as Juno was to Theban royalty (5.599–602).

Other characters in the poem reiterate the claims of erotic determinism, though to somewhat different effect. Pandarus announces that the universal inclination to love takes two distinctive forms: 'Was nevere man or womman yet bigete / That was unapt to suffren loves hete, / Celestial, or elles love of kynde' (1.977–9). He posits this difference only in order to confuse it again in the universal law of 'loves hete.' As she reproves him for his feigned jealousy, Criseyde allows that no one should resist love (3.988–90). In her soliloquoy after learning she must leave Troy, she blames the 'corsed constellacioun' (4.745) under which she was born. But in the Greek camp with Venus and other planets in auspicious position (5.1015–29), she contemplates Diomede in the same terms by which she earlier regarded Troilus. Diomede protests that Greeks and Trojans serve the same God of Love (5.143) and underscores the point by affirming his obedience in the same language as the Trojans: 'Ek I am nat of power for to stryve / Ayeyns the god of Love, but hym obeye / I wole alwey' (5.166–8).

Surely the most problematic aspect of erotic determinism lies in the alliance of creaturely with divine love. This dualism haunts authors important to Chaucer like Alan of Lille, whose *De planctu naturae* tries to integrate kinds of love on a metaphysical scale yet still has recourse to distinguishing the discrete operations of God, Nature, and Venus. The differences remain incompletely articulated in the *Roman de la rose*, and Boccaccio reproduces them in his gloss on the two Venuses in the *Teseida* (7.50 gloss). For Chaucer, the poetic and conceptual difficulty stems from Boethius's hymn to cosmic unity (*Consolation* 2.m.8). As we have seen in the Knight's Tale, Boethius's idea that love unifies levels of being and existence is applied to the species but only obliquely and tacitly to the individual. In *Troilus and Criseyde*, this complication acquires a heightened prominence as Chaucer moves and supplements the portion of the *Filostrato* celebrating the consummation of love. Troiolo's original song serves as the Proem to Book 3, while Chaucer turns to its source in Boethius and inserts his poetic rendering of *Consolation* 2.m.8 to replace the song. Noting that Chaucer introduces religious terms before connecting cosmic and sexual love in the Proem, Wetherbee points out that its Boethian subtext includes a conflict between nature and will.[35]

In appropriating Troiolo's song as the proem to his central book, Chaucer reshapes the theme of Venus's erotic power. Boccaccio's opening phrase 'O luce eterna' is transformed to 'O blisful light' (3.1). The social virtues that flow from Venus – pleasure, grace, piety, and love – are made her own attributes: 'Plesance of love, O goodly debonaire' (3.4). Boccaccio's conceit that Venus is the lady of gentle hearts prompts Chaucer's allusion to Guido Guinizelli's more philosophically charged poem 'Al cor gentil rempaira sempre amore,' a signature piece for the Dolce Stilnuovo which defines love through the Aristotelian analysis of potency and act operating in the physical and emotional worlds together.[36] Chaucer follows Boccaccio in proclaiming Venus's power over plant, animal, and human life – the vegetative, animal, and rational souls in man and the sources of Dante's three great poetic topics. Venus confers both existence and meaning: 'in this world no lyves creature /

Withouten love is worth, or may endure' (3.13–14). In both poems she transforms Jupiter and Mars and then moves to a human scale, holding together in unity the social institutions of the kingdom, city, and friendship. In Boccaccio, Venus sets in place a universal law that confers being: 'per la quale esso in esser si mantiene' (3.79.2). Chaucer changes this reference into the law of universal obedience to Venus: 'Ye folk a lawe han set in universe, / And this knowe I by hem that lovers be, / That whoso stryveth with yow hath the werse' (3.36–8).

As an overture to the book in which Troilus and Criseyde most fully realize their love, the Proem frames human action within beneficent necessity. The middle stanzas of the Proem try to balance compulsion with moderation. Boccaccio has Venus incline Jupiter to love and consequently to show mercy for human offenses (3.76.3–6). Chaucer suppresses this motif to emphasize Venus's influence over her father: '[Ye] amorous him made / On mortal thyng, and as yow list, ay ye / Yeve hym in love ese or adversitee' (3.17–19).[37] With the taming of fierce Mars, as with the social reform of Troilus, love instills not only social virtues but also moral consciousness: 'Algates hem that ye wol sette a-fyre, / They dreden shame, and vices they resygne' (3.24–5). But as Venus effects unity in human institutions and friendships, her power to join individuals is suddenly mystified. Boccaccio says, 'tu sola le nascose qualitadi / delle cose conosci' ('you alone know the hidden properties of things' [2.78.5–6]). Chaucer explains what this 'covered qualitee / Of thynges' means to people: 'how it may jo / She loveth hym, or whi he loveth here, / As whi this fissh, and naught that, comth to were' (3.33–5). Venus's power works transparently through the political and personal structures of male attachments – *regne, hous, frendship*. The examples in Boccaccio are still more overtly patriarchal, referring to distinct yet interlocking spheres of male action – *case, cittadi, regni, provincie, amistadi*. It is only when Boccaccio and Chaucer come to the topic of their poem, the intersecting passions of a man and woman, that Love's coercive power is covered and rendered opaque.

The Proem to Book 3 honors Venus by celebrating the effects she causes, and in this way it forecasts the lovers' impending union as well as the interim of felicity they enjoy before destiny overtakes them. The translation of Boethius that replaces Troiolo's original song later in Book 3 offers a slightly different perspective but reveals the same complications. In the Proem (3.8–9), Venus affects sentient creation situated within all parts of the physical universe, while cosmic love in Boethius's poem governs the physical elements of earth, sea, and heavens themselves. In the first stanza of Chaucer's replacement poem, which is rearranged considerably from the topical and stylistic sequence of *Consolation* 2.m.8, this cosmic order immediately connects the metaphysical to the social sphere. Troilus's four-fold repetition of 'Love' refers twice to the physical world and twice to the social world, where love imposes on human experience. Love, says Troilus, '[h]alt peples joyned, as hym lest hem gye' and it 'knetteth lawe of compaignie / And couples doth in vertu for to dwelle' (3.1747–9).[38] Chaucer does not mention Boethius's 'holy boond' ('sancto foedere') joining people together but stresses instead Love's power to direct them as it wishes. He suppresses Boethius's reference to the 'sacrement of mariages of chaste loues' ('coniugii sacrum / Castis...amoribus'). The social bonds of friendship apparently stand-in for marriage under the 'lawe of compaignie' so that couples are made to dwell together by moral virtue rather than sacred ritual. This unifying power, working by proxy for individuals, Troilus invokes to bind his 'acord' with Criseyde.

Troilus's song is consistent with the situation in Chaucer's narrative. As the narrator remarks, Troilus's heart is caught in 'Criseydes net'; he is 'narwe ymasked and yknet' (3.1733–4). In the final stanza of his song, where Boethius hopes for the congruence of divine order and the human soul, Troilus prays for the subjugation of lovers: 'hem wolde I that he twiste / to make hem love' (3.1769–70). As with the narrator's praise of Love's power in Book 1, the meaning of love shifts from Boethian harmony to love between the sexes.[39] But even taken on its own terms, the love Troilus praises carries ominous implications. Boethian love postulates a form of necessity that exists before the possibility of choice and agency. Foregrounding concord, stability, and perpetual bonds, it paints a dark background, for love is the means to contain conflict within the bonds of law and harmony. Boethius chooses metaphors of violent struggle: the 'contrarious qualite[s] of elementz' ('pugnantia semina') and 'batayle' ('bellum'). Troilus gives voice to only part of the underlying fear: 'And if that Love aught lete his bridel go, / Al that now loveth asondre sholde lepe' (3.1762–3). Under the assurance lies terror. The larger threat is that everything would collapse. By celebrating the encompassing power of love at the apogee of Troilus's good fortune, then, Chaucer brings into sight what love controls, and he subtly prepares for the ensuing failure of the love affair and the destruction of the city.

Like his broader view of destiny, Chaucer's portrayal of erotic determinism encompasses some measure of choice. But choice in this instance does not entail alternatives within history or purposive action taken within unseen constraints. Under Love's compulsion, choice centers on consent. Troilus is staggered by the initial sight of Criseyde, and her image impresses itself and fixes in his heart and imagination (1.295–8). The source of love is external, but Troilus's response is to assent and amplify. He subsequently makes a mirror of his mind to contemplate Criseyde's visual image (1.365–7). These two scenes represent, in scholastic terms, the movements of the sensitive and rational souls, first in apprehending Criseyde and then in exercising will.[40] While Boccaccio insists that Troiolo is disposed to love Criseida, Chaucer's narrator gives a markedly different formulation: 'took he purpos loves craft to suwe' (1.379). His phrasing recalls both the courtly diction of the Man in Black from the *Book of the Duchess* – 'I ches love to my firste craft' (791) – and Ovid's image of an erotic tactician in the *Ars amatoria*. He goes on to report in confirmation, 'with good hope he gan fully assente / Criseyde for to love' (1.391–2).

Volition is reiterated in the sonnet translated from Petrarch and added by Chaucer as Troilus's first song. Troilus asks Love, 'How may of the in me swich quantite, / But if that I consente that it be?' (1.412–13). Immediately thereafter, he consigns himself to the God of Love: 'now youres is / My spirit' (1.422–3). His next step, equally decisive, is to delegate the conduct of the love affair to Pandarus. In his mock repentance to Love, with Pandarus acting as his confessor, he formally consents (1.936), echoing his earlier apostrophe to Love. As he agrees to Pandarus's management of the affair, his language parallels his assent to love: 'now do right as the leste' (1.1029). What follows on from this is agreement to the practical steps Pandarus takes on his behalf – letter writing, the feigned suit against Criseyde by Poliphete, the stratagem of supposed jealousy over Horaste that brings the lovers together at Pandarus's house.

Criseyde's consent emerges through resistance and deliberation punctuated by the chance intervention of love. In his embassy to her in Book 2, Pandarus ostensibly seeks 'love of frendshipe' (2.371) and plays on her fears and vulnerability. Trying to set a limit to her uncle's demands, Criseyde concedes his first request in a line with portentious ambiguity, 'I shal myn herte ayeins my lust constreyne' (2.476). As Criseyde anatomizes her passion, she momentarily resembles Boccaccio's Criseida, who hides her latent desire behind social codes and the fear of public disclosure.[41] Troilus's appearance in the street below, unplanned but impelled by necessity, sets her change of heart and intent in motion. The narrator anticipates objections that Criseyde gave Troilus her love suddenly – and therefore lightly. His defense answers the immediate objection yet raises other questions: 'For I sey nought that she so sodeynly / Yaf hym hire love, but that she gan enclyne / To like hym first' (2.673–5). In other words, Criseyde appropriates Troiolo's original disposition, and Troilus wins her love over time through the cumulative weight of his good service. But by identifying her inclination the narrator concedes at the same time that Criseyde's habit of character leads her toward love. As Derek Pearsall remarks, Chaucer takes us into 'the marketplace of the will,' where the self both seeks what it wants and obscures its wish.[42]

Criseyde's internal debate over Troilus's love, much reworked from the *Filostrato*, displays psychological process and practical deliberation, while finally leaving her as mysterious as the cosmic love ostensibly governing human passion.[43] As in Boccaccio (2.73.1–3), the debate is premised on her agency. Criseyde insists repeatedly on her freedom to accept or reject love – 'I am myn owene womman' (2.750). It is Antigone's song (2.827–75), compiled from Machaut's courtly verses and inserted by Chaucer into the story, that answers her objections and begins a process that repeats Troilus's change.[44] Just as Criseyde's figure impresses itself on Troilus's mind, Antigone's words 'synken in hire herte, / That she wex somwhat able to converte' (2.902–3). Her dream in which the royal eagle violently removes her heart to insert his own (2.925–31) externalizes a process that is likewise internal. At Troilus's second entrance, a spectacle planned by Pandarus, love again overcomes intention. Though Criseyde has just written him to pledge only sisterly love (2.1224), the sight of Troilus draws forth deeper emotions. The narrator comments, 'she hath now kaught a thorn, / She shal nat pulle it out this nexte wyke' (2.1272–3). Criseyde, in other words, consents to what she desires and resists. Her final intentions are nowhere clearer than in the consummation scene, where Troilus asks her to yield herself and she replies that she already has: 'Ne hadde I er now, my swete herte deere, / Ben yolde, ywis, I were now nought heere!' (3.1210–11). How she arrives at them may be hidden from our sight, but in the emotional center of the poem, the alignment of act and will is not at all in doubt.

Escaping desire

I have been arguing that the twin necessities of history and desire unfold in a significant tension with poetic assertions of choice in *Troilus and Criseyde*. Chaucer's ancient pagans are historical agents whose choices give shape to their destiny, both by what they do and what they elect not to do. Though known to the narrator, his audience, and readers from the outset, their political and personal fates follow from their judgments in council and on the battlefield. Meanwhile, Troy's city of friends remains under the sway of a more complete internal necessity. Love, however diversely it may be defined or perceived, compels obedience from all the characters, and choice therefore amounts to consent. To understand the poem's depiction of love, by which it largely means Troilus's love, modern interpretation has worked within an equivalent hermeneutic constraint. Its questions reproduce the multiplicity of erotic determinism. Does love *paramours* have any moral standing? Does *trouthe* redeem passion and thereby make sexual love a virtue? How does 'false felicity' apparently give way, in the end, to some grasp of divine love? To understand how Chaucer stages the predicaments of his pagan characters, we need to look beyond how the characters accommodate eros and ask as well whether they have any capacity to escape erotic determinism. By escape I mean a shift in perspective or understanding that allows them to remove themselves from the steadily closing pattern of doomed passion. Pandarus, I propose, uncovers one such alternative in his Ovidian approach to love. Troilus discovers another in the power of desire. One method consciously falls short of the concept of love that commentators have struggled to integrate; the other overshoots it.

Pandarus has long been recognized as Ovid's *praeceptor amoris*, refracted in part through the Lover's counselors in the *Roman de la rose*, who are the lineal descendants of the erotic teacher. John Fyler calls Pandarus 'the expert in the Ovidian *ars amatoria*' and notes that in the pursuit of love he takes on the role of 'an artificer of situations, a deviser of fictions.'[45] Wetherbee carries this characterization further, arguing, 'Pandarus can be said to perform the function of sexual desire and of that Ovidian ingenuity that desire stimulates.'[46] On this view, Troilus's wish for physical love does not direct Pandarus's creative efforts; instead, those efforts themselves create and determine Troilus's love. The hermeneutics of Pandarus's Ovidian heritage depend, in large measure, on a reading of the *Ars amatoria* that stresses its literary irony, moral cynicism, and emotional detachment. Ovid's claim at the start of his pseudo-didactic poem is, however, that his craft causes no harm: 'Nos venerem tutam concessaque furta canemus, / Inque meo nullum carmine crimen erit' ('Of safe love-making do I sing, and permitted secrecy, and in my verse shall be no wrong-doing' [*Ars amatoria* 1.33–4]). In addition, he writes a measure of self-criticism into the poem. The story of Daedalus and Icarus (2.21–96) is a monitory example of misdirected artfulness; Apollo intervenes, only half-comically, to urge the wisdom of self-knowledge on aspirant lovers: 'Qui sibi notus erit, solus sapienter amabit'

(2.501). Love in the *Metamorphoses* may be a volatile, transforming force of nature, but it is represented differently in Ovid's elegies, which define Pandarus's role most significantly.

Pandarus holds out the prospect of escaping love's coercive power through art and its corollary, self-regulation. The language Chaucer gives to him is the idiom of the artisan, expressed most insistently in Ovid's repetition of the word *arte* at the opening of the *Ars amatoria* (1.3–4). Pandarus takes over the idiom in bringing Troilus and Criseyde together at three crucial times. He 'shapes' their first meeting at Deiphebus's house (2.1361–5), the consummation of their love at his house (3.193–6), and their meeting after the Trojan parliament (4.651–7). Criseyde's seduction is the 'werk' (1.1066, 1.1071) he undertakes as a counterpart to poetic invention.[47] Pandarus refers to this 'werk' after Troilus's sudden appearance before Criseyde's window (2.960). He instructs Troilus, 'Now lat m'alone, and werken as I may' (2.1401), when he plots the meeting at Deiphebus's house and later when he plans to bring the distraught couple together (4.651). The narrator takes up the term at the crucial moment when Pandarus releases Troilus from the stew (3.697, 3.702).

By itself, the craft Pandarus exercises is limited and contingent. His schemes, as Fyler notes, ironically forecast and blindly further destiny. His tactics can be transferred readily: Diomede acts out Ovid's prime metaphor of hunting as he ponders '[h]ow he may best, with shortest taryinge, / Into his net Criseydes herte brynge' (5.774–5). The corollary to art, as Ovid makes clear, is internal control. The *Ars amatoria* opens with both a celebration of art and a repeated imagery of control. Just as wild Cupid must be subdued (*regi* [1.10]) and made to yield, the lover must internalize the discipline he would impose on his love objects. The persistent fears are that he might become a victim of his own game or allow true intentions to slip the control of dissimulation. Ovid reiterates the need for internal discipline at the beginning of the *Remedia amoris*, where he offers the means to escape the tyranny (*regna*) of an unworthy mistress, a project Troilus never conceives. The moral aim of his teaching, he says, is to preserve control and to regulate the self: 'Utile propositum est saevas extinguere flammas, / Nec servum vitii pectus habere sui' ('A profitable aim it is to extinguish savage flames, and have a heart not enslaved to its own frailty' [53–4]). Boccaccio introduces just this lesson when Pandaro advises, 'ponghi freno alla mente amorosa' (3.60.5). Chaucer translates that advice as a proverb after the lovers' consummation: 'Bridle alwey wel thi speche and thi desir, / For worldly joie halt nought but by a wir' (3.1635–6).

The clearest example of Pandarus's Ovidian perspective occurs when destiny has taken over and love no longer directs events. After the Trojan parliament agrees to exchange Criseyde for Antenor, Pandarus offers consolation to Troilus in a speech significantly expanded and transformed from its original in the *Filostrato*. Pandarus describes Troilus's loss as a shift in Fortune (4.384–5) but quickly points out that Fortune's gifts are 'comune' (4.392) rather than vested in individuals. He admonishes Troilus, 'thi desir al holly hastow had, / So that, by right, it oughte ynough suffise' (4.395–6). He addresses him, in other words, as the Ovidian adept who can control himself while capturing his prey. Pandarus reminds Troilus that Troy is replete with beautiful and desirable women – implicitly, that it is as rich a hunting ground as Ovid portrays Rome to be:

> This town is ful of ladys al aboute;
> And, to my doom, fairer than swiche twelve
> As evere she was, shal I fynde in som route –
> Yee, on or two, withouten any doute.
> Forthi be glad, myn owen deere brother!
> If she be lost, we shal recover an other.
>
> (4.401–6)

Pandarus promises Troilus a capable substitute for Criseyde, and he specifically invokes the language of chance that earlier abets his stratagems for bringing the lovers together: 'syn it is but casuel plesaunce, / Som cas shal putte it out of remembraunce' (4.419–20). Thus new love will alleviate Troilus's pain, and Criseyde's absence will at length remove her from his heart. Ovid's equivalent precept, though we have no evidence Chaucer read it, is to displace passion: 'Quamlibet invenias, in qua tua prima voluptas / Desinat' ('find someone in whom the first bliss may spend itself' [*Remedia amoris* 403–4]).

Pandarus's stance and his advice derive remotely from Ovid's elegies, but Chaucer consciously amplifies the *Filostrato* in ways that reflect his invention of Boccaccio's poem. In the *Filostrato*, Troiolo complains, 'Fortuna insidiosa se ne 'l mena, / e con lui 'nsieme il sollazzo e 'l diporto' ('Envious fortune leads [my sweet comfort] away, and with it my solace and pleasure' [4.45.5–6]). Chaucer removes this vague reference to Fortune from Troiolo and assigns it to Pandarus, and he gives Fortune a philosophical rather than courtly meaning. Pandarus advises, in lines added by Chaucer, 'Ne trust no wight to fynden in Fortune / Ay propretee; hire yiftes ben comune' (4.391–2). He thus associates the 'hap' of Troilus's love with the doctrine in Boethius's *Consolation of Philosophy*, which denies 'that ever any mortel man hath resceyved ony of tho thynges to ben hise in propre' and asserts instead that man is put 'in the comune realme of alle' (*Boece* 2.pr.2.10–12, 84–5). He also draws on the view of earthly love expounded in the *Roman de la rose*, specifically in the speeches of Reason and Ami in Jean de Meun's continuation of the poem.[48]

The shift in speaker and reference from the *Filostrato* is paralleled by a second enhancement of meaning. Pandarus identifies Fortune's gifts as Troilus's desire (4.395), and this equation of common gifts and desire points in turn toward the Old Woman's famous remarks about sexual appetite in the *Rose*. She contends that every man and every woman hold their love commonly and that desire operates across the species without differentiating individuals except on the basis of gender. Her speech plays rhetorically on grammatical and gender distinctions (*touz* / *toutes*, *commun* / *commune*, *chascun* / *chascune*) which connect rather than divide men and women in a single appetite.

> [Nature] Ains nous a fait, biau fix, n'en doutes,
> Toutes por touz et touz pour toutes,
> Chascune por chascun commune
> Et commun chascun por chascune.
>
> (13885–8)

Instead, fair son, never doubt that she [Nature] has made all us women for all men and all men for all women, each woman common to every man and every man common to each woman.

Pandarus's formulation of erotic desire is another change wrought in the speech. Boccaccio's text describes Troiolo as the intending subject and author of his desire; Pandaro tells him, 'Ciò che disideravi avuto l'hai' ('You have had what you desired' [4.47.3]). The line is recast by Chaucer, however, so that Troilus's desire becomes identical to the object of his desire: 'thi desir al holly hastow had' (4.395). Desire is hypostasized as both sign and referent. At the same time, the *Filostrato*'s aristocratic social vision of Troy as a city 'piena di belle donne e graziose' ('full of beautiful and gracious ladies') acquires a new structure and function. Troy is besieged on the outside and Hector has just told the Trojan parliament, in another passage of Chaucer's invention, 'We usen here no wommen for to selle' (4.182). The city's encirclement and isolation serve, however, to define it as the site for a closed system of domestic exchange. Pandarus envisions an economy of desire internal to Troy, in which men, bound to each other by friendship and kinship (the two are convertible for Pandarus), lose and regain Troy's beautiful women.[49] In Boccaccio this exchange involves surplus and increments. Pandaro tells his friend, 'però se noi perdemo / costei, molte altre ne ritroveremo' ('Thus if we lose this one, we shall find many others' [4.48.8]). Chaucer's version calls for an erotic equilibrium in Troy: 'Forthi be glad, myn owen deere brother! / If she be lost, we shal recovere an other' (4.405–6). This circulation also permits, as Pandarus says in a stanza added to the *Filostrato*, the distribution of specific qualities associated with different women: 'If oon kan synge, an other kan wel daunce; / If this be goodly, she is glad and light; / And this is fair, and that kan good aright' (4.409–11).[50] In this way, as in Ovid and Andreas Capellanus, 'newe love' and 'newe cas' work against the declining arc of appetite by permitting 'newe avys' (4.416) – that is, a continuation of sexual appetite by finding new objects of contemplation and thought.

Pandarus's speech is notable for its links to other parts of the poem. Structurally, it is the final element of a narrative sequence (public event, private response, and interview) that parallels the action in Book 1.[51] Thematically, Pandarus makes the same argument about Fortune in Book 1, when Troilus sees Fortune as his foe and Criseyde as an unobtainable object. There Pandarus reminds his friend 'that Fortune is comune / To everi manere wight in som degree' (1.843–4). Just as joys pass away, he assures Troilus, so do sorrows. After the lovers' consummation, Pandarus warns that the 'worste kynde of infortune' is to have been in prosperity and remember it when it is lost (3.1625–8). On both these occasions, as in Book 4, Chaucer adds to Boccaccio's text to let Pandarus make the same point: Fortune is by turns the mechanism of comedy and tragedy. By maintaining the emotional distance of the Ovidian tactician of love, Troilus can take advantage of the turns in his favor and take assurance in his loss that Fortune will turn around again for him.

Pandarus's advice is, of course, repudiated in the narration and narrative alike. The narrator dismisses it as an 'unthrift' (4.431), nonsense or an impropriety.[52] In lines that have no counterpart in Boccaccio, he assures us and the audience of courtly lovers to whom he addresses his work, 'Thise wordes seyde he for the nones alle, / To help his frend' (4.428–9). He would thus have us believe that, as in his first interview with Troilus (1.561), Pandarus spontaneously makes up something merely to shake his friend out of his lethargy. In Boccaccio, Troiolo rejects Pandarus's advice, refusing to commit 'un tale eccesso' (4.50.4), and for Chaucer's Troilus, the advice literally goes in one ear and out the

other (4.434). When Troilus recovers himself, he offers a lengthy refutation (4.435–516) of Pandarus's advice. Ida Gordon says that Pandarus's
words raise the problem of 'what constitutes "trouthe" in love,' when
such love is a gift of fortune.[53] R.A. Shoaf contends that Troilus finally
elects death over Pandarus's version of love.[54] Narrow and pragmatic,
Pandarus's advice reveals one level on which love can proceed apart
from erotic determinism. By defining love as appetite, it disperses love's
power by shifting among its objects. By requiring internal regulation as
the corollary of art, it disciplines the intending subject. Pandarus's
description of Troilus's love as 'casuel plesaunce,' blunt and uncom-
promising as it is, looks forward to the perspective that Troilus and the
narrator will adopt at the end of the poem. The most successful embodiment of Pandarus's Ovidian principles, however, is Diomede, the second
Troilus, who not only uses art and self-discipline to take Troilus's place as
Criseyde's lover but also takes his place in chronicle history as the city's
defender after its destruction.

Chaucer offers a second way to escape love's constraints by sketching
the emergence of desire as a force that carries beyond physical appetite,
social practice, and erotic reciprocity. While Pandarus pursues love
through art and self-regulation, Troilus uncovers an emotional drive
that resists containment and control. To one extent or another, most
interpretations of Troilus's love present it as sexual passion directed by
trouthe, the virtue of fidelity, and thereby redeemed from mere sensuality. Late medieval and Renaissance reception of Chaucer's poem clearly
identifies Troilus with truth.[55] If we look closely at the nature of Troilus's
love, however, we find an emotional force different from the kinds and
gradations of love that the poem gives us to analyze other erotic attachments. Though fate and fortune conspire to rob Troilus of his lover and
his life, his desire remains significantly and defiantly beyond their
power. In the end, it is the means to escape both a closed history and
antiquity itself.

The defining characteristic of Troilus's desire is excess. Love wreaks his
vengeance on Troilus by compelling him to fall in love, but what Love
sets in motion is radically different from the Lover's appetitive quest in
the *Rose* and from Troiolo's frankly sexual attachment in the *Filostrato*.
Troilus's desire is constituted in the moment he first encounters Criseyde in the temple. Troilus's 'lokynge' (1.269) among the women
gathered in the temple is seemingly more casual than Troiolo's roving
eye ('l'occhio suo vago' [1.26.5]), but it penetrates the crowd more
forcefully and strikes Criseyde.[56] In this scene, Boccaccio and Chaucer
restage the Lover's experience with the 'mirrour perilous' in the *Rose*,

where he sees a 'roser chargid full of rosis' (*Romaunt* 1651) and arbitrarily fixes on one. Chaucer adds a stanza to Boccaccio that makes explicit the connection between sight and desire. The relevant lines are the following:

> And of hire look in him ther gan to quyken
> So gret desir and such affeccioun,
> That in his herte botme gan to stiken
> Of hir his fixe and depe impressioun.
>
> (1.295–8)

The precise nature of this impression is indicated by the *Consolation*. Boethius presents the Stoic contention that 'ymages and sensibili-ties...weren enprientid into soules fro bodyes withoute-forth' (*Boece* 5.m.4.6–10) much like letters written on parchment or figures reflected in a mirror. The soul, 'naked of itself' as Nicholas Trivet says in his gloss to the passage, receives the sense impressions brought to it whether by chance or design. But the limitation of this view, as Boethius points out, is that it allows the soul no capacity for knowledge or for moral discrimination. In other words, the mechanism of desire that Chaucer elaborates and ascribes to Troilus comes from a position that Boethius discredits.[57] Thus seen in the context of Chaucer's sources, the Trojans' festive worship of the image of Pallas is recreated in Troilus's idolatrous and solipsistic desire.

Chaucer effects a second change in this scene by reducing Boccaccio's rhetorical echoes of the Dolce Stilnuovo in portraying Criseyde and thereby removing her from associations with a divine miracle like Dan-te's Beatrice. His thematic stress falls on the blackness Criseyde inhabits. Chaucer fashions Boccaccio's phrase 'sotto candido velo in bruna vesta' ('under a white veil in a black habit' [1.26.8]), which echoes Beatrice's approach to Dante in *Purgatorio* 30, into a space of negativity that Troilus's desire penetrates, much as the dreamer in the *Rose* arbitrarily fixes his desire on a bud in the rose bush.[58] Criseyde, dressed in 'widewes habit blak' (1.170), stands near the door of the temple 'in hir blake wede' (1.177), and '[s]he, this in blak, likynge to Troilus / Over alle thing, he stood for to biholde' (1.309–10).

Troilus's love begins, then, with his eye piercing the darkness and seizing an image. The source of the image, as the poem makes clear, is not in itself passive, for Criseyde strikes a confident pose and asserts her right to stand where she wishes.[59] Nonetheless, she is experienced throughout the passage as an object seen, an image imprinted on the

soul from without. The narrator undertakes to recreate Troilus's subjective experience for us, telling us that Criseyde is 'so good a syghte' (294)
that 'hire look' (295) – but not 'l'angelico viso' as in Boccaccio (1.28.8) –
kindles desire and makes Troilus feel that his spirit dies in his heart
(307). Afterwards Troilus returns to his palace like the dreamer in the
Rose: 'Right with hire look thorugh-shoten and thorugh-darted' (325).
Even the brief physical description of Criseyde in this scene (281–7)
contributes to the experience of seeing. Chaucer renders the descriptive
passage without Boccaccio's references to 'bellezza / celestiale' (1.27.3–
4), and he rhetorically frames it as if it were a moment of attention
suspended within Troilus's gaze. In that specular moment, her graceful
limbs answer to womanhood, and she moves in such a way 'that men
myght in hire gesse / Honour, estat, and wommanly noblesse' (286–7). It
is this figure of his subjectivity that Troilus subsequently contemplates,
as he sits waking in his bed:

> . . . his spirit mette
> That he hire saugh a-temple, and al the wise
> Right of hire look, and gan it newe avise.
>
> Thus gan he make a mirour of his mynde,
> In which he saugh al holly hire figure. . . .
>   (1.362–6)

The phrase 'make a mirour of his mynde' appears in Love's description
of Swete-Thought (*Romaunt* 2804–8).[60] But in the *Rose* Love specifies
that Swete-Thought evokes the memory of past events to assuage the
lover's pain (2801–3, 2815–20). Troilus as yet shares no history with
Criseyde from which he might draw memories. It is, rather, the Boethian
overtone in the passage that conveys the essential idea of his desire: the
figure is insubstantial, its arrival analogous to the execution of a text on
a neutral medium – 'ryght as we ben wont somtyme by a swift poyntel to
fycchen lettres empriendid in the smothnesse or in the pleynesse of the
table of wex or in parchemyn that ne hath no figure ne note in it' (*Boece*
5.m.4.16–20). Criseyde is textualized at the moment Troilus moves from
sensuous apprehension to judgment and the mobilization of the will.

If Troilus's desire is somehow independent from its immediate object,
it continues on its own trajectory, gathering force beyond the reluctant
reinforcement Criseyde allows him in the first part of the poem. Troilus
remarks to Pandarus in their first meeting how 'desir so brennyngly me
assailleth' (1.607). Criseyde's letter to him increases his desire so that he

'gan to desiren moore / Thanne he did erst' (2.1339–40). Book 3 explores Troilus's experience most deeply. Chaucer adds a passage in which, after his first interview with Criseyde at Deiphebus's house, Troilus assimilates at least the outward appearance of Ovidian self governance, 'though as the fir he brende / For sharp desir of hope and of plesaunce' (3.425–6). In the consummation scene, he adds the allusion to St. Bernard's prayer to the Virgin from *Paradiso* 33, which not only provides the image of desire flying without wings but also connects erotic excess to theological grace: 'thi grace passed oure desertes' (3.1267). Parting from Criseyde, Troilus feels the compulsion of desire: 'desir right now so streyneth me / That I am ded anon, but I retourne' (3.1482–3).[61] Desire immediately aligns with the memory of pleasure (3.1531–3). Returning to his palace, Troilus realizes the vast and unforseen extent of his feelings: 'she for whom desir hym brende, / A thousand fold was worth more than he wende' (3.1539–40). Here, as in Boccaccio (3.53.7–8), desire runs ahead of its object, and memory drives it further: 'And verraylich of thilke remembraunce / Desir al newe hym brende, and lust to brede / Gan more than erst, and yet took he non hede' (3.1545–7).

We can delineate Troilus's desire further by its parallels in Criseyde and its final difference. Her first sight of Troilus, occurring like his by chance, largely replays Troilus's experience in the temple. Criseyde sees the outer figure and infers the inner virtues. But the complex process of her change from resistance to acceptance follows a different path from Troilus's increments of desire. The narrator refuses to identify the point at which she decides to love. As we have seen, when Pandarus brings them together at his house, Criseyde remarks that she has already decided to yield herself to Troilus. The difference between them becomes apparent after the lovers part in Book 3. As desire continues to grow in Troilus, Criseyde contemplates his virtues: 'His worthynesse, his lust, his dedes wise, / His gentilesse, and how she with hym mette' (3.1550–1). Chaucer presents this scene as a counterpart to Troilus's reflection in the palace, following Boccaccio who signals the parallel directly: 'Criseida seco facea il simigliante' (3.55.1). Yet while Troilus's desire moves forward, Criseyde remains in the same emotional register as earlier.[62] Each finds 'suffisaunce' (3.1309, 3.1716) in the other and reciprocates the other's pleasure (3.1690), but what they experience remains fundamentally distinct. Besides pleasure, Troilus feels 'a newe qualitee' (3.1654). Richard Firth Green proposes that this new quality is *trouthe*, which keeps the stylized game of love from becoming anarchy.[63] The context of the passage suggests, however, that Troilus is voicing his recognition of desire. He has just told Pandarus, 'ay the more that desir me biteth / To love hire best, the more it me deliteth' (3.1651–2). Pandarus affirms that the experience of 'hevene blisse' (3.1657) transforms one utterly. Troilus's new quality emerges internally as a state of erotic desire, not a moral virtue.

Set as it is within the tradition of the *Rose* and the *Consolation*, Troilus's desire is finally impoverished as an object of moral speculation. By comparison to Dante's analysis of desire in *Purgatorio* 17–18, it falls short of the synthesizing power that connects natural and elective love. Working within the terms of his authors, Chaucer depicts a love that must operate through absence, through the demand for another who cannot be fully present and available. His love for Criseyde is directed to what she herself identifies as a 'fals felicitee' (3.814), and those critics who have interpreted it as the confusion of a lower for a higher good accurately reproduce the assumptions that Chaucer writes into the poem through his sources. Under the pressure of history, love for Criseyde proves inadequate; as an object of desire, it signifies something else, which he reads, if only darkly, in other venues such as the house left desolate by her parting or the social world he cannot join with Sarpedon.[64]

The discrepancy between the object of Troilus's desire and desire itself nonetheless offers some suggestion of how he might escape the closed history of pagan antiquity. We have seen that, from its originary moment, Troilus's love is independent from Criseyde. Desire runs ahead of its object and connects with it in the center of the poem when Criseyde is moved to reciprocate through a process never wholly revealed to us and kept mysterious to her. After she leaves Troy for the Greek camp, Troilus suffers melancholy and struggles with doubts about her fidelity, but he does not abandon his desire. In a second echo of Guinizelli's doctrinal *canzone*, his only other use of the verb, the narrator remarks, 'ay on hire his herte gan repaire' (5.1571). Guinizelli's poem, we recall, ends with a fortuitous misperception as the speaker addresses God to apologize for mistaking his beloved for a heavenly angel. The object may be false, but the validity of his desire is not in doubt. Guinizelli's speaker insists, 'non me fu fallo, s'in lei posi amanza' ('It's not my fault if I fell in love with her' [4.60]). In the same way, Troilus's desire stands apart from and beyond Criseyde. When his brooch is discovered on Diomede's tunic and he cannot no longer resist consciousness and acknowledgment of Criseyde's betrayal, Troilus insists, 'I ne kan nor may, / For al this world, withinne myn herte fynde / To unloven yow a quarter of a day' (5.1696–8). Desire, too, has gone somewhere else, past capacity and will in a paradoxical liberation.

To many readers, the escape through desire must seem empty. It looks like an assertion of the self's most precious investment just when it can have no effect. Moreover, desire continues apace with the search for death, which Troilus, in fact, recognizes as soon as Criseyde leaves. 'Deth' is the first word he utters when he returns to his chamber (5.205). His frustrated quest to slay Diomede is an effort to kill not only his rival but also his new second self. Yet the problem of escaping history, as Patterson indicates, is the problem of escaping repetition. Troilus's perfunctory death at the hands of Achilles, occurring as it does in Chaucer with no supporting narrative or historical context, places desire beyond history. The narrator consciously eschews history, the record of heroic deeds and action: 'if I hadde ytaken for to write / The armes of this ilke worthi man, / Than wolde ich of his batailles endite' (5.1765–7). The topic, stressed emphatically at the end, is 'his love' (5.1769), not his 'worthi dedes' (5.1770) already textualized in Dares and the historians who follow on from him.

Troilus's escape from history is staged as his spirit rises up to the eighth sphere. It achieves, as E. Talbot Donaldson observed, 'that reward which medieval Christianity allowed to the righteous heathen' presumably because of his virtue, a human value transcending human life.[65] And like Trajan (the paradigmatic case in Dante and Langland), Troilus escapes not just the circumstances of his historical moment but the circumstances of history itself. We might say, however, that Troilus does not escape the textuality that releases him from history. His apotheosis is heavily overdetermined, with strands from Cicero's *Somnium Scipionis*, Dante's *Paradiso* 22, and Lucan's *Pharsalia*.[66] Its immediate source is Arcita's upward flight in the *Teseida*, which contains three distinct actions. His soul first apprehends the order of the universe, then judges the earth with respect to the heavens, and finally dismisses the funeral rites in his honor.

Chaucer follows this pattern, using *avysement* (5.1811) and *avyse* (5.1814) for Boccaccio's verbs *ammirava* (11.1.6) and *rimirare* (11.2.1) in the first two parts and giving these terms a meaning of perception through the intellect that is quite distinct from his usage elsewhere in the poem.[67] But he makes a significant change to the third action. In the *Teseida*, turning his eyes down to where he had left his body, Arcita laughs when he sees the mourners gathered round his corpse, which is the sign of his mortality and their blindness ('tenebrosa cechitate'). Chaucer creates a far more abstract scene by altering one essential detail: there is no corpse but only a place '[t]her he was slayn' (5.1820). His last sight of himself, like his first sight of Criseyde, penetrates to an empty locus.[68] What he sees there in the place of his death and the laments for him that represent culture and its human attachments thus follows 'blynde lust' (5.1824). 'Lust,' which designates everything from natural love to appetite, intention, pleasure, manners, and civic friendship, is defined at the last moment of Troilus's consciousness not by its being an inferior or lower good but by its being temporal – 'the which that may nat laste' (5.1824). History is where desire is blind because it is foreshortened.

Like Boccaccio in the *Teseida*, Chaucer exploits the ambiguity of Troilus's final disposition. Mercury decides where he is to go, but we are given no indication of where that might be. It is at this point that Troilus vanishes into exemplarity of two sorts. The first makes him a monitory figure for the audience of 'yonge, fresshe folkes' (5.1835), warning them to abandon worldly vanity and discover in Christ an object beyond 'feynede loves' (5.1848). Though Troilus is their ostensible antitype, they are, like him, to look up to their source of ultimate meaning: 'of youre herte up casteth the visage / To thilke God that after his ymage / Yow made' (5.1838–40). It is here that desire cannot be foreshortened: 'he nyl falsen no wight' (5.1845). The second kind of exemplarity redirects literary tradition, rejecting antiquity in its manifold cultural practices (rituals, gods, and the substance of its poetry) for Dante's hymn of praise to the Trinity. Those readers who regard the final stanzas as intrinsic to the poem argue plausibly that we are to see the limitation of Troilus's desire here measured against the only real standards of love, Christ's sacrifice and the Virgin's intercession. But I would propose that with Mercury's disposition Troilus's desire has already disappeared as a point of reference and topic of speculation. It persists only as a monitory and literary example, a shadow figure pointing to truths beyond itself. Troilus's escape from the twin necessity of history and love serves as an analogy, not a model of redemption through grace. Its most powerful lesson is to show us how the past can open up and interrogate the present but not solve its most profound concerns.

3
The 'confusioun of gentil wemen': Antiquity and the Short Side of History

In the narratives of Thebes and Troy, Chaucer displays antiquity from a dominant position. Virtually all his characters are noble; the common story they enact is the fall of an ancient city; the themes that organize their thoughts and actions are necessity and choice. Above all, the predicaments his poems explore with extraordinary subtlety are those of male aristocratic subjects facing the convergence of history and desire.[1] What lends a tragic, exemplary, and moral dimension to these poems is the element of human agency, which holds out the possibility of resisting necessity. At one level, this resistance portrays antiquity heroically and nobly at its limit, as reason and human abilities encounter history and destiny. At another, the gestures of resistance preserve the ideological fiction that necessity finally bears down on ancient heroic culture and, by extension, on medieval chivalric culture. The alternative raised in the historiographical tradition behind Chaucer's poems of antiquity – namely, that catastrophe is not external but at least partly generated from within – is thus obscured or aestheticized. The discourse of antique epic and tragedy drives from consciousness the very agency that Gower acknowledges in Chaucer's contemporary moment: 'For man is cause of that schal falle' (*Confessio Amantis* Prologue 528).[2]

The characters who most fully register alternatives to the dominant view of antiquity are the aristocratic women subordinated to historical necessity in the heroic narratives of Thebes and Troy. Emily scarcely speaks in the Knight's Tale; her Amazon sisters, living under authority delegated to Hippolyta, have been left behind in Boccaccio's preamble to the story of Arcita and Palemone. Anelida articulates the question that hovers over Theban and Trojan history – 'Wher is the trouthe of man?' (312) – but the poem, if completed, would evidently sever erotic deceit from history and treat it as the fit topic only for static complaint. For all our apparent intimacy with Criseyde's thoughts, speech, and writing, she remains somehow obscured from our understanding. She rightly predicts that, isolated even from women's sympathy, she will be a victim of history written to uphold a dominant position: 'thise bokes wol me shende' (5.1060). She is hostage, in Carolyn Dinshaw's phrase, to reading like a man – the narrow understanding of a text that controls its potentially disruptive elements and leads to an overall impoverishment of meaning.[3]

The poem that challenges the dominant perspective on antiquity is the *Legend of Good Women*, but the challenge has largely gone unrecognized. For the most part, the stories of the *Legend* have been read through the optic that Alceste furnishes and Cupid confirms in the Prologue: Chaucer is to write of women who 'weren trewe in lovyng al hire lives; / And telle of false men that hem bytraien' (F 485–6).[4] Comparison of the stories and their sources has shown that the narrator, as John Fyler says, 'passes on distorted versions of the stories he learns from others,' presumably to further this program.[5] Florence Percival contends that in the legends 'Ovidian sympathy for women is mingled with Ovidian cynicism.'[6] Chaucer's representation of women and his wondrously ambivalent exhortation to them, 'trusteth, as in love, no man but me' (2559–61) inevitably raise questions about what is at stake in his voicing of feminine subjects within Cupid's social text of 'fyn lovyng.' In this chapter, I want to argue a different reading of the stories. Though the narratives recounted in the *Legend* cannot reverse history, they can offer a view of it that locates the causes of catastrophe internally – that is, within characters and within ideology, institutions, and cultural values. The women of antiquity demonstrate the vulnerability of the dominant position, most notably in its imperial projects, the protocols regulating courtly culture, and the patriarchal family that underwrites social, political, and cultural institutions. Through them, Chaucer shows us antiquity from the short side of history.

In this respect, the *Legend* diverges from medieval narratives whose focus is ostensibly on women's virtue. The most renowned collection of such narratives, Boccaccio's *De mulieribus claris*, was once thought to be a source for the *Legend*, and it remains a useful contrast in form and treatment. Boccaccio, taking Petrarch's *De viris illustribus* and the tradition of male anecdotal biography as his starting point, proposes to remedy the neglect of women by writers. He treats virtuous men and women as identical in kind but different in their natural endowments. Women, he says, are naturally frailer in body and more sluggish of mind, and for this reason the deeds of women who have acquired the 'manly spirit' to perform great deeds deserve even more to be remembered. Fame rather than virtue is his criterion of inclusion, but Boccaccio's writing remains firmly within the aims of the middle style, which is to blame vice and praise virtue.

In the *De mulieribus claris*, Boccaccio's discourse of feminine virtue stands precisely beside the misogyny that generated it and seeks to deny itself. Semiramis's political shrewdness is overshadowed by sexual appetite and incest (ch. 2), while Cleopatra's appetite furthers her political ends (ch. 86). The story of Piramus and Thisbe (ch. 12) illustrates the need for temperance. Medea's wanderings (ch. 17) are a monitory example against the lust of the eyes. Boccaccio, unlike Chaucer, tells the full story of Hypermnestra, in which Danaus is killed and she is freed from prison, restored as Lynceus's queen, and made a priestess of Juno. Hypsipyle's full story (ch. 15) is a romance of separation and reunion with her sons by Jason. The story of Dido (ch. 40) aims to restore the reputation of her widowhood and chastity – even to the point of staging Dido's suicide as Aeneas first arrives in Carthage. Boccaccio comes closest to Chaucer's treatment in his stories of Lucretia (ch. 46) and Virginia (ch. 56), which acknowledge the social and political threats of the state to patriarchy and family by clearly placing their heroines within the twin regimens of fatherly power and marriage. But Chaucer, as we shall see, goes beyond the pathos of women's tragic deaths to reveal the failures within antiquity as a model for ideology and social relations.

Alternatives to empire: two African queens

Chaucer's iconic portrayal of the *Aeneid* in Book I of the *House of Fame* is a richly suggestive rehearsal of the predicament and themes that he will develop in the *Legend of Good Women* and set against the epic world of Thebes, Troy, and Rome. Eros literally and symbolically moves into history in the glass temple described at the start of the narrator's dream. There the narrator encounters an array of visual images, portraits, and figures standing for narratives. Marilynn Desmond has argued that the narrator's account reveals 'the unrepresentability of woman, except as representation' – that is, as a figure talked about rather than speaking, one who functions in another's discourse of power.[7] Yet the figure of Venus '[n]aked fletynge in a see' (133), surrounded by iconographical details such as her doves and attended by Cupid and Vulcan, focuses and dominates the visual images. This *ekphrasis* is a static emblem of natural appetite glossed by figures associated with three different narratives: the courtly pursuit overseen by Cupid in the *Roman de la rose*, domestic life represented by Venus's lawful if unsatisfying marriage to Vulcan, and the suppressed example of Venus's betrayal of Vulcan with Mars. All three modes – courtly, domestic, and martial – variously recur in the *Legend*. The story that gives them life and resonance in the *House of Fame* is a retelling of the *Aeneid* that jettisons Vergil's imperial design in order to privilege the subjectivity sacrificed to destiny.

The narrator's rehearsal of images and story gives a special prominence to Venus's intervention in history.[8] Venus descends from heaven to urge Aeneas to flee Troy (162–5), intervenes with Jupiter to save Aeneas and his fleet from Aeolus's winds (212–18), directs him to Carthage and reunion with his men (225–38), and causes Dido to fall in love with Aeneas (239–44). Though these episodes have their sources in Vergil, Chaucer adapts them to a different design. In Vergil, Neptune acts alone when he calms the winds threatening Aeneas's destruction at sea.[9] Juno devises the love affair with Dido as a plot to thwart Aeneas's destiny, while here Venus is the sole author. At the end of his summary, the narrator places Venus's role in high relief against Juno and the 'alle the mervelous signals / Of the goddys celestials' (459–60): 'Jupiter took of hym cure / At the prayer of Venus' (464–5).

An equally prominent feature of Chaucer's rewriting is the theme of duplicitous language. The narrator's confident iteration of his visual witness – 'I saugh' and 'sawgh I grave' – stands over and against the deceitful speech and dissembling that drive the tale he relates.[10] Language and social performance complement one another in a scenario of deception and betrayal. Synon causes the destruction of Troy 'with his false forswerynge, / And his chere and his lesynge' (153–4). Dido bestows her beneficence on Aeneas '[w]enynge hyt had al be so / As he hir swor' (262–3). Soon enough she has cause to complain not just of Aeneas but of male duplicity in general: 'O, have ye men such godlyhede / In speche, and never a del of trouthe?' (330–1). Chaucer omits one detail that implicates Dido in verbal fraud – her deception of Anna as she plans her suicide (*Aeneid* 4.474–503) – and he appends a list of men who practice an 'untrouthe' (384) similar in kind to Aeneas's: Demophon, Achilles, Paris, Jason, Hercules, and Theseus. All are false lovers addressed in Ovid's *Heroides* and mentioned variously in the *Rose*, Machaut's *Jugement du Roy de Navarre*, and the *Ovide moralisé*. It is not coincidental that they are also characters in the master narrative of Theban and Trojan history. Deception remains the same in the public and private sphere alike.

The corollary of false speech, as Dido recognizes, is injurious Fame. Like Criseyde (5.1058–64), she laments that her reputation will be lost through rumor and textualized in consequence of heroic exploits not her own: 'For thorgh yow is my name lorn, / And alle myne actes red and songe / Over al thys londe, on every tonge' (346–8). Yet the books that preserve reputation and cultural memory are themselves the products of authorial intention and hermeneutics; they are thus located in history, too. Chaucer gives two examples of this transcription, which register his uneasy tie to Vergilian authority. When Dido realizes that Aeneas will betray her, Chaucer invents a speech in which Dido rehearses the various motives for male perfidy while lamenting Aeneas's betrayal and her loss of reputation (300–60). As he moves from the first topic to the second, he asserts the place of his dream and memory within Vergil's overall narrative: 'Non other auctour alegge I' (314). Later, he suggests that Vergil's own story is a convenience. The book, he says, has Mercury appear 'to excusen Eneas / Fullyche of al his grete trespas' (427–8). At the moment Vergil's narrative is about to write her into its tale as an icon of love sacrificed to duty, Chaucer raises questions about its capacity to tell an adequate or reliable story.[11]

Chaucer's authorial resistence to Vergil has a shape and a previous textual warrant. Fyler notes that Geffrey is first a passive observer, then a commentator and participant who reshapes his source in the Dido story, and finally an observer again as he summarizes the *Aeneid*'s last eight books.[12] In the tradition emanating from Fulgentius, Dido signifies lust and the episode represents Aeneas's moral adolescence.[13] Though Sheila Delany has argued that medieval Orientalism works to the same moralizing effect in the *Legend*, Chaucer largely ignores this hermeneutic tradition.[14] He turns instead to Ovid's *Heroides*, a collection of verse epistles by women to men who have abandoned them in one fashion or another. The *Heroides* provide both a literary model and a direct source for the Dido Chaucer sympathetically portrays. As Ovid's allusions to his *Amores* indicate, these letters are associated with a conscious turn from epic in both form and subject matter. Modern readers have seen in them a sustained exercise in poetic indeterminacy and instability.[15] For Chaucer, they underwrite the effort to see classical heroism from the other side. E.K. Rand notes that the Dido story in the *House of Fame* reads as if it were composed by Ovid. By that he means the Ovid of the elegies for whom heroism is a foil for erotic poetry.[16]

Chaucer's interpolation of Dido's perspective into the *Aeneid* is only one modification of Vergilian history. Equally important for the *Legend* is his exploitation of the rhetorical and dramatic situation developed in the *Heroides*. Ovid's epistles employ the conventions of the *suasoriae*, speeches directed to historical and mythological personnages at their moment of crucial decision, and *ethopoeia*, speeches supposedly by famous figures. From these models, Ovid creates a situation of address in which a woman speaker fated to suffer a great loss or tragic end tries to persuade a man not to follow a course whose outcome we already know. The disparity between what we know and what we pretend the speaker does not yet know allows pathos, aesthetic distance, and moral deliberation. No reader of the poems actually believes that the speech will have an effect. The figures the speakers ostensibly seek to persuade, Warren Ginsberg notes, are absent.[17] The poems therefore feature emotion and rhetorical ethos drawn from a consciously literary world.[18] Nonetheless we are intensely curious to see what arguments might be mustered if choice were real instead of hypothetical or, as in Ovid's case, fictitious and fictional. In *Heroides* 7, Chaucer found, I would argue, a still further use of the form: rather than portray the lover's complaint as psychological portraiture and aesthetic choice, he uses it as a way to represent history as it is experienced.

Ovid's Dido speaks from the paradoxical strength of concession. Having lost her achievements, fame, and her chastity of body and soul, what does it matter now, she asks, if she wastes her words trying to move Aeneas by her prayers? She thus turns her subordination to rhetorical advantage. In particular, she is able to depict history outside the constraints of imperial destiny. Viewed on its own terms, Dido argues, Aeneas's departure trades the certainty of her love for flux and repetition. In *Heroides* 7, the imagery of wind and waves signifies instability, while the contrasts between Carthage and Italy convey cyclical history. Aeneas has abandoned his secure position as her consort to resume his role as a foreigner and exile. *Hospes* ('guest'), the term that describes his position as Dido takes him in, comes to denote the rootlessness and alienation that await him (7.146 *hospes* 'foreigner'). Leaving what he has done for what must be begun anew, Dido reminds him, he searches for a realm he cannot at the moment even locate. His ambitions there are to raise another city and find another wife ('altera Dido' [7.19]); his means, as before, will be bad faith. As Dido recites her own story of founding Carthage while fleeing her brother and then fending off enemies and suitors, she offers it as the stable achievement that Aeneas abandons for an uncertain reception. With an irony she seems not to appreciate fully, she juxtaposes her dead husband Sychaeus, a constant husband with an inconstant wife, to Aeneas, an inconstant husband with a constant wife.

The story of Dido recounted in the *Legend* absorbs a number of themes developed in the *House of Fame* and *Heroides* 7. The narrator's suggestion in the *House of Fame* that there are alternatives to the Vergilian account emerges as full-scale authorial ambivalence. Taking the 'tenor' from Vergil and Ovid but reserving the 'grete effectes' to himself (929), the narrator insistently stages his resistance. In half a dozen places, he overtly suppresses portions of Vergil's account as extraneous to his aims or wasteful of time. The doubt expressed earlier in the *House of Fame* about Mercury's intervention becomes skepticism first about Venus's making Aeneas invisible (1020–2) and then, even more emphatically, about the substitution of Cupid for Ascanius: 'as of that scripture / Be as be may, I take of it no cure' (1144–5). As Vergil declines as an authority, he takes with him the apparatus of authorship that Chaucer seemingly venerates elsewhere in his poetry. When the narrator mentions him as 'oure autour' (1139) and '[t]he autour' (1228), his tone is distant. He refers to the 'bok' and 'scripture' as sources to be challenged. By contrast, 'myn auctour' (1352) is Ovid, and the poem ends with a close translation of the opening of *Heroides* 7, along with directions on where to find the rest of Dido's letter.[19]

As in Chaucer's earlier version of Dido's story, the narrator associates Aeneas with duplicitous speech, but the *Legend* supplies a context of action to the emblem of Dido as a betrayed lover. In one sense, Aeneas's vivid account of his exploits to the queen is a prelude to his deception, and though Dido will lament her loss of fame at the end (1361), it is Aeneas who complains that the story of Troy's fall from prosperity is widely known: 'Thourghout the world oure shame is kid so wyde' (1028). The decisive point occurs with Aeneas's promises to Dido in the cave, where he 'swore so depe to hire to be trewe / For wel or wo and chaunge hire for no newe' (1234–5). When Dido accepts him as her husband, a detail not in Vergil, he is already seen retrospectively as a 'fals lovere' (1236). The narrator immediately denounces him to the 'sely wemen' (1254) who presumably profit from the lesson of 'sely Dido' (1237). They are to see through the elaborate social performance that accompanies his double speech (1264–76) and represents Chaucer's wholesale interpolation of chivalric courtliness and gentility into the story. Aeneas quickly wearies of Dido and his pretense, secretly prepares his departure, and, mustering 'his false teres' (1301), tells her of the prophetic message from Anchises and Mercury. The details of the dream accord with Vergil and Chaucer makes no effort here to discredit the dream directly, but the sequence of events leading to it – disaffection, preparations, disclosure – marks the dream as a strategem.

Beyond deconstructing Vergil's narrative of empire and destiny, Chaucer consciously recontextualizes the story. We have seen how he casts Aeneas as a duplicitous courtly lover repeating the pattern of Arcite in *Anelida and Arcite*. Dido is a courtly heroine, 'holden of alle queenes flour / Of gentillesse, of fredom, of beaute' (1009–10). In a striking passage not fully explained (1035–43), the narrator claims that her beauty and moral virtues would make her a fit love for God. In succouring Aeneas and his men, she exercises 'fredom' (1127), the aristocratic virtue of both generosity and magnificence. Her love for Aeneas, as Robert Worth Frank, Jr., points out, develops in 'a kind of double time,' for she falls in love both immediately and gradually.[20] The larger forces driving her love are fortune and erotic necessity, not Vergil's Fate. Chaucer inserts a passage with the Boethian tones of the Knight's Tale and *Troilus and Criseyde* to make it clear that Fortune discloses Aeneas's presence as his men make supplication to Dido in the temple: 'Fortune, that hath the world in governaunce, / Hath sodeynly brought in so newe a chaunce / That nevere was ther yit so fremde a cas' (1044–6). When the narrator comes 'to th'effect, now to the fruyt of al, / Whi I have told this story' (1160–1), his topic is Dido's passion, whose source is Love's compelling power: 'finaly, it may nat ben withstonde; / Love wol love, for nothing wol it wonde' (1186–7).

The most revealing context of Dido's story is one not available in Chaucer's earlier version. The story in the *Legend* foregrounds *Troilus and Criseyde* as a means for reading Aeneas and Dido. The narrative proper begins with mention of Troy's fall through Greek deception (930–45), and Chaucer evokes the frame of chronicle history for Aeneas's journey. As in Vergil, the *ekphrasis* of the city's destruction and Aeneas's own account of its fall are the emotional focus. But the echoes of *Troilus and Criseyde* show that the Troy story does not necessarily continue directly into Roman history in the steady progress of the *translatio imperii*; it can be diverted or forced back into repetition. As Dido sees Aeneas 'lyk a knyght' (1066), she re-enacts Criseyde's first sight of Troilus (2.624–37). His place in her thought (1172), which she discloses to Anna, recalls Criseyde's subsequent contemplation of Troilus (2.659–62). Using a pervasive rhyme from *Troilus and Criseyde*, the narrator collapses Troilus's double sorrow into the single event of the nuptials in the cave: 'this was the firste morwe / Of hire gladnesse, and gynning of hire sorwe' (1230–1). Similarly, the rhyming of 'joye' and 'Troye' signals the imminent betrayal of Dido's love as well as the tragic cycle of destruction. For Aeneas and his men, Dido's generosity and the interlude in Carthage are a remedy for what they have lost: 'This Eneas is come to paradys / Out of the swolow of helle, and thus in joye / Remembreth hym of his estat in Troye' (1103–5). Dido shares 'in plesaunce and in joye, / With alle these newe lusty folk of Troye' (1150–1). When he succeeds in wooing her, Aeneas finds an erotic and material surplus: 'Now laugheth Eneas and is in joye / And more richesse than evere he was in Troye' (1252–3). As Frank points out, Dido's lavish giftgiving represents 'her heedless giving of self' and continues the process of falling in love.[21] Yet as in *Troilus and Criseyde*, the consequences of betrayal are political as well as personal. Amidst her appeals to pity and obligation when Aeneas announces his monitory dream, Dido recognizes the threat that her love has made actual: 'These lordes, which that wonen me besyde, / Wole me distroyen only for youre sake' (1317–18). The prospect of political alliance (*foedus*) with the Trojans mitigates her encirclement by barbarians and the threats that remain from her earlier conflict with Pygmalion.[22] Her death ends the pregnancy that would complicate but also broaden the power of a Trojan dynasty in Africa.

In the end, Dido succumbs to history as both a destinal force and textual authority. Aeneas steals away to Italy and Lavinia, his 'altera terra' and 'altera Dido.' The cloth and sword he leaves behind are symbols of his absence, and it is significant that Chaucer selects them as the 'exuviae' ('relics') in the last lines he quotes from Vergil. The final word is from Ovid in a text whose opening enters Chaucer's poem while the body remains to be read outside. But if Dido's story loses to the narrative of empire, it nonetheless succeeds in showing what that narrative must hold contained within itself. The *gentilesse* that Aeneas shows as a lover serves, as Lee Patterson observes, as an attraction to deceive women and dignify an appetite that will undo the noble world.[23] Dido's protest, 'I am a gentil woman and a queen' (1306), discloses an aristocratic world at the mercy of itself.[24] 'Dischevele' (1315), pleading for mercy from Aeneas, Dido is the image abroad that Lucrece later becomes at home, first in her vulnerability within an aristocratic Roman household (1720) and then in her public dishonor (1829). Dido's story warns that Aeneas not only abandons the erotic but simultaneously embraces a history where the public, domestic, and private spheres continue at risk.

Much of what Dido's story teaches is replayed in the story of Cleopatra, which opens the *Legend*. Chaucer's narrator insists that the tale is 'storyal soth, it is no fable' (702). We might interpret his remark as not just the conventional distinction between actual events (*res gestae*) and fiction (*fabula*) but also as a recognition of the historical implications of the story. All Chaucer's 'storial' tales are about Roman topics. The intersection of history and eros occurs immediately in the Cleopatra story and may reflect the influence of Boccaccio's *De casibus virorum illustrium*, which emphasizes Antony's exchange of Roman titles and triumphs for sensuality and sloth.[25] Love's coercive power, which brings Antony in a 'rage' and holds him 'so narwe bounden in his las' (600) leads him to reverse Aeneas's earlier path. He abandons his Roman wife, the 'altera Dido' whom Aeneas seeks, for an African lover. Antony becomes '[r]ebel unto the toun of Rome' (591) because he leaves 'the suster of Cesar' (592). That he does so in imitation of Aeneas's stealing away from Dido at night (1326) is indicated by Chaucer's phrasing: 'He lafte hire falsly, or that she was war' (593). By marrying Cleopatra, Antony threatens to take Aeneas's *translatio* a step further, removing imperial destiny from Rome and installing it in yet another locale. Desire and marriage, the private and domestic are already in the political sphere.[26] For that reason, the mechanism for both Antony's falling in love and his loss of worldly prosperity is Fortune. Moreover, Antony's reversal of Aeneas suggests that the imperial enterprise itself may be contained within repetition. If Aeneas leaves behind a potential rival in Carthage, Antony and Cleopatra create a potential successor in Ptolemaic Egypt.

In Antony, Chaucer creates an erotic hero who realizes what Aeneas cuts short, yet the narrative structure of the poem lays the emphasis finally on Cleopatra. Antony assumes that desire can be separated from its historical consequences: 'al the world he sette at no value' (602). He undertakes the courtly project of service to Cleopatra, and she loves him in return as a reward for service ('[t]hourgh his desert') and 'for his chyvalrye' (608). Delany contends that Antony does everything wrong except being a lover, while Frank argues, 'Antony is *almost* a chivalric figure.'[27] In any event, the battle scene that demonstrates his martial qualities is notable for its shift away from him toward the tumult of naval warfare. And after that scene the focus rests on Cleopatra, whom Chaucer portrays as an icon of 'trouthe' (668) against the traditions of misogyny. Chaucer's likely source, a short entry in Vincent of Beauvais's *Speculum Historiale*, portrays her as inconstant in battle and in love, but she acts explicitly as Antony's wife in the *Legend*.[28] She therefore claims fully the role that Chaucer had secured for Dido by way of Ovid.

The proof of Cleopatra's fidelity – the truth in her loving – comes in the admixture of sexuality and death that ends her story in the *Legend*. Cleopatra orders a tomb constructed for Antony's body. In one respect, she carries out what Dido thinks she intends in remaining faithful to Sychaeus: 'ille meos, primus qui me sibi iunxit, amores / abstulit; ille habeat secum seruetque sepulcro' ('He who married me first stole my love; let him keep it with him and preserve it in the grave' [*Aeneid* 4.28–9]). In another respect, her gesture locates Antony within the tradition of chronicle histories. Like the tomb Priam constructs for Hector in the Troy stories, Antony's shrine is an aesthetic object made '[o]f all the rubyes and the stones fyne / In al Egypte that she coude espie' (673–4); this wondrous structure contains a second aesthetic object, the embalmed corpse that simulates the living man, which is a source of memory and wonder in Benoît, Guido, and Lydgate. The grave she chooses for herself is set next to Antony's monument; it is the snake pit that she enters 'naked, with ful good herte' (696). She is clothed only in her good intentions and wifely fidelity – precisely as Cupid understands the world of authors in the Prologue to the *Legend*.

The composite image of her death gives us a figure of desire channeled into devoted marriage, a wife physically subordinated to her husband, and a shrine of Roman courtly chivalry founded on an African female body through her agency. The speech Cleopatra makes before descending shows how fully integrated and internalized eros and history have become. Antony is the 'love' and 'knyght' whom she has chosen to obey. Cleopatra has taken on within herself the 'covenaunt' (688, 695) to match his feelings, subject only to the limits of propriety – '[u]nreprovable unto my wyfhod' (691) – of a Roman *matrona*. Claiming with her last words, 'Was nevere unto hire love a trewer quene' (695), she repeats Dido's suicide within a licit and recognized marriage. Just as Troilus maintains *trouthe* to his desire, Cleopatra preserves fidelity to a marriage founded on desire. But where Troilus escapes history, Chaucer's Cleopatra remains within it as a figure of resistance to the mythological and historical claims of imperial narrative.

Courtly culture and 'foul delyt'

Aeneas's deception exemplifies the sacrifice of eros to history. Charting the course of Dido's infatuation, her 'nyce lest' (287), the sympathetic narrator of the *House of Fame* adds apostrophes and proverbs that lead to a single conclusion: 'Therfore be no wyght so nyce / To take a love oonly for chere, / Or speche, or for frendly manere' (276–8). On the one hand, his counsel seems directed to a timeless realm of practical advice, and its persuasive power depends on the force of worldly wisdom. As the noun 'wyght' indicates, the lesson applies to men and women alike. On the other hand, his remark addresses a chivalric world whose origins and protocols Chaucer situates in antiquity. Appearance, speech, and manner are the social and rhetorical facets composing the courtly subject; through them a vast array of public events is negotiated and decided – history follows from artfulness. His advice, then, is not just general but historically specific and culturally resonant. If antiquity allows philosophical speculation about destiny and choice for heroic men, it permits in the *Legend* an internal critique of courtly culture. The authorizing sources of medieval aristocratic myth and practice show themselves already compromised at their origins.

Jason is the figure around whom this critique is organized. The pattern that Chaucer associates with Jason as the mark of his treachery is repetition. Jason's betrayal of love links the stories of Hypsipyle and Medea in a single legend, and it is repeated in the stories of Ariadne and Phyllis, where erotic treachery reaches across generations, from father to son, in the examples of Theseus and Demophon. In the sequence of Chaucer's legends, Jason is the first male lover for whom there are no excuses or narrative alibis. Antony's incontinence in abandoning Octavia is testimony to his passion for Cleopatra; Piramus simply misreads the sign of Thisbe's wimple; Aeneas has the pretext of divine warnings to leave Dido. By contrast, in the twin story of Hypsipyle and Medea, the fourth in Chaucer's *Legend*, Jason is the 'rote of false lovers' (1368). He is both the originating source and the prime example for all erotic betrayals. His duplicity reaches, however, significantly beyond the private sphere of his love affairs, for it threatens not just 'gentil wemen, tendre creatures' (1370) but the cultural practices through which an aristocratic world functions. Putting love at risk, he also risks the public realm that love dignifies conceptually and maintains practically.

Jason devalues love and desire by reducing them to appetite. As Chaucer represents it here, appetite is concerned with immediate objects of sensuous gratification, and these objects are replaceable and interchangeable.[29] The governing metaphor of Jason's appetite is ravenous consumption. At the start of Hypsipyle's tale, the narrator rebukes him as a 'sly devourere / Of gentil wemen' (1369–70) and names his passion as 'foul delyt' (1380). He makes a point of contrasting Jason's passion with 'the loveris maladye / Of Hereos' and the 'manye' (I.1373–4) which Arcite suffers in the Knight's Tale. At the start of Medea's tale, the same terms recur. Jason is 'of love devourer and dragoun' (1581); these two facets of appetite – the general and the specific – will be brought together later in the devouring Minotaur whom Theseus must face in the labyrinth (1937, 1947, 1976). For the moment, Chaucer insists on the parallelism and repetition, hence the equivalence of any one woman among the class of 'gentil wemen.' The importance of this equivalence becomes even more apparent when we recall that Chaucer suppresses the hostility of Hypsipyle and Medea in the *Heroides*.[30] With Medea as with Hypsipyle, Jason is focused on erotic consumption: 'For to desyren thourgh his apetit / To don with gentil women his delyt, / This is his lust and his felicite' (1586–8).

The appetite that Jason embodies is obsessive, defective, and feminine. Though it shares with the Ovidian lover a common metaphor of hunting, it differs by having no control and no sense of real pleasure. Jason enjoys no peace, the narrator insists, because his appetite is insatiable 'as a welle that were botomles' (1584) and because it is migratory – 'As mater apetiteth forme alwey / And from forme into forme it passen may' (1582–3). Moving from one object to another, he exists only moment by moment. He is continually in a state of coming-to-be and passing-away, unable to sustain himself independently from the women who become his projects of seduction. As mere matter, he lacks the definition of form, hence an authentic state of being. He can come into being only through the agency of the women he victimizes. Chaucer's description of Jason's marriage to Hypsipyle gives a revealing expression to his deficieny: 'Jason wedded was / Unto this queen and tok of hir substaunce / What so hym leste unto his purveyaunce' (1559–61). Her 'substaunce' is both her possessions and her essential qualities.

Chaucer's source for depicting Jason's appetite marks it as specifically feminine. In Guido delle Colonne, it is Medea who is described in this way: 'Scimus enim mulieris animum semper virum appetere, sicut appetit materia semper formam.'[31] In his translation of this passage in the *Troy Book*, Lydgate manages to synthesize Guido's concept and Chaucer's language:

> For as matere by naturel appetit,
> Kynd[e]ly desyreth after forme,
> Til he his course by processe may parforme,
> So þis wommen restreyn[en] hem ne can
> To sue her lust ay fro man to man.
>
> (1.1876–80)

Jason is doubly feminized by Chaucer's relocation of the passage from its source in Guido. In the logic of comparison, he is subordinated to his appetitive objects, as matter is to form. At the same time, he takes on the prime features of women in misogynistic literature – mutability and instability ('semper mutabile femina').

If Jason's appetite calls into question a fundamental value of Chaucer's classicized aristocratic culture, his practice as a lover erodes the conventions that allow it to operate. The exemplary power of classical heroes and heroines depends on their remaining fundamentally identical across time and custom. To be intelligible, the courtly world must employ a coherent code so that the signs of gentility can be read immediately. In practice, this means accepting appearance at face value, without the interference of ambiguity, irony, or dissembling. Aeneas, we have noted, is seen by Dido in much the same way as Criseyde sees Troilus – 'lyk a knyght.' Jason's repeated deception threatens these protocols. At the start of Hypsipyle's story, the narrator of the *Legend* highlights the means of Jason's subversion. He denounces his appearance, language, 'feyned trouthe' and manner, his obedience, deference, and 'contrefeted peyne and wo' (1372–6) – in short, the outward signs ostensibly denoting his inner gentility and signifying his membership in the company of ancient heroes. These traits reappear in Medea's story, as she first sees him. Jason is 'a semely man withalle'; he is 'lyk a lord' and 'goodly of his speche,' and 'coude of love al craft and art pleyner / Withoute bok' (1603–8). In her complaint, translated from *Heroides* 12.11–12, Medea again remarks the signs of his apperance: 'Why lykede me thy yelwe her to se.... Why lykede me thy youthe and thy fayrnesse, / And of thy tonge, the infynyt graciousnesse?' (1672–5).

It would miss the point of Chaucer's revision of Guido and Ovid to argue merely that Jason simply dissembles and simulates courtly values. In Guido, Jason is first portrayed as an honest and innocent figure, and the force of Chaucer's critique depends on these qualities. Under Pelleus's regency, Jason is described, without irony, as 'a famous knyght of gentilesse, / Of fredom, and of strengthe and lustynesse' (1404–5). His virtues confer on Jason the popular affection that makes Pelleus see in him a potential rival. We are never told what causes Jason to become duplicitous. The essential point, then, is that Jason begins from and remains within the values of chivalric culture. His duplicity does not mimic qualities he does not possess; rather, it suppresses those honorable traits which we see in him initially. In this way, Chaucer mounts an internal critique rather than an external challenge. Furthermore, if he obscures the moment of Jason's transformation from chivalric hero to erotic traitor, he sets out a sequence of events that connect public and private deception. Pelleus sends Jason on the quest for the Golden

Fleece, feigning '[g]ret chere of love and of affeccioun' (1421) to cover his stratagem for destroying Jason. From this perspective, the betrayals of Hypsipyle and Medea, which occur as incidents in Jason's heroic endeavour, are repetitions of the duplicity which launched it.

Jason's seduction and betrayal of Hypsiple take place against the twin backdrop of epic history and a chivalric social code. As Hypsipyle recounts in *Thebaid* 5 (49–498), the Lemnian women murder their husbands and children in retribution for the men's abandoning them in order to pursue war in Thrace. Hypsipyle alone saves her father from the slaughter; at the end of the episode she must take flight from the vengeance of the other women. In the background story, Jason arrives with Hercules and the rest of the Argonauts to an island that has been depopulated of men and stripped of its families: 'non arva viri, non aequora vertunt, / conticuere domus' ('No men are left to plough the fields or cleave the waves, silent are the homes' [5.309–10]). The women have acted on Venus's promise of better marriages ('melioraque foedera iungam' [5.138]), but have since repented their crimes.[32] Chaucer's *Legend* suppresses this background in order to insert a different narrative with an alternate ending. In Statius, the Lemnian women mistake the arriving Argonauts for Thracians and frantically resist their landing in an almost comic grotesque (5.356–7) that is his view of heroic warfare elsewhere with the Argive and Theban armies. In Chaucer, Hypsipyle is at leisure; she has gone 'pleying' and 'romynge on the clyves by the se' (1469–70), when she first sees Jason's ship. She sends her messenger to offer comfort to the storm-tossed sailors, 'as was hire usaunce / To fortheren every wight, and don plesaunce / Of verrey bounte and of curteysye' (1476–8). Jason likewise has come 'for to pleye out of the se' (1495). While her messenger talks with him, Hypsiple and her 'meyne' (1498) encounter the visitors and conduct them to the castle where they show them 'gret honour' (1508). What Chaucer has done is to inject elements of the story of Jason and Lamedon from Guido's *Historia*, which is the remote cause of the Trojan War. Far from continuing violence, Hypsipyle takes the steps that could have avoided tragic history.

Hypsipyle's natural courtesy establishes the social horizon and moral values of the story, suppressing along the way Ovid's disclosure of a darker, more menacing self.[33] Her instinctive response to Jason and his party demonstrates the Chaucerian aristocratic precept 'pitee renneth soone in gentil herte.' Hypsipyle assumes, too, that the signs of gentility will translate directly from one people to another, as Diomede insisted to Criseyde. She appraises Jason and his companions not only by their appearance but by what their appearance signifies: 'she tok hed, and knew by hyre manere, / By hire aray, by wordes, and by chere, / That it were gentil-men of gret degre' (1504–6). Social rather than personal identity is her concern; only after extended conversation does she learn that the renowned Jason and Hercules are her guests. Likewise, Jason's seduction is a social performance that depends on the transparency of signs. Hypsipyle opens her heart to Hercules without guile, while Jason and Hercules concoct the 'shrewed lees' that betrays her innocence. In the *Thebaid*, the Argonauts are revealed to the Lemnian women by the light of Jupiter's thunderbolt; their sudden appearance transforms the women from warriors and returns their sexuality: 'rediit in pectora sexus' (5.397). Chaucer's Hypsipyle is the victim of mediated desire and polished stagecraft. Hercules praises Jason to her for his personal and social attributes, and attributes to him a discretion about love that corresponds to the assurances that Criseyde seeks about Troilus. He is Pandarus bent on malice. Meanwhile, Jason makes good the deception, acting 'as coy as is a mayde,' looking 'pitously,' and conferring gifts on Hypsipyle's courtiers that might be construed as either signs of generosity or bribes. Statius's Hypsipyle suggests that she is the unwilling victim of Jason's rough and foreign manners (5.455–8, 463–5). In Chaucer's *Legend*, she is victimized through the social conventions and cultural practices they ostensibly share.

The fragility of convention and courtly semiotics is equally apparent in the repetition of Jason's betrayal across generations by Theseus and Demophon. Ariadne's story offers the richer narrative of the two, though Phyllis's serves as a summary. Patterson argues that the legend of Ariadne furnishes a critique of the Knight's Tale and implicates Theseus directly in the tragic pattern of recursive history.[34] At the same time, however, it shares important links with Hypsiple's tale. Ariadne acts on the same precept as Hypsipyle; she saves Theseus '[a]s evere of gentil women is the wone / To save a gentyl man, emforth hire myght, / In honest cause, and namely in his ryght' (2131–3). But as in Lemnos, the social sphere is unstable and tacitly at risk. Minos's son, Androgeus, is killed in Athens, where he has gone to study philosophy. Minos's campaign of vengeance leads him to besiege Alcathoe, where Scylla, King Nysus's daughter, betrays the city '[f]or his beaute and for his chyvalrye' (1912) and Minos in turn casts her aside. Conquering Athens, he imposes a tribute by which Athens will offer its children for destruction by the Minotaur. After Ariadne and Phedra secure Theseus's rescue and abandon Minos, Theseus abandons Ariadne for her sister and then inadvertently causes his own father's death by hoisting the wrong sail to signal his return. Betrayal is the governing dynamic, and, as with Jason, the chief metaphor is consumption. The Minotaur's appetite (1947) and the compassion of Minos's daughters (1974–6) are linked by devouring. Ariadne saves Theseus as he waits to be 'freten' ('eaten like an animal' [1951]). When she is left behind, she ironically invokes his intended fate, complaining to Theseus, 'Meker than ye fynde I the bestes wilde' (2198).

In Ariadne's story, Chaucer reverses the priority of sight over speech, which characterizes the encounter of eros with imperial narrative. Scylla falls in love with the sight of Minos, but it is Theseus's language – his complaint heard echoing up the wall joining the tower and a privy – that enlists Ariadne's and Phedra's pity. It will be echoed at the end in the answer of the hollow rocks to Ariadne's complaint when she is left alone on the island, speaking to the vanishing sail and then to the bed she has shared with Theseus. The sisters' response to Theseus's complaint, like their subsequent interview with him, is situated within a social rather than psychological context. Ariadne is moved by Theseus's plight as a 'woful lordes sone' reduced to the 'povre estat that he is in, / And gilteles' (1979–81): an aristocratic victim of Fortune's wheel. Phedra, though much more tactically minded about ways to kill the Minotaur and effect an escape, concludes her speech with the same observation – 'so gret a lordes sone is he' (2023). The interview they subsequently conduct with Theseus to test his intentions and mettle tracks unsteadily between the signs and social referents of courtly language.

Theseus seeks to literalize courtly language, to take its metaphors of service and subordination at face value, not just acting as a servant but actually becoming one. The 'grace' he seeks is 'my mete and drynke' (2040). He promises, 'for my sustenaunce yit wol I swynke' (2041), and for that he is willing to shift identities as needed: 'So slyly and so wel I shal me guye, / And me so wel disfigure and so lowe, / That in this world ther shal no man me knowe' (2045–7). As critics have long recognized, the allusion here is to Arcite's disguise in the Knight's Tale, but the differences are as instructive as the parallels.[35] Arcite's change is an involuntary effect of love, and it is an authentic transformation. Theseus's offer is a stratagem, and his abasement in Crete stands over and against his identity in Athens. Troping Dido's assertion, he reminds the women, 'I am a kynges sone and ek a knyght' (2055), and calls down curses on himself if he does not act his true role at home as faithfully as his feigned identity abroad. At the end of the interview, he takes on another form of courtly identity, professing that he has loved Ariadne unknown to her in his own country for seven years.

Theseus thus demonstrates the power of courtly discourse to destabil-ize social and political structures from within. The servant in love, faced with the terror of savage death, threatens to become a servant in fact – and a servant as circumstances require. Theseus is able to manage his identities, or at least the languages that create them, *seriatim* – aristocrat and unknown lover at home and serving man at Minos's court. In the end, of course, he literally becomes the base-born man, the *villain*, he is willing to impersonate for love and advantage. Ariadne goes even fur-ther to suggest that he becomes something like the creature she has helped him escape, a monster below the beasts. The two daughters, meanwhile, are interested in regulating the metaphoric qualities of language and maintaining the stability of its meanings. Like Emily and Criseyde, Ariadne knows what she sees: 'A kynges sone, and ek a kynght' (2080). For him '[t]o ben my servaunt in so low degre' (2081) would shame all women because it inverts the social realm. It also works at cross-purposes to her aim of becoming his wife, uniting the realms, and marrying Phedra to Theseus's son. A version of her last wish ironically comes true, outside the scope of the legend here, in the tragic story of Hippolytus and Phaedra; but the essentially conservative, aristocratic cast of her intentions is not in doubt, nor is Phedra's loyalty at this point. Ariadne foresees herself and Phedra in roles that restore social stability and repair the initial break of Androgeus's death: 'Now be we duchesses, bothe I and ye / And sekered to the regals of Athenes, / And bothe hereafter likly to ben quenes' (2127–9). They are true believers in the social forms that encompass them.

Chaucer recapitulates his study of the vulnerability of courtly society to its own conventions in the story of Phyllis, the penultimate legend and the last one fully narrated. Demophon is a figure of erotic belated-ness, who can only repeat the treachery of other men. The narrator of the *Legend* imputes a genealogical determinism to him. He is 'lyk his fader of face and of stature, / And fals of love; it com hym of nature' (2446–7): 'At shorte wordes, ryght so Demophon / The same wey, the same path hath gon, / That dide his false fader Theseus' (2462–4). But the repetition is more extensive and more significant than the emblem-atic sense of betrayal. In the background to this story, Demophon is returning to Athens from Troy so that he may reassume the throne taken by Mnestheus during Theseus's exile.[36] His journey is part of the final phase of the Troy story, in which the Greek leaders return home tri-umphantly to treachery and catastrophe. Shipwrecked on his journey, Demophon resembles Aeneas and tacitly assumes his own imperial project. Reference to Reynard the fox associates him with the hunting imagery applied to Jason. The advice he receives to seek 'socour' and to 'loke what his grace myghte been' with the queen (2432–3) evokes Hypsipyle's natural courtesy to Jason and his men. When Demophon leaves Phyllis, having 'piked of hire al the good he myghte' (2466), he reenacts Jason's taking Hypsipyle's 'substaunce' (1560). If Demophon becomes, as Frank argues, the focus of the tale, he does so not because of his own story but because the other stories have overdetermined him.

Phyllis's complaint, which Chaucer allows greater amplitude than any other in the *Legend*, reinforces the lesson that erotic betrayal carries with it social as well as personal consequences. In Ovid, Phyllis protests that oaths made with the gods as witnesses have been broken. Chaucer omits the pagan deities to focus on the elements that bind human beings to one another. The 'term' (2499, 2510) and 'forward' (2500) agreed on by Phyllis and Demophon are casualties of his betrayal. In Ovid, Phyllis's crime is to have accepted Demophon in his social identity: 'unum in me scelus est, quod te, scelerate, recepi, / sed scelus hoc meriti pondus et instar habet' ('The one crime which may be charged to me is that I took you, O faithless, to myself; but this crime has all the weight and seeming of good desert' [2.29–30]). In Chaucer, her fault shades into virtue: 'For I was of my love to yow to fre' (2521). Phyllis is careless in loving, to be sure, but also, as Ovid recounts (2.108–16), generous. Demophon's betrayal of her thus calls into question all the signs of gentility. She laments, 'To moche trusted I, wel may I pleyne, / Upon youre lynage and youre fayre tonge, / And on youre teres falsly out yronge' (2525–7). Chaucer follows Ovid (2.49–53) in this list, omitting only trust in the gods.

Filippo Ceffi's translation, which Chaucer may have known and used, supplements Ovid in ways that reveal the courtly overlay on the classical text. Ceffi's prologue, summarizing the narrative background, describes Phyllis's seduction in a courtly vocabulary: 'facendogli ancora lieta cortesia della sua propria persona.'[37] Phyllis retains that vocabulary in reproving Demophon: 'io credetti alle tue lusinghevoli parole, delle quali tu eri molto copioso; e ancora credetti alla tua nobile schiatta, ed alli tuoi Iddii, ed alle tue lagrime.'[38] Demophon's 'lusinghevoli parole' mark him as the antithesis of the courtly lover, the *losengeour* whom Queen Alceste tells Cupid haunts his court, retailing slander for amusement and malice (F 352). Demophon's 'copious' speech shows him to be an orator as well as a lover. *Schiatta* is the term for noble descent that Guido Guinizelli and Dante made central to debates on aristocratic values and character.[39]

'Hire frendes alle': the patriarchal family and the political order

In the stories we have been examining, the betrayal of love occurs through precisely the same conventions that construct the courtly and chivalric sphere. Lemnos, Colchis, Crete, and Thrace are put in jeopardy by erotic duplicity whose corollary is political deception and civic turmoil. These threats exact a cost not only from the social and political order but also from the family structures that finally stand behind aristocratic culture. Jason's betrayals, for example, have consequences for the children and potential dynasties he leaves behind with Hypsipyle and Medea. With her dismemberment of her brother, mentioned obliquely by Hypsipyle, Medea also destroys her father's family as she is leaving Colchis. Antony's love for Cleopatra breaks up his political marriage within an imperial family. Theseus not only takes Minos's daughters but subsequently turns the sisters against each other and indirectly exacts the vengeance against children that Minos had imposed on Athens. Elsewhere in the *Legend*, Chaucer explores the intersection of eros with the familial dimension of culture still further. His treatment of the topic is by no means uniform. Family structures are the background of some tales about love and the thematic focus in others. Taken together, the tales reveal how powerfully eros affects not only the individual subject and the couple pitted against history but also the aristocratic self in its relations to others.

Literary interest in Piramus and Thisbe rightly falls on the semiotics that foster desire and on the tragic misreading of signs that leads to the lovers' double suicide. Their story plays out, however, against a mythological background in which the family, city, and political power are major concerns. Chaucer opens the story by presenting Semiramis as an urban and political architect, not unlike Dido. Ninus, whose grave is to be the meeting point for Piramus and Thisbe, is the actual founder of the city, but Semiramis, his queen, builds the city walls.[40] The importance of her act can be seen in the discussion of community (*civitas*) in Isidore of Seville's *Etymologiae* (15.2).[41] Human community, says Isidore, is a gathering of men held together by the chain of fellowship, which takes the forms of family, city, and people. A city is distinguished from other forms of human habitation by its having walls for safety and by not being dedicated solely to agricultural work – it is a place of social life, not merely subsistence. On this view, Semiramis transforms Ninus's creation into a center of culture. To maintain her power, she crosses the barrier of gender by putting on men's clothes, and she commits incest by marry-

ing Ninus's son after his death.[42] The twelfth-century *Speculum virginum*
depicts her as a composite of man and woman ('habitu et sexu femina
uir animo'), who reigns for forty-two years, carries on wars, and increases the power of Babylon.[43] Though an emblem of sexual indulgence, Semiramis uses eros in the service of the political order. It is
during the period of her dominion as a sexualized ruler that Piramus
and Thisbe fall in love. This interweaving of sexuality and politics adds
an important social resonance to the romantic story.

The city and its walls are the defining locale for Chaucer's story and its
source, Ovid's *Metamorphoses* 4.55–166. Only a stone wall separates the
two patriarchs, who are the object of civic fame ('gret renoun' [711]) to
the same extent that their children are the topic of domestic reputation
circulating through 'women that were neighebores aboute' (720). This
balancing of the public and private spheres is Chaucer's invention. The
wall both divides and joins the aristocratic families, and it is the medium
through which the lovers' discourse must pass. In Ovid the lovers know
and talk to each other and in Gower they make a hole in the wall to
communicate (*Confessio Amantis* 3.1371), but Chaucer makes their
desire eminently symbolic and even adds the sentimental and comic
detail that they kiss the stone dividing them (768). The issue raised by
both the topography and the narrative is a fundamental question for
patriarchy: who shall control access to a family's young women? That
question signifies, in turn, the problem of succession. Semiramis offers
the example of sexuality used to political ends, and her example becomes at once warning and policy in the tale: 'For in that contre yit,
withouten doute, / Maydenes been ykept, for jelosye, / Ful streyte, lest
they diden som folye' (721–3). The 'folye' is, of course, for women to act
autonomously on desire and thereby destabilize the stages of patriarchal
succession.

The fathers will not agree to Piramus and Thisbe's marriage, and the
wall symbolizes their prohibition. But their denial is not of the lovers'
desire in itself: they refuse to relocate the authority for controlling
Thisbe to Piramus, thus to effect a transition of power across generations. As Chaucer's language shows, Piramus and Thisbe envision an
alternative to this stasis. Their flight removes the obstacles to desire,
while replacing patriarchal authority with erotic investments that serve
as their 'trouthe' (778, 798) and 'convenaunt' (790) with one another. If
their flight shows them acting as Troilus and Criseyde do not, the
language of attachment uses the terms that sanction Antony and Cleopatra as a licit couple. When Thisbe fatally wounds herself, she reproves
'ye wrechede jelos fadres oure' (900) and asks '[t]hat in o grave yfere we

moten lye, / Sith love hath brought us to this pitous ende' (903–4).[44] At one level, she requests the grim nuptials already darkly forecast by their planning to meet at Ninus's grave; at another, she asks for the legitimation of her 'convenaunt' as a form of power within families. The lords who 'woneden so nygh' (713) head families joined finally by their children's common grave.

The question of access raised by the tale of Piramus and Thisbe recurs on a larger scale in the legends of Philomela and Hypermnestra, where the ominous forebodings are intensified by the Furies and by destiny respectively. By marrying Procne, Tereus ostensibly joins Thrace to Athens and establishes his relation to Pandion, the king of Athens. In *Metamorphoses* 6, he is the defender of Athens and gains Procne as his prize. The network of filiation is revealed clearly in the *Legend* by Pandion's transfer of Philomela, Procne's sister, to Tereus's authority. Pandion addresses Tereus as his 'sone' and sends his greetings to 'my doughter and thy wife' (2299). It is Philomela, Pandion says, who 'bereth the keye of al myn hertes lyf' (2298), and he asks to see her before he dies. When Tereus consequently rapes her, his offense is against not just her innocence and person but all the other family bonds as well – marriage, sisterly affection, the pledge to Pandion and alliance with Athens. Chaucer, unlike Chrétien de Troyes and Gower, coyly omits the vengeance that Philomela and Procne exact by having Tereus unwittingly consume his son's dismembered body: 'The remenaunt is no charge for to telle' (2383). His Procne does not waver, as in Ovid, between her roles as avenging sister and mother. What results, though, is the eradication of two noble families. While Ovid draws on the background of the Bacchante, the woman who acts as if she were a Fury, Chaucer reassigns blame to men who have failed their duties as patriarchs. Tereus, as the opening of the tale asserts, is the corrosive extension of Jason's appetite; Pandion wrongly assumes that he is his 'sone' and so will protect women in his family. Gower makes Tereus's deed explicitly political: he is a 'tirant' (*Confessio Amantis* 5.5627, 5646), and his rape of Philomene is 'tirannye' (5.5921).

In the story of Hypermnestra, the threat to aristocratic families is not from outside males but from internal rivalries in love and power. Danaus and Aegyptus are figures of wanton appetite and competitors in war and sexual license. Their decision to marry Lynceus and Hypermnestra does not violate an incest taboo – 'thilke tyme was spared no lynage' (2602) – but it locates the competition for access to women, hence for succession, completely within the family structure. Ovid's language gives some hint of these complexities in its elastic terms for kinship. Hypermnestra's lament, for example, reveals the repetition and confusions of war between father and uncle: 'Bella pater patruusque gerunt' [14.111]). When she urges Lynceus to think of the peril he has left her in by fleeing alone, she uses the term *soror* to mean both sister and cousin: 'tibi cura sororis' (14.123).

Chaucer modifies the background myth to the story, in which Danaus's fifty sons marry Aegyptus's fifty daughters, all of whom, except Hypermnestra, then murder their new husbands on Aegyptus's orders. Focusing on Hypermnestra alone, he accentuates her predicament in the face of her double subordination as daughter and wife. He also adds the theme of determinism by which Hypermnestra's character, particularly her compassion and fidelity, is given by the Fates (2580–99) rather than shaped by her conflict between fear and tenderness (*Heroides* 14.49–50). Like Philomela, she is the object in which her father invests his love, the 'tresor of myn herte' (2628). The rivalry between the patriarchal brothers is thus fought through their favored children. Aegyptus accurately forecasts that his son-in-law and nephew will be his downfall (2659), and his order for Hypermnestra to kill Lynceus aims to forestall succession and escape destiny at the same time. For Hypermnestra, Aegyptus's order sets the duties of wife and daughter at odds. What makes her decision is the 'feyth' (2700) she has pledged as Lynceus's wife. She acts, in other words, on the same basis as Piramus and Thisbe. Though Lynceus abandons her in his headlong flight, she honors her promise over the commands of patriarchy.

The family conflicts of Greek mythology take on a distinct historical cast when Chaucer writes about their Roman counterparts. Dido and Cleopatra, as we have seen, have an immediate political rather than exemplary context. In the Physician's Tale of Virginia and the legend of Lucrece, Chaucer examines a peculiarly Roman theme with a strong resonance for his own age, for he explores the power of the state over aristocratic families. Virginia's tale stands apart from those of the virtuous women in the *Legend* because she is a maiden who both eschews sexuality and obediently suffers death to preserve her innocence. Yet there are significant linkages between her tale and the *Legend*. Virginia shares Hypermnestra's amalgam of beauty and virtue. She flees those occasions of 'folye' (VI.64) to which Thisbe succumbs. The false judge, Apius, is inflamed by her beauty in the same way that Tereus is inflamed by his desire for Philomela; each man seeks possession rather than love (VI.129 and *Legend* 2293). Most important, each abuses the duties of power. Tereus is responsible for Philomela's safeconduct to visit her sister, while Apius betrays his responsibilities as a 'governour' (VI.122).

In the *Rose*, Chaucer's immediate source for Virginia's story, Jean de Meun makes it clear that her father recognizes the point at which the family and patrician rights of a 'bons chevaliers' cannot prevail against perverted state justice: '[Il] bien sot que vers Apius / Ne puet pas sa fille deffendre' (*Rose* 5624–5). Chaucer reformulates the scene by describing how Virginius '[m]oste by force his deere doghter yiven / Unto the juge, in lecherie to lyven' (VI.205–6). In both versions, the betrayal of political trust, the 'comune profyt,' for private appetite provokes the popular revolt leading to Apius's imprisonment and Claudius's exile. A 'thousand peple' (VI.260), representing the body of Roman citizens, hence the source of all Roman political authority, break into Apius's consistory 'for routhe and for pitee, / For knowen was the false iniquitee' (VI. 261–2). It might be argued that the 'peple' are moved to action too late and therefore share some complicity in Virginia's death, but the cultural tensions written into the tale suggest another reading. Apius's design to gain control of Virginia depends on Claudius's false claim, an inversion of the romance theme of unknown identity, that Virginia is his 'servant, which that is my thral by right' (VI.183). As a 'thral' (VI.189) rather than a nobleman's daughter she can be a possession without the attendant political or social consequence. Political action mobilizes around the head of Virginia, struck off when Virginius exercises his right as a *paterfamilias* to control access to her body. The apparatus of imperial government, perversely imposed on the family sphere, falls before the interests of oligarchy sustained by the people. Gower's version of the tale makes the conflict of family and state even more apparent.[45] Apius intervenes in the planned marriage of Virginia to Ilicius, '[a] worthi kniht of gret lignage' (*Confessio Amantis* 7.5150), while Virginius fulfills his patrician duty to wage war 'for the comun riht' (7.5190). After Virginius slays his daughter, he returns to the Roman forces and exhorts them to redress injustice at home rather than abroad: 'For thus stant every mannes lif / In jeupartie for his wif / Or for his dowhter' (*Confessio Amantis* 7.5273–5).

Lucrece's tale in the *Legend* carries this conflict a step further, in a narrative that depicts the political reascendance of aristocratic families over despotic and capricious monarchy. Though it is not his ostensible aim, Chaucer nonetheless describes the historical backgrounds at the very start of the tale: 'Now mot I seyn the exilynge of kynges / Of Rome, for here horible doinges' (1680–1).[46] As in the tale of Virginia, his tale depicts misgovernance working to the detriment of patrician families. Lucrece, as the narrator insists, is a 'verray wif, the verray trewe Lucresse' (1686), a pagan 'seynt' honored by a day in the Roman calendar (1871).

But her story is not a celebration of her virtue so much as a monitory narrative of governance and the assertion of patriarchal rights. Whatever her value as an emblem of marital fidelity, her importance lies in serving the interests of family, which her kinsmen eventually pursue through the control and display of her body. The linkage between the political and domestic is apparent in the structural parallelism of the poem's two locales. Unlike Gower, who starts the tale with the deception and slaughter of the Gabii, Chaucer begins his narrative with the siege of Ardea, the capital of the Rutuli, who resist the Romans and force the conflict into stasis: 'Ful longe lay the sege and lytel wroughten' (1696).[47] In the interim of warfare, a space of 'pley' (1698) opened unexpectedly by their 'ydel lyf' (1700) of frustrated conquest, the warriors shift conflict toward verbal competition – namely, the rivalrous praise of their wives.[48] Idleness, as the Second Nun proclaims in the Prologue to her tale, is 'roten slogardye / Of which ther nevere comth no good n'encrees' (VIII.17–18). In this case, it foils the royal strategy of directing aggression outward and allows the tensions between freeborn men to surface; Gower calls it 'strif' (*Confessio Amantis* 7.4772). The static siege of Ardea prompts the assault on the Roman household.

When Colatyn and Tarquinius surreptitiously visit the household, penetrating the 'estris' that represent its architectural design and social intimacy, they witness precisely the sort of 'besynesse' and order that they fail to practice on the battlefield. Lucrece demonstrates the ideal self-regulation of a Roman subject, spinning wool '[t]o kepen hire from slouthe and idelnesse' (1722), while directing her servants to 'don hire besynesse' (1722). The domestic scene is disciplined and stable, while the political is seemingly thwarted. In Ovid and the First Vatican Mythographer, the contrast is even greater. Arruns, the figure Chaucer changes to his father Tarquinius, visits his home and finds his wife singing and dancing.[49] In the *Confessio Amantis*, she is '[a]ll full of merthes and of bordes; / Bot among alle hire othre wordes / Sche spak noght of hire housebonde' (7.4799–801). Chaucer omits this local contrast between wives to highlight the larger one between the public and private spheres.

Chaucer describes what Colatyn and Tarquin observe in their surveillaunce of Lucrece as a perfect linguistic sign. The figure under their gaze combines semblance and reality: 'Hyre contenaunce is to hire herte dygne, / For they acorde bothe in dede and sygne' (1738–9). But Lucrece functions throughout the tale as a sign moving through various discursive fields, construed in each instance according to different needs. The visual image of her 'wifly chastite' (1737) inflames Tarquinius's desire. The brief *effictio* that Chaucer offers (1746–9) is Tarquinius's visual inventory of her face, hair, shape, and bearing. The passage translates Lucrece from her domestic scene into a courtly domain. Like Troilus after his first sight of Criseyde, Tarquinius replays the image, all the while renewing his desire as he dwells on the figure: 'thogh that hire forme were absent, / The plesaunce of hire forme was present' (1768–9). The narrator intervenes to say his obsession is 'nat plesaunce but delit, / Or an unrightful talent, with dispit' (1770–1), and he punctuates this correction by reporting Tarquinius's real intention – 'she shal my leman be!' (1772). The overlay of courtly rhetoric is inescapable and at the same time problematic. When Tarquinius rapes the inert body of Lucrece, desensitized so that it will not experience even involuntary pleasure ('She feleth no thyng, neyther foul ne fayr' [1818]), he acts as a distorted version of a courtly lover. In the most reductive way possible, he has 'plesaunce of hire forme' (1769). And doing 'vilanye' to her, he does 'dispit to chivalrye' (1822–3).

At the start of the tale, Chaucer situates Lucrece in another discursive frame, though the hermeneutic framework is confused, if not wholly ironic. St. Augustine, as the narrator remarks, has compassion for Lucrece; but in *De civitate Dei* 1.19, he is critical of her suicide and points to the example of Christian women who suffer violation without killing themselves and offer examples of the true 'gloriam castitatis.'[50] Augustine may be responding to a more neutral description of Lucrece's suicide in Tertullian, who says Lucrece kills herself, motivated by the desire to show the glory of her chastity to her kinsmen after enduring defilement ('quae uim stupri passa cultrum sibi adegit in conspectu propinquorum, ut gloriam castitati suae pareret').[51] Though St. Jerome places her at the head of his list of Roman women who commit suicide to remove the stain to their bodies, Abelard follows Augustine's authority and sees Lucrece as entirely too concerned with her reputation ('laudis nimium auida').[52]

The question of fame debated by Christian exegetes serves a complex thematic end in Chaucer's tale. Tarquinius forces Lucrece's silence by the twin menace of death and infamy. He threatens to kill her serving man and throw him in her bed, to create the appearance of finding her in 'avouterye': 'And thus thow shalt be ded and also lese / Thy name' (1810–11). Lucrece loses consciouness 'for fer of sclaundre and drede of deth' (1814). The key element of Tarquinius's threat is display. The narrator remarks how Roman wives loved their reputations and dreaded shame; Cupid had argued the same point for all the women recorded in the world of authors (G 296–300). This commitment to virtue becomes the ironic means by which Tarquinius imposes his sexual will on Lucrece. Display is the means by which Lucrece is doubly victimized. Dressed for death, she reports her shame to her husband, father, mother, and friends, and kills herself despite their assurance that she is guiltless. Though Gower limits Lucrece's disclosure to Colatyn, her father, and Brutus her cousin, Chaucer makes the family in its full affinity a witness and victim of her violation.

Lucrece's motive, as Tertullian argues, is ostentive, for her death in the sight of those close to her is the warrant for her claim of chastity. Though she dies making the decorous gesture of covering herself, she is victimized again by her male kinsmen who publish her humiliation and display her body as proof of '[t]he horryble dede of hir oppressyoun' (1868). In its syntactic ambiguity, 'hir oppressyoun' – the trespass Lucrece and her male kinsmen have suffered at the hands of the Tarquins – perfectly expresses the appropriation of feminine virtue in the service of the patriarchal family. Brutus's report and the showing of Lucrece's corpse are both made 'openly' (1865, 1866). The ostentive is immediately political; Lucrece's shame is revealed to a community of citizens – 'al the toun of Rome' (1861) and 'the peple' (1864). The political, in turn, is familial: Brutus banishes not only Tarquin but all his kinsmen, thereby ending kingship and installing republican rule.

In the background narrative recorded by Ranulph Higden's *Polychronicon* and translated by John Trevisa, kingship is founded on violence to families, citizens, and community. Tarquin has come to power by slaying his father-in-law, and during his twenty-five years of kingship he introduces torture to the Romans.[53] The narrator of the *Legend* asserts that his purpose in telling Lucrece's story is to tell how true and constant she was in love (1874–6), and he shows no awareness that he has, in effect, published her shame yet again. But the true beneficiaries of Lucrece's fidelity are the freeborn men of her family whose rights have not only been recognized but also given political and cultural primacy. What Chaucer omits is the inglorious sequel to republican politics, also recorded in Higden and Trevisa. Lucrece's husband is removed from the consul's office within a year 'by fraude of his felawe þe oþere consul,' Tarquin mounts a campaign to recapture the city, and Brutus and Aruns (Tarquin's son and Lucrece's attacker in Ovid and Gower) kill one another in battle. Trevisa adds that Brutus dies in poverty, and money for his burial must be gathered from the people. The return to patrician rule, like the political ascendancy of magnates in the 1380s, may offer a respite from royal tyranny, but it does not escape its own history.

Coda: Christian antiquity

Chaucer's project of writing antiquity finds its endpoint in the women who are the victims of pagan myth and history. Their stories and complaints dismantle the poetic ideology of the classical heroic world – its heroic struggle between choice and destiny, its protocols uniting cities and nations in a uniform courtly practice, its investments in family, kinship, and political order. Women are, paradoxically, the most revealing subjects of antiquity because of their subordination: unlike Boccaccio's Arcita or Chaucer's Palamon and Troilus, they have no way of transcending their predicaments in the stories told about them. By the 'confusion' of its good women – their downfall as well as their misunderstandings of fidelity – the ancient world plays itself out not because its heroes reach the limits of secular virtue, like Arcite and Troilus, but because they fail its values for their own desires. It is not surprising, then, that for 'gentil wemen' the dramatic situation of complaint is essentially static or that Chaucer's *Legend*, the most focused portrayal of them, should diminish to silence.

In a larger view, however, the *Legend* and its critique of antiquity reach completion in two other works of the 1380s – the lives of Saint Cecilia and Custance. These stories lie to the side of Chaucer's major project of composition; at the same time, they stand apart from the contexts later devised for them in the *Canterbury Tales*. Both stories feature Christian antitypes who effect the structural changes not allowed to the classical heroines. They embody a 'Christian feminism' that looks beyond the moral and political order.[54] Cecilia inhabits the domestic patrician world of Virginia and Lucrece, whose deaths underwrite republican values. Her marriage is not thwarted, like Virginia's, but transformed beyond the patriarchal Roman model of Lucrece to the spiritual ideal of the *familia Christi*. She represents new affinities and protocols for men and women independent from courtliness and patriarchy in a body of faith. Her confrontation with the judge Almachius in her martyr's *passio* turns specifically on the contrast between the 'dombe' idols (VIII.284–7) that blind pagans and the power of her language and example to convert through the word of revelation. The issue, as for Virginia and Lucrece, is the power of the state to impose its will over its citizens, notably its female dependents. As Cecilia remarks, the magistrate has only the power to slay, not to give life.

In Chaucer's tales of Christian antiquity, women renegotiate the question of allegiance. Cecilia converts her husband and his brother, the Roman officer Maximus, and the crowd that witnesses her three days of torment. She intends for each of them to become 'myne allye' (VIII.297), her spiritual kinsman in the dispersed family of believers presided over by Pope Urban. Custance in the Man of Law's Tale, though usually seen as an allegorical rather than hagiographic figure, transforms empire from the top. She relives the voyages of quest and return in Theban and Trojan history. Understood in their historical and political dimensions, her forced journeys align Church and empire. The quest that faithless Jason begins in the Troy story has its counterpart in faithful Custance. The translation of empire begun by Aeneas reaches fulfillment in the reunion of Custance and Alla, a Roman matron and her foreign, English husband. Their son Marius is made emperor by the pope 'and lyved cristenly' (II.1122). This synthesis of pagan and Christian culture has a predecessor in Boccaccio's ending to the *Filocolo*. Critical opinion divides over its meaning in Chaucer. Stephen Knight argues, 'The Man of Law's Tale establishes both secular Christian morality and conservative political order together.'[55] Barbara Nolan locates the meaning of the poem in spiritual transcendence.[56] It would misrepresent the cultural work of religious writing among Chaucer and his contemporaries to separate the spiritual from the social or to reduce one to the other. In Chaucer's grand narrative of antiquity, the classical past finds its accommodation with history outside itself in a new spiritual order.

4
The 'Cherles Tale' and Chaucerian Modernity

Modernity in the late Middle Ages is not an historical period or cultural imaginary but a form of consciousness. In recent literary scholarship, it is virtually inseparable from concerns with subjectivity and the construction of selfhood. The most influential criticism rejects the notion of an autonomous individual and argues instead that external forces at once generate and control inwardness, reflection, and identity.[1] The description of modernity I want to offer for Chaucer and Boccaccio differs somewhat in its emphases from this account. What modernity registers most profoundly in the narratives of Chaucer and Boccaccio is the experience of change. Both writers see modernity as heterogeneous and hybrid, improvisational and uncertain. In the *Canterbury Tales*, Chaucer's pilgrims establish an artificial, temporary community last shown moving toward but still falling short of its symbolic and spiritual destination, which will also mark its dissolution as an imagined social body. In the *Decameron*, Boccaccio's young women and men return at the end of their retreat to a city that remains in the political, social, and moral crisis they had earlier fled. In the stories that Chaucer and Boccaccio locate within these narrative frames, the dynamics of modernity center on human agency and social relations within structures that are themselves transforming.

The social bases for modernity differ for Chaucer and Boccaccio in significant respects, of course. Boccaccio celebrates an urban, mercantile ethos in which desires, appetites, and ambitions are held in check by complex institutional arrangements designed to assure the circulation rather than concentration of cultural, social, and political energy. Merchant citizens negotiate rivalry and cooperation among themselves at the same time that they hold off feudal patricians from above and a disenfranchised laboring class from below. The subject who emerges from these forces, like the characters of Boccaccio's *novelle*, is a mobile, adaptive agent of his own interests. Civic virtues like Florentine *libertas* give an ideological coherence and political rationale for individual and collective action in public life and fictional narrative. Yet the practical means for negotiating subjectivity are wit, cunning, and verbal agility. It is not by chance that in Days Three, Six, Seven, and Eight of the *Decameron*, stories of sexual gratification, quick thinking, and rhetorical self-presence all play out on the same ground.

We do not possess a framework for Chaucer that corresponds exactly to the mercantile ethos that Vittore Branca has applied so decisively to Boccaccio.[2] Chaucer's modernity, by most accounts, develops from in-novations within feudal, hierarchical structures rather than civic trad-itions. To this extent, our understanding works from the top down, as if changes in the aristocratic and noble worlds were a synecdoche for developments in other social strata. The social and cultural forces of this modernity are to be found in what K.B. McFarlane termed 'bastard feudalism.'[3] Though challenged and debated in the half-century since he coined it, McFarlane's term nonetheless captures a sense of change that does not reject earlier medieval structures altogether, and in this respect it resonates with the multiplicity of positions within Chaucer's portrayal of modernity.[4] Without abandoning the dominant ideology, forms, and conventions of traditional hierarchies, bastard feudalism shifts the basis on which social classes and individual agents negotiate their economic, social, political, and cultural lives. 'Its quintessence,' says McFarlane, 'was payment for service.'[5] The principal effect is to replace landholding, indentured service, and the subordination of vassal to lord with cash exchange and to supplant sworn oaths of fealty with contracts. While a vertical framework of hierarchy remains intact, nego-tiations occur laterally with individual subjects of the feudal structure acting out of relative autonomy and self-interest.

Vertical and horizontal structures overlap and intersect in late medi-eval England. The power of feudal hierarchy is mediated by associational forms that prove flexible, adaptive, and often complementary. These new forms accommodate merchants and mercantile life, both of which are poorly assimilated in the traditional structure of three feudal estates (nobles, clergy, and laborers), and they find places for groups of gentry dislodged from their accustomed positions by social and economic pressures in the fourteenth century. Lateral connections produce associ-ational forms – guilds, fraternities, and other affinities with religious and secular aims – that operate within social strata and at times reach across rank, social class, and occupation in the shared interest of realizing common objectives. Taking the guild as a paradigm of associational forms, David Wallace emphasizes that it is not so much a specific institution as a mentality.[6] These new forms consequently produce, as Paul Strohm notes, 'a partial redirection of personal loyalty, from vertical commitment to a single lord in a hierarchical system to a more horizontal dispersal of loyalties among the members of one's own social group.'[7]

Feudal hierarchy depends on landholding, the ritual power of sworn oaths, and social patterns of dominance and subordination. By contrast, the associational forms that help construct Chaucerian modernity are based on exchange, contract, and self-authorization. The hallmark of these new forms is contract. Individual agents bind themselves to each other and to the social structures they invent. They enter voluntary agreements and thereby act as agents who disclose their intents and desires – in other words, their subjectivity – through their social practice and performance. Contract also implies a distinct orientation toward time and authority. The feudal oath imagines a relationship independent of time, sanctioned by traditional authority, and sacralized by ritual. Its tragic situation, staged repeatedly, for instance, in Arthurian romance, grows out of the conflict between a timeless sworn promise and concrete circumstances. Contract is time-bound and contingent, however. It creates temporary alliances specified by language and intent rather than custom or ritual. Its tragic mode is not a conflict of values but the potential for anomie, the fear that nothing stands outside improvisation and the negotiation of desires among independent agents.

The literary genres that give expressive form to modernity in Chaucer and Boccaccio are the fabliau and novella. Both are minor genres situated on the margins of literary discourse, and both draw on traditions of exemplary narrative – the stories of illustrious men and women, saints, and notable figures located in their occupations, social roles, classes, and communities. Chaucer and Boccaccio transform exemplary narrative by complicating moralization, testing the common values that underlie it, and emphasizing verbal wit and play. Their tales become what Anne Middleton has called 'speculative anecdotes': 'Stories of experience without transcendent authority for their instructive claims.'[8] Such writing, says Middleton, encourages comparative rather than absolute judgments and rewards practical ethical improvisation. In this decentered exemplarity, conventional truths prove to be misreadings of experience, or they furnish the materials of comic irony and inversion. It is the contingent truths of fiction, negotiated by agents within a changing social sphere, that constitute and give voice to modernity.

In Chaucer criticism, the fabliau has been a privileged form because it best represents Chaucer's realism. Our understanding of it has been largely shaped, however, by Josph Bédier's succinct definition of the French fabliaux – 'contes à rire en vers' – and by extensions of Bédier's definition, which value Chaucer's fabliaux as the greatest aesthetic achievement of the form. This long-standing view has been challenged in at least two respects. Omer Jodogne contends that Bédier's definition is narrow and misplaced, and he proposes instead that *aventure*, comic or exemplary, is the defining trait of the genre.[9] N.S. Thompson argues that the *novelle* rather than the fabliaux provided Chaucer with his literary model because they emphasize place, language, and characterization. Chaucer and Boccaccio, he says, share proximate narrative worlds: 'Stock types and plots become miraculously transformed by local settings and particularized individuals who occupy worlds of surprising moral ambiguity, although a complex response will show how a moral perspective is implied or where the narrative forms a case for examination.'[10] Thompson's argument for the *novelle* is part of a larger case for the 'collective' influence of the *Decameron* on the *Canterbury Tales* based on internal evidence.

The fabliaux present a stronger claim than the *novelle*, I believe, because their fundamental structure – a love triangle – recurs in various guises in the *Canterbury Tales*. Derek Pearsall observes, 'Intrigue and trickery is the central feature of the plot, and the instigator of the plot is the third member of the triangle' (169) who 'does not belong to the same class as the wedded pair.'[11] As Derek Brewer points out, the fabliau was a dead form when Chaucer took it over.[12] Its very obsolescence, in fact, makes possible the narrative and cultural work that Chaucer assigns to it. Such adaptations draw on features of genre that lie below comic effects and give voice to modernity. R. Howard Bloch emphasizes that 'the fabliaux are rooted in scandal' and their scandal goes beyond social inversion to self-critique and a general critique of representation: 'they insist incessantly that the coat of representation is to some degree always ill-fitting, always torn and dirty.'[13]

'Harlotrie' and the poetics of exchange

The Miller's Tale and the Reeve's Tale present modernity by showing the pressure of change beneath an imaginative world constructed out of earlier narrative conventions and traditional social roles. Both tales have partial analogues in the *Decameron* for their action, but Chaucer seems directly engaged here in reviving the fabliau and extending its thematic and conceptual range. He sets the action in a narrative present, incorporates comic love triangles, and exploits the rivalry between established occupational types. Yet he goes beyond deploying fabliau conventions in contemporary guise by situating the characters, especially the comic victims, in an economic and social frame outside their accustomed place. Though lodged squarely in the third estate, the carpenter and miller in the stories complement their work by the accumulation of property and capital. They are unlike the Plowman of the General Prologue, the 'trewe swynkere' (I.531) who works and does good works, paying his tithes out of 'his propre swynk and his catel' (I.540) in a fixed equilibrium of temporal and spiritual exchange. For them, the important values are gain and mobility. Both values establish, in turn, a set of social relations based on individual agency and self-interest.

In his Prologue (I.3142), the Miller identifies John as a carpenter, and his trade is essential to both the plot and the dramatic rivalry between the Miller and the Reeve. But in the tale Chaucer complicates the occupational type. He introduces John first as a comic enigma – a 'riche gnof' (I.3188) – and then by his trade as a carpenter. John has acquired the economic base to sustain a house large enough to accommodate boarders and to require an unofficial staff. He has his 'knave' Robin break down the door to Nicholas's chamber, and he is prepared to accept Nicholas's judgment that Gille the maid must be sacrificed in the coming flood. In his gulling of John, Nicholas entices the old man partly by the promise that after the second flood, all three characters will enjoy a new social status: 'thanne shul we be lordes al oure lyf / Of al the world' (I.3581–2). What he does not say is that, under this fictitious new covenant, human history will begin again on the model of a fabliau about an old man, his young wife, and a young man without a wife or lover.

The opening of the tale contrasts John's 'craft' (I.3189) with Nicholas's 'art' (I.3191). In this way, the tale seems to follow the fabliau convention of privileging wit; it also prepares for the 'queynte case' (I.3605) that dupes the aged husband and provides a thematic link to the Reeve's Tale. Similarly, a justification for John's betrayal and rough treatment might be found in the Miller's claims that 'his wit was rude' (I.3227). But the nature and limits of John's wit have to do with more than the proverbial wisdom of marrying his 'simylitude' (I.3228) according to his age and status. John's position challenges the fixity of status, for Cato's dictum about men marrying 'after hire estaat' (I.3229) conceals and mystifies the more urgent question of agency. John can marry Alisoun not because he is an old carpenter but because his social position is mobile rather than fixed. He is a counterpart to January in the Merchant's Tale, without the ambiguous honorific of Lombard knight.

The other characters of the Miller's Tale share John's mobility to a greater or lesser degree. Alisoun is described predominantly by the imagery of nature and animals in the Miller's *effictio*. Yet her personal properties have a value in the world of mercantile exchange: 'Ful brighter was the shynyng of hir hewe / Than in the Tour the noble yforged newe' (I.3255-6). When she turns to 'Cristes owene werkes' (I.3308) and goes to church to display her worth on a holy day, the economic image of Alisoun as a shining coin is repeated. We see her in circulation as '[h]ir forheed shoon as bright as any day' (I.3310). Nicholas is both the stock type of the devious student and a character whose income derives from 'his freendes fyndyng and his rente' (I.3220). Through these sources he enjoys a room by himself that he inhabits, in an ironic echo of Arcite's burial in the Knight's Tale, '[a]llone, withouten any compaignye' (I.3204; cf. I.2779) but surrounded by scent and ornament, astrological gear and books. Absolon, the parish clerk, has diversified his skills by adding barbering, blood-letting, and drafting legal documents to his clerical duties.[14] While the characters belong to the fixed types of the fabliaux, the fictional world they move in is more heterogeneous and fluid than the traditional estate model.[15]

Social relations in this world show older forms operating in the service of a heightened sense of agency. Nicholas's initial address to Alisoun is at once lyric complaint and comic performance: 'Ywis, but if ich have my wille, / For deerne love of thee, lemman, I spille' (I.3277-8).[16] Absolon adopts the rhetoric of the Song of Songs.[17] John's first reaction to Nicholas's revelation about the impending flood is to cry, 'Allas, my wyf!' (I.3522), and he obligingly acts out the paradigm of Noah and his wife that Nicholas suggests. The central relation of Nicholas and Alisoun hovers uncertainly between mock-courtliness and contract. She grants him her love and swears an oath to be at his 'comandement' (I.3292), thereby confusing the roles of lover and beloved in courtly service. They are bound, however, by their common aim of deceiving her husband, which is made explicit by the contracts and oaths between them: 'And thus they been accorded and ysworn / To wayte a tyme, as I have told biforn' (I.3301-2). When John leaves for Osney, they are again '[a]corded' (I.3402) to devise a means of tricking him and satisfying their wishes. Chaucer makes it clear that the wish is mutual and reciprocal: 'this was his desir and hire also' (I.3407).

Nicholas and Alisoun abed '[i]n bisynesse of myrthe and of solas' (I.3654) present an icon of desire mutually negotiated by characters acting freely apart from but still inside traditional relations of marriage and herberage. They are pledged to each other not in perpetuity but for the time required to satisfy their desires. In this way, they differ from characters like Dom Felice and the wife of Frate Puccio, who create a kind of protracted domesticity by maintaining their intrigue: 'con discrezione lungamente ne prese il suo piacere' (*Decameron* 3.4.32). Unlike the mystery of 'Goddes pryvetee' (I.3164, 3454, 3558), the 'pryvetee' Nicholas and Alisoun share is the means and immediate aim of their transactions.[18] Moreover, their 'accord' is governed by a principle of economic equilibrium: each party risks discovery in return for satisfaction. John and Absolon ironically illustrate the same principle. John invests in illusion and suffers his loss and pain. Absolon pledges 'at the leeste wey I shal hire kisse' (I.3680) and redeems his pledge by kissing Alisoun in the lowest bodily orifice ('the leeste wey').[19] His vengeance at being duped asserts the principle of equilibrium that motivates the Miller to answer the Knight's Tale and devolves to revenge for John and Aleyn in the Reeve's Tale: 'I shal thee quyte' (I.3746; cf. I.3119). When Nicholas tries to extend the joke, he finds himself one of its victims because another cycle of exchange has begun. The cultor Absolon selects as his weapon is offered to Alisoun as a gold ring, and when the smith Gervase loans it to Absolon, he imbues it with economic worth: 'were it gold, / Or in a poke nobles alle untold' (I.3779–80). Absolon promises to repay the loan by recounting the story to Gervase the next day (I.3784).

The ending of the Miller's Tale forces closure on these private transactions through social consensus. The Miller insists on an equilibrium that serves as poetic justice for excess. Thus, John's jealousy is repaid by his being cuckolded, Absolon's fastidiousness by his disgust, and Nicholas's wit by his being outwitted. Alisoun is the famous exception. In some readings, she escapes because she is free of illusions and acts (faithfully, as it were) out of natural appetite.[20] In another reading, she, like Emily in the Knight's Tale, is the largely passive feminine object around which male desire circulates. Wetherbee rightly observes that Alisoun escapes the narrow cage of old John's jealousy only to be held fast in Nicholas's arms.[21] Even her spontaneous 'jape' is amended by Nicholas. In seeking to resolve the tale, however, we should not accept the Miller's hermeneutics any more than we credit the Host's literary judgments elsewhere in the *Canterbury Tales*. The ending of the Miller's Tale shows the improvisational and temporal qualities of contracts and accords. The folk who laugh at John's 'fantasye' (I.3840) wish to textualize loss and physical pain, to turn 'al his harm unto a jape' (I.3842), to make it into another story told retrospectively. The clerks who close ranks and declare him mad swear 'othes grete' (I.3845) that drive out his 'reson' (I.3844), his competing narrative. Not just comic laughter but the covenants of social reality end the tale, and they differ markedly from what we know has happened.

The modernity portrayed in the Reeve's Tale builds directly on the exchanges that the Miller's Tale locates within literary conventions and traditional social relations. As in the Miller's Tale, occupational rivalries provide a motive. Just as the Miller contrasts John's 'craft' as a carpenter (I.3189) to Nicholas's 'art' as a student and cleric (I.3191), so the Reeve portrays the social tensions between Symkin the miller and the Cambridge students John and Aleyn. The miller notices their wariness about him and their efforts to thwart his theft, and he takes up the challenge: 'Yet kan a millere make a clerkes berd, / For al his art' (I.4096–7). These rivalries are generated, of course, by the conflict in the dramatic frame. The Reeve follows the Miller's example of 'quiting' the Knight's Tale, but in the meantime he changes the meaning of quiting. The Miller matches the Knight's Tale; Chaucer's comedy depends on the unexpected equivalence of antique epic and fabliau. As Derek Pearsall argues, ' "Quite" means "repay" ("make return for something with something of the equivalent value"), and the Miller is speaking of the tale-telling competition and not about the contents of the tales.'[22] The Reeve means to match in the same way and to get even: 'I shal hym quite anoon; / Right in his cherles termes wol I speke' (I.3916–17).[23]

This difference in quiting reaches back to the Aristotelian distinction between distributive and rectificatory justice. Aristotle explains that distributive justice is a geometrical proportion that holds between persons of different social rank (*Nicomachean Ethics* 5.3).[24] The just share each receives from a transaction is determined by the individual's status and worth. Because a knight and a miller are not equivalent socially or politically, the miller's fabliau (a minor, anti-courtly form) can proportionally balance the Knight's epic (a major, courtly form), so long as each teller adheres to his own mean. By contrast, rectificatory justice obtains in transactions where the social differences between persons are not a factor, and the two persons can be treated as equals. Justice in this instance is the mean between loss and gain; each person has an equal amount before and after the transaction. The Reeve's 'quiting' the Miller in his own terms assumes this kind of justice. At the same time, the Reeve depletes the idea of 'quiting' of its intellectual and moral force. Justice, as Aristotle insists, has to do with virtue and with questions of law and fairness; it is defined according to agents. The Reeve, identifying himself, reveals, 'Oure wyl desireth folie evere in oon' (I.3880). The principle that guides him is like-for-like, and it takes the form not of negotiation but force: 'For leveful is with force force of-showve' (I.3912). Ellesmere and other manuscripts of the *Canterbury Tales* mark this passage with the Latin proverb to the same effect: 'Vim Vi repellere.'[25] The idea is restated at the end of the tale when the Reeve claims to have 'quyt' the Miller (I.4324), and it carries forward in Fragment I to the Cook's promise that he will 'quit' the Host (I.4362).

The dramatic links in Fragment I of the *Tales* force us to view the Reeve's Tale as a counterpart to the Miller's Tale, and they prepare us as well to see how rivalry and grievance diminish the concept of human agency. Here the difference from the closest analogue in Boccaccio (*Decameron* 9.6) is instructive. The tale of Pinuccio's desire for the innkeeper's daughter in Mugnone begins, like the Griselda story, with a young nobleman wandering in the countryside; the bedroom antics that lead to their lovemaking and to Adriano's impromptu romp with the innkeeper's wife (*Decameron* 9.6) are driven by mutual desire. By contrast, the main sphere of action in the Reeve's Tale is economic exchange, and the point of exchange is to realize social ambition great and small. Symkin's pride in his status has its counterpart in the local reputation that John and Aleyn hope to secure by not allowing the miller to swindle them, when they stand in for the college manciple and bring grain to be milled. Symkin is related semantically to both *simia* (Latin 'ape') and simony. The first term portrays him as a parody of a human – a creature with appetite but not reason and judgment. The second term reveals his source of wealth. Symkin's marriage to the parson's illegitimate daughter shows his social ambitions, particularly his wish '[t]o saven his estaat of yomanrye' (I.3949) by display, public performance, and outright menace. Their daughter, an ironic refiguring of the Miller's Alisoun, is the heir of a spiritual donation brought into mercantile exchange as disposable property. The parson bestows 'his catel and his mesuage' (I.3979) on Malyne in order to secure the social advancement of his lineage, and the Reeve's commentary makes it clear that, like the gluttonous theologian in *Piers Plowman* (B 13.25–202), he sacrifices a spiritual institution for his own gratification: 'Therfore he wolde his hooly blood honoure, / Though that he hooly chirche sholde devoure' (I.3985–6).

The action of the Reeve's Tale takes place, then, among institutions shown predominantly in their economic functions. Holy church has become a source for family capital. Soler Hall, the students' college, gathers wheat and malt, and consumes the refined products. The miller enjoys a monopoly – a '[g]reet sokene' (I.3987) – in the middle of this chain of production. His transgression, at the start of the story, is not the fact but the style of his thievery. After the manciple falls ill, Symkin goes beyond the bounds of even sharp business practices: 'For therbiforn he stal but curteisly, / But now he was a theef outrageously' (I.3997–8). The Reeve's story of retribution against the Miller is ostensibly the narrative of his punishment for a breach in the decorum of exchange.

The action of the tale is a record of transactions, and the items exchanged (grain, bread, sexual favors) signify the intangible but real values of social status and individual worth. In the Reeve's imagined world of rectificatory justice, the books have to balance. The amount of grain brought to the mill is the same that eventually returns with the students, including the half bushel baked into a loaf of bread. John and Aleyn pay for their night's lodging and food 'trewely atte fulle' (I.4133; cf. 4119). But it is the abstract exchanges that matter most and convey the negotiations of Chaucer's modernity. John and Aleyn fear the social consequences of losing the grain:

> 'Allas,' quod John, 'the day that I was born!
> Now are we dryve til hethyng and til scorn.
> Oure corn is stoln; men wil us fooles calle,
> Bathe the wardeyn and oure felawes alle,
> And namely the millere, weylaway!'
> (I.4109–13)

Their humiliation costs them reputation among superiors, equals, and inferiors, and it potentially carries a literary penalty as well: they will become characters in a satirical narrative of their misadventure. Thus while Aleyn seeks compensation with the miller's daughter, John returns to the same calculation about reputation lost and regained. He reasons, 'Yet has my felawe somwhat for his harm' (I.4203). A *felawe* is originally someone who puts up a share to fund an enterprise, and the sense of being bound to a common project carries over to both the college fellows and the two students who have acted in their interest. John enhances the mercantile element of his calculation by contrasting his passivity to Aleyn's entrepreneurial spirit: 'He auntred hym, and has his nedes sped' (I.4205). John's fear is shame and a comic literary role: 'when this jape is tald another day, / I sal been halde a daf, a cokenay!' (I.4207–8). His remedy is to imitate Aleyn and so to undertake risk in terms that look forward to the merchant in the Shipman's Tale rather than a courtly lover: 'I wil arise and auntre it, by my fayth!' (I.4209). His 'faith' is an asseveration but also a pledge of reputation in the social sphere.[26]

The quest for compensation that John and Aleyn undertake has its dramatic rationale outside the tale in the Reeve's alleged grievance with the Miller and his transformation of what 'quiting' will mean for other pilgrims and their stories. Aleyn expresses the Reeve's principle as the miller, his wife, and daughter snore in their grotesque imitation of liturgical song:

> 'For, John,' seyde he, 'als evere moot I thryve,
> If that I may, yon wenche wil I swyve.
> Some esement has lawe yshapen us,
> For, John, ther is a lawe that says thus:
> That gif a man in a point be agreved,
> That in another he sal be releved.
> Oure corn is stoln, sothly, it is na nay,
> And we han had an il fit al this day;
> And syn I sal have neen amendement
> Agayn my los, I will have esement.
> By Goddes sale, it sal neen other bee!'
>   (I.4177–87)

Though some manuscripts add the Latin phrase corresponding to Aleyn's reading of the law ('Qui in uno gravatur in alio debet relevari'), commentators point out that he announces a principle of vengeance rather than justice.[27] The relief he seeks for his loss must be appropriate, not arbitrary. *Esement* is directed to the subjective experience of loss rather than replacing what has been lost.[28] Moreover, Aleyn's claim is false in its own terms. He alleges two kinds of loss – the stolen grain and the suffering he and John have endured ('we han had an il fit al this day' [I.4184]). The grain is restored in full measure at the end of the story. The 'il fit' is compensated by Malyne's favors to Aleyn and the wife's *myrie fit* (I.4230) with John.

The economic exchanges of the Reeve's Tale probably derive generally from Chaucer's fabliau source. The closest analogue, 'Le Meunier et les II Clers,' casts the clerks as poor, hungry men living in a forest. They become entrepreneurs by necessity, borrowing wheat at full market price along with a horse so they can become bakers. Their eventual recovery of the wheat allows them to survive over the coming year. Chaucer locates the story in a more fully imagined social landscape, and he uses wit rather than deceit and physical force as the means for the students' vengeance. The philosophical basis of this wit is the power of predication, which allows things to have properties and values experientially and socially. Chaucer introduces the theme of wit in the miller's disparaging remark about a clerk's 'art' (I.4097). He then exploits it as a comic premise in the miller's description of his house when the forlorn, swindled students ask for lodging for the night:

> Myn hous is streit, but ye han lerned art;
> Ye konne by argumentes make a place
> A myle brood of twenty foot of space.
> Lat se now if this place may suffise,
> Or make it rowm with speche, as is youre guise.
>
> (I.4122–6)

The sophistical arguments he attributes to the students represent the new intellectual technology of the high and late Middle Ages.[29] Symkin claims commonsensically that things subsist in themselves with an established and steady value. And his challenge is for the students to use their art not merely to transform space but to make it 'suffise,' to be adequate to their purposes. John answers his challenge with a proverb that accurately forecasts the outcome. He tells the miller that things exist both as they are and as they are perceived: 'Man sal taa of twa thynges: / Slyk as he fyndes, or taa slyk as he bryngmore' (I.4129–30). The baby's cradle is the device that demonstrates his distinction, for its shifting location allows John to sleep with the miller's wife and leads Aleyn to disclose his love-making with Malyne to the miller. Chaucer's emphasis on perception and arbitrary predication is conscious. In the fabliau analogue, the daughter is locked away in another room and the miller discovers his wife sleeping with the student.[30] As Helen Cooper points out, the theme of arbitrary meaning receives extended treatment elsewhere in the tales of the Merchant, Franklin, Second Nun, and Canon's Yeoman.[31]

The Reeve, like the Miller, offers a summary by way of imposing closure on his story. His theme is the ironic justice of a deceiver deceived. By his reckoning, the proud miller suffers the triple humiliation of being beaten, losing his ill-got gains, and compensating John and Aleyn for the cost of their meal by furnishing his wife and daughter for their sexual enjoyment. But the Reeve offers only a partial accounting. Eager to quit the Miller and still more eager to be seen by the pilgrims as having done so, he misreads the details and scope of his story. The balancing out that counts as justice for him involves a wider range of

conversions than the Reeve realizes. Reversals occur for all the characters. The decisive transaction is not, however, sex for food; it is pleasure
for distress. Intangible values in the social sphere outweigh material
gains and losses. Equally important, the wit that makes such exchanges
possible legitimates individual agency acting on desire. John and Aleyn
return to Cambridge from Trumpington with the story they want to tell,
and Malyne escapes, if only temporarily and vicariously, from the family
history that the miller and her parson grandfather, acting like Theseus,
have scripted for her.

'Curious bisynesse'

The agency partially registered in the Reeve's hermeneutics informs the
Shipman's story of the merchant, his wife, and the monk Daun John,
which is arguably the most modern and Boccaccian of the *Canterbury
Tales*. Its modernity lies topographically in the mercantile landscape
plotted for the story. Like Milan in Neifile's story of the German mercenary Gulfrado (*Decameron* 8.1), Saint-Denis, Paris, and Bruges mark off
a geography of commerce. Though the principal characters of the Shipman's Tale differ in their occupational roles, they are joined on a single
plane as economic agents. The unnamed merchant is a financier who
speculates on mercantile ventures and currencies.[32] The wife is chiefly
concerned with 'dispence' both personal and domestic (VII.16). The
outrider Daun John is an 'officer' (VII.65) superintending farms and
landholdings for his monastery. If the Miller's Tale and the Reeve's
Tale stage a rivalry over which occupation exercises the superior 'art,'
the Shipman's Tale insistently portrays its characters in a common
pursuit of economic exchange. They are all traders in the marketplace.
The tale's modernity reaches, however, well beyond an urban setting
and a mechanism of exchange. If we look at the transactions within the
Shipman's Tale and their corollary in linguistic signification, we see that
they represent the negotiation of appetite within traditional structures
and institutions. Chaucer's modernity emerges, then, from the pressure
of economic agency on established social relations and from the accom-
modations these transactions require.

Critics have long recognized that economic transactions are the chief
action of the Shipman's Tale.[33] The opening section elaborates the
themes of 'dispence' and payment in a preamble that, in the feminine
references of the pronouns, may retain evidence of Chaucer's original
plan of assigning the tale to the Wife of Bath. The action itself begins
from a transaction stipulated but not shown – the wife's purchase of

clothing. She trades sex with Daun John for the hundred francs required to pay her debt. The monk in turn borrows the money from her husband and, when asked by the merchant to repay the loan, tells him that he has already returned the sum to his wife. In outline, the tale follows the main action of its closest analogues, the stories told by Neifile and Panfilo in *Decameron* 8.1 and 8.2, which likewise turn on lovers' swindling wives who trade sex for money. But in Boccaccio, the transactions aim to produce equilibrium, to balance gain and loss in the way the Reeve conceives exchange as a means of rectificatory justice. Neifile says her story is not about 'beffo' ('trickery') but 'merito,' and she distinguishes women who give their chastity for money ('per prezzo') from those who do so for love ('per amor'). The former, she says, deserve the justice of being burned alive and the later the mercy of a lenient judge.

The paradigm behind Neifile's story is one Chaucer refuses to invoke in the Shipman's Tale. Gulfardo, a loyal mercenary, is a paradox in the capitalized militarism of the late Middle Ages. His loyalty makes him a good credit risk, and he enjoys access to large sums at low interest. His friendship with Guasparruolo Cagatraccio ('assai suo conoscente e amico') masks his love for Guasparruolo's wife, Madonna Ambruogia. When Gulfardo professes his love and learns that Ambruogia will return his affection for the promise of secrecy and the payment of two hundred gold florins, his love turns to hatred ('odio'), and Gulfardo resolves to pay her back ('pensò di doverla beffare'). Neifile explains the change as outrage; Gulfardo 'was incensed by her lack of decorum' ('isdegnato per la viltà'). His anger also has an explanation within Boccaccio's own literary authorship. Ambruogia's greed has turned the tale away from the narrative model of Menedon's story in the Love Questions of the *Filocolo* and its retelling in *Decameron* 10.5, the source and analogue respectively of the Franklin's Tale. Gulfardo, the loyal mercenary, expects the story in which a valorous young man importunes a wealthy man's wife only to face an impossible task to gain the pleasure that she has no intention of granting him. Denied the exemplary narrative that will elevate commercial loyalty to true gentility, he settles for the fabliau, enjoying his 'avara donna' free of charge ('senza costo') while preserving the illusion of chivalric honor as a bankable item in a mercantile world.

Besides focusing directly on commerce rather than honor, Chaucer expands the scope and meaning of economic exchanges over Boccaccio's stories. In Neifile's tale, Galfardo 'quits' Ambruogia for her indecorous suggestion ('viltà'); in Panfilo's rustic tale of 'uno amorazzo contadino' in *Decameron* 8.2 the priest of Varlungo has his way with

Monna Belcolore while regaining the cloak he left as security for the five lire he promised her. Panfilo's story introduces secondary exchanges that structurally resemble the merchant's dealings with other traders and bankers in the Shipman's Tale. But Chaucer's chief interest is to exploit the narrative devices in order to create the dense texture of mercantile life. The 'riche' merchant pays for his wife's 'dispence' or faces the threat of a rival: 'Thanne moot another payen for oure cost, / Or lene us gold, and that is perilous' (VII.18–19). The merchant's house is primarily a site of economic exchange. It is there that he displays his 'largesse' (VII.22) to his guests, that Daun John shows his generosity to the merchant's *meynee* 'after hir degree' (VII.47), that the merchant has his counting house, that the wife exercises domestic governance over a 'thrifty houshold' (VII.246), that the private space of the garden becomes a place for striking a bargain. There is no internal space that is not already suffused with exchange. Meanwhile, the external world is comprised of urban markets and populated by other merchants, Lombard bankers, and clerical administrators like the monk and his abbot.

Commodification is the most prominent feature in the imaginative texture that Chaucer gives to mercantile life. The trade of sex for money is an example at once obvious and subtle. The merchant's wife asks the monk for the loan of one hundred francs and promises in return, 'at a certeyn day I wol yow paye, / And doon to yow what plesance and service / That I may doon, right as yow list devise' (VII.190–2). The bargain she proposes differs from the simple exchange of sex for money suggested by Madonna Ambruogia to Galfardo. The wife is closer to Monna Belcolore in asking for a loan. The difference seems at first glance to be a mere euphemism, and Daun John clearly understands it as such. Grabbing her flanks, he promises her the hundred franks and subsequently arranges the necessary financing by telling the merchant, 'certein beestes...I moste beye' (VII.272). The subtlety of the transaction enters with the equation between the loan and 'plesance and service' (VII.191). It is the promise of payment that secures the corresponding abstract qualities of pleasure and service. Chaucer marks its contractual rather than merely transactional nature by having the wife specify the temporality of exchange: 'at a certeyn day I wol yow paye' (VII.190). When the wife and monk subsequently act on their 'acord,' sex and money redeem their pledges.

That Chaucer describes their love-making in thoroughly abstract terms – 'this acord parfourned was in dede' (VII.317) – indicates the power of exchange to transmute substance and value. Earlier, the monk had given another example by counterposing exertion and repose as he salaciously imagines the sexual labor the merchant brings to satisfying his wife (VII.106–11). In response, the wife's close echo ('how that it stant with me' [VII.120; cf. 114]) of her husband's accounting ('how that it with hym stood' [VII.79]) equates marital with fiscal well-being. Later, she transforms the Pauline marriage debt shared by all husbands and wives to a system of house credits and debits tallied metaphorically on her body (VII.413–26). In his analysis of Chaucerian commerce, Lee Patterson draws attention to the Patristic backgrounds of medieval economic theory and especially to the troubling fact that exchange supplants natural value. Economic order, he observes, 'is a system of exchange driven by an *indigentia* caused by man's fall away from the original perfection of the order of nature.'[34] In the discussion of the Golden Age in the *Roman de la rose*, economics, positive law, and secular institutions are founded to compensate for man's original, undifferentiated participation in natural bounty; Chaucer makes the same point in 'The Former Age.' Yet the Shipman's Tale does not harken back to this nostalgic origin, even in its garden scene. On the contrary, its relentless commodification makes it impossible to imagine that any time without exchange ever existed. In his most generous moment, offering the monk his gold and 'nat oonly my gold, but my chaffare' (VII.285), the merchant extolls not bounty but his confidence that the monk is a good credit risk.

Chaucer's analogues in the *Decameron* hold to the fabliau convention of balancing accounts at the end of trading, but the Shipman's Tale conceives an exchange economy operating apart from traditional symmetries. It introduces the question of adequacy, which is never resolved here and continues to resonate in different ways in the Clerk's Tale.[35] After striking her bargain with Daun John, the wife rebukes her husband for his obsessive reckoning. 'Ye have ynough, pardee, of Goddes sonde' (VII.219), she tells him. Her remark guilelessly contrasts natural and exchange value, divine bounty ('Goddes sonde') and economic production, which simulates divine creation. Without equating himself with God, the merchant turns the remark back on his wife when he delivers instructions about her role in domestic economy: 'Thou hast ynough, in every maner wise, / That to a thrifty houshold may suffise' (VII.245–6). Facing no material lack, she is to regulate the internal economy of the household, just as the merchant sustains the household in the external world. As Eustache Deschamps prescribes in his *Miroir de mariage*, 'Homs doit par dehors ordonner, / Femme doit dedenz gouverner' (221–2).[36] Later, the husband returns home invigorated by his trading adventures and insists on his conjugal rights. The wife complains, 'Namoore . . . by

God, ye have ynough' (VII.380). Her subsequent renegotiation of the marriage debt connects the merchant's pleasure in reckoning with his rediscovered sexual appetite: 'score it upon my taille' (VII.416). The tally stick equated here with her sexual organ allows the husband to quantify and measure sexuality, hence to regulate his wife's management of the marriage *debitum* and his own claim over that debt. But it raises a further question, as R.A. Shoaf points out: 'In whose keeping is the other part of her "taille"? Who puts notches in it and when?'[37] The Shipman's concluding prayer is a plea for natural bounty and good credit that deflects the unresolved ambiguity: 'God us sende / Taillynge ynough unto oure lyves ende' (VII.434).

The question of adequacy in the Shipman's Tale is closely linked to surplus and abstract value, two of most troubling features of modernity in the late Middle Ages. In his final reckoning, the merchant comes out ahead in his venture. Echoing the earlier language of self-accounting, the Shipman says, 'wel he knew he stood in swich array / That nedes moste he wynne in that viage / A thousand frankes aboven al his costage' (VII.370–2). The merchant has not only redistributed goods and services but also produced new wealth, which takes its appropriate form in quantifiable currency. Similarly, the loan and return of the hundred franks has produced an increment of pleasure, while the marriage debt between the merchant and his wife works as well to pay off the wife's original debt for her clothes. As Patterson observes, 'Somehow, by a process we can only with difficulty specify, the very fact of exchange has produced a surplus value: something has come of nothing.'[38] Surplus value has its counterpart in linguistic ambiguity and instability, where words mean more than they denote and thereby constitute a semiotic surplus. Critics have noted the widespread play on double meanings and the convertibility of economic and sexual metaphors. Cooper aptly summarizes the scholarship: 'The tale is riddled with words misused, abused, and misapplied, with speeches in which one thing is said and another intended. It is one of the clearest examples in the whole work [the *Canterbury Tales*] of the shaping of an entire reading of life through the manipulation of language.'[39]

Surplus value is unforeseen value in the Shipman's Tale, and its characteristic form is abstract rather than concrete. The merchant brings home a profit above cost, not a collection of new possessions with intrinsic value or usefulness. Rather, his transactions produce a credit. The wife and monk enjoy whatever incremental pleasure they find in their perfunctory coupling. The wife has begun the sequence of transactions by buying array that signifies honor. As the feminine voice of the preamble says of a husband, 'He moot us clothe, and he moot us arraye, / Al for his owene worshipe richely' (VII.12–13). So understood, clothing is the social and linguistic sign that defines the wife's value as currency, but her significance lies in a husband's standing in the public sphere, the community of potent men who assess his social worth. This explanation may obscure the wife's own motives and acquisitiveness, but it is the same rationale that she offers in asking Daun John for the loan: 'For his honour, myself for to arraye, / A Sonday next I moste nedes paye / An hundred frankes, or ellis I am lorn' (VII.179–81). She repeats this rationale at the end of the tale under the ethic of value for money: 'I have on myn array, / And nat on wast, bistowed every deel' (VII.418–19). She then goes on to claim that her husband is the beneficiary of her consumption; his worth is the social product and linguistic referent of her array: 'for I have bistowed it so weel / For youre honour' (VII.420–1).

The opening of the tale provides a framework for analyzing the social display that ostensibly comprises this husbandly honor and worship. The wife's beauty and sociability, we are told, cause 'more dispence / Than worth is al the chiere and reverence / That men hem doon at festes and at daunces' (VII.5–7). In other words, array is a bad investment. At best, it only confirms misogynist beliefs about the appetitiveness and superficiality of women. By way of clarification, the speaker appends a disturbing simile: 'Swiche salutaciouns and contenaunces / Passen as dooth a shadwe upon the wal' (VII.8–9). Scholars identify the simile as proverbial and note its appearance in the Merchant's Tale (IV.1314–15) and the Parson's Tale (X.1068).[40] Its biblical source is Job 14:2, which compares the brevity of human life to a flower's blooming and fading and to the flight of a shadow ('fugit velut umbra et numquam in eodem statu permanet').[41] Chaucer's other uses of the simile are consistent with the Shipman's primary meaning, referring in both instances to the transience of worldly goods. But there is a further sense to the simile – namely, that the public acknowledgment secured by display is itself insubstantial. In this sense, the world of abstract value generated by surplus has no grounding outside the dynamics of exchange. Honor and worship are social fictions and human constructions, artifacts without even the mystifying claims to natural or divine origins.

The tale thus holds out the bleak prospect that abstract value is merely insubstantial and illusory. This prospect is confirmed dramatically in two brief speeches made by the merchant on the topic of his craft. Though Daun John plays on the reputation of his 'professioun' as a monk in swearing his love to the wife (VII.155), the merchant takes his occupation in earnest. Not only does accountancy occupy his home life; when he is abroad in Bruges, he acts 'as a marchaunt' (VII.305), which means that he concentrates on business alone. Consequently, we incline to take him at his word when he describes the interior experience of commerce. Expounding the 'curious bisynesse' of chapmen to his wife, he explains, 'Scarsly amonges twelve tweye shul thryve / Continuelly, lastynge unto oure age' (VII.228–9). Exchange and surplus run ahead of death, just as in the *Roman de la rose* natural love stays ahead of death to preserve the species (15891–976). The merchant ventures forward into an uncertain world sustained by a public face ('chiere and good visage') that warrants his credit and with a capacity for improvisation that allows him to 'dryve forth the world as it may be' (VII.230–1). His occupation requires alertness and adaptation against continual mutability:

> And therfore have I greet necessitee
> Upon this queynte world t'avyse me,
> For everemoore we moote stonde in drede
> Of hap and fortune in oure chapmanhede.
>   (VII.235–8)

Chaucer's language at once deflates and elevates the merchant's account. The 'queynte world' means one thing in the sphere of mercantile exchange, as the merchant intends it, and another at home, as we know from our privileged position as readers – or perhaps it means the same thing in different guises. As the Wife of Bath says, 'al is for to selle' (III.414). But there is nonetheless an unselfconscious heroic claim in this account. Like the chivalric hero of romance, the merchant ventures forward into a realm of 'hap and fortune' in a quest that tests his nerve and judgment. Here the chapman comes close to the merchant-hero that Vittore Branca imagines as the subject and audience of the *Decameron*.

The merchant's second speech reiterates his claims about his occupation, while shifting the terms of comparison. When Daun John approaches him for the loan that will yield his wife's sexual services, the merchant equates commerce and fertility: 'ye knowe it wel ynogh / Of chapmen, that hir moneie is hir plogh' (VII.287–8). Having witnessed the private scene between the monk and the wife, we know that money is both the instrument of economic productivity and the means toward private pleasure. The implication that the merchant draws, however, betrays the insubstantiality of exchange. He immediately adds, 'We may creaunce whil we have a name, / But goldlees for to be, it is no game'

(VII.289–90). The merchant assumes that his public value ('name') allows him to obtain loans and credit and that this nominal value is underwritten by coin. It does not occur to him that gold itself has only nominal value; its worth resides in the shifting equivalence of goods and services that people ascribe to it.[42] His wife has, in the meantime, delivered a different assessment of his worth: 'he is noght worth at al / In no degree the value of a flye' (VII.170–1).

The poetic importance Chaucer derives from this emerging world of commerce and exchange value lies chiefly in its social implications. If he has captured the penetration of a mercantile ethos into late medieval institutions, his modernity is most apparent in the ways his characters deal with one another. The tale seems to give us an array of established institutions and relations. The merchant maintains a household with attendant personnel – a 'meynee' that includes a messenger, apprentice, cooks, and a maid-child to accompany the wife. His marriage divides between a masculine outer world of commerce and a feminine interior world of domestic governance; man and wife are bound to each other by their shared marriage debt. The merchant and Daun John share a common origin in the same village. An extensive social language describes these relations. The merchant and his wife address each other in their marriage roles as 'sire,' 'wife,' and 'spouse.' The monk is a 'famulier' (VII.31) and 'freend' (VII.32). Claiming each other as 'cosyn,' they join in 'eterne alliaunce' (VII.40) and assure each other of eternal 'bretherhede' (VII.42). At the start of her interview with Daun John, the wife addresses the monk as 'deere cosyn myn' (VII.99), and he speaks to her as his '[n]ece' (VII.100, 106, 125). Events prove, of course, how insubstantial the relations and accompanying language are.[43] The wife proclaims, 'Myn housbonde is to me the worste man / That evere was sith that the world bigan' (VII.161–2). The monk repudiates the merchant, 'He is na moore cosyn unto me' (VII.149). The colloquy between the two subsequently shifts to a mock-courtly idiom. The wife addresses the monk as 'My deere love' (VII.158), and the monk responds to her as 'myn owene lady deere' (VII.196).

Beneath its collocations of kinship and affinity, the social world of the Shipman's Tale is a place for transactions between pairs of individual agents. No one acts apart from the convergence of self-interest. Patterson describes the condition as a degradation of natural relations because of commodification.[44] The problem, however, is that the relations among the merchant, wife, and monk are not natural but cultural; marriage, the ties of a common homeland, and the duties of pastoral counsel are the compensatory relations of a fallen world rather than the products of commodification alone. Chaucer's poem explores the pressures on social life of radical agency. Its central icon is the portrait of the merchant isolated in his counting house, reckoning his own condition by tabulating the year's transactions. Whether commercial or sexual, these exchanges produce alienation. Pearsall observes, 'The characters have no obsessions or fantasies, as does January, no lusts that cause them to move heaven and earth to gain their desires, as does Nicholas, no passions of rage and revenge such as motivate the action in the Reeve's Tale.'[45] Commerce does the work of intimacy, not just in the sexual 'acord' between the wife and monk but also in the wider sphere of relations. The merchant pays off his loan in Bruges by borrowing from 'freendes' in Paris (VII.333). When he returns home, he seeks Daun John 'to tellen hym of his chaffare, / As freendes doon whan they been met yfeere' (VII.340–1). The 'pryvytee' withheld from the world and ostensibly kept secure and hidden within the household is a selfhood that finally must be put in circulation, too.

In sketching the pressure of mercantile exchange on traditional structures of household, marriage, and friendship, the Shipman's Tale stops noticeably short of portraying their collapse. Unlike the Miller's Tale, it reaches no point of narrative crisis, nor does it invoke closure through a comic resolution. To some degree, it shares the moral ambiguity of Panfilo's tale of the priest and Monna Belcolore, which reestablishes an equilibrium without censuring the characters.[46] A closer and more revealing parallel is with the Merchant's Tale, where the contradictions between lateral agreements and established hierarchy are more intense and the resolution potentially more disquieting. What the Shipman's Tale brings to an understanding of Chaucerian modernity is an ethic of accommodation. There is no element of providence at work in the tale; characters act out of effort and calculation alone. They are content to live as agents within hierarchies that no longer directly determine selfhood, values, or behavior. They manage to do so, moreover, without disenchantment, exploiting mutability moment by moment under the cover of convention.

The Pardoner's 'moral tale'

In Chaucer's fabliaux, we see the workings of associational relations largely apart from any corresponding social forms. Contract, improvisation, and temporality establish the bonds between individual agents rather than forge a corporate or group identity in which individuals participate. In the fragmentary Cook's Tale, Chaucer seems to be prepar-

ing some analysis of corporate identity when he describes Perkyn Reve-
lour as both apprentice and 'riotous servaunt' (I.4408) at the center of a
'meynee' of like-minded scoundrels.[47] But the tale ends with Perkyn's
removal from his master's house to the lodgings of 'a compeer of his
owene sort' (I.4419) and the man's prostitute wife. Chaucer's analysis of
the relations in associational forms lies elsewhere, in a different repre-
sentational mode from the mimetic realism of the fabliau and its low-
life urban setting. We find it, I believe, in the stark allegory of the
Pardoner's Tale.

The Pardoner's Tale is widely regarded as the most compelling
emblem of the aesthetic and moral complications of Chaucer's art.[48] It
is a 'moral tale' told by 'a ful vicious man' (VI.459–60) whose 'entente is
nat but for to wynne' (VI.403): 'I preche of no thyng but for coveityse'
(VI.424). The Pardoner has absorbed a mercantile ethic and carried it to
its spiritual conclusion. Dramatic performance and narrative combine
inextricably in his tale, for the imaginative world portrayed by the
Pardoner for the Canterbury pilgrims overlaps with the exemplary and
complex performance of his own role as preacher to the gullible and
unwary. The social domain of his tale is a hyper-realistic, hence allegorical, version of the commercial world of consumption and exchange in
the Shipman's Tale. Chaucer locates the Pardoner's Tale in the social
crisis and confusion of the plague, where there is seemingly no other
framework than temporary association and false kinship.

The tavern setting where the tale begins is not only the 'develes
temple' (VI.470) but also the marketplace of desire and appetite stripped
to the essentials. Its defining characteristic is a 'superfluytee abhomynable' (VI.471), objectified in the 'cursed superfluitee' (VI.528) of gluttony. Thematically, Chaucer's phrase evokes the mystery of surplus at
the center of economic exchange in the Shipman's Tale. Rhetorically, it
slips between the moral censure of 'abominable excess' and the suggestion of neutral description – excess characteristic of mankind, that is,
'abhomynable' because 'ab hominibus.' The excess of gluttony is linked
in the Pardoner's other homiletic topics, gaming and swearing, which
are forms of false signification that squander assets both material and
intangible. Gambling, which aims to produce bounty from sheer
chance, is 'wast also / Of catel and of tyme' (VI.593–4) and, in the
example of Demetrius, of 'his glorie or his renoun' (VI.625). Swearing,
the 'fruyt' that comes along with anger, betrayal, and violence from
gambling, reenacts the falsification of idolatry. At one level, these
three vices show the reduction of all values to matter, but at another,
they reveal an equally sinister process. Rather than outstrip poverty, as

the Shipman imagines in his two speeches on chapmanhood, consumption and exchange accelerate it.

Like the motives driving them, the bonds that connect the rioters are falsified and reductive. The corpse they see being carried to its grave is and is not 'an olde felawe' of theirs (VI.672). It is a symbol of their moral and spiritual dissipation and a foreshadowing of what they will become at the end of the story, but the corpse has no value in itself.[49] What they construct on these material remains is an improvised, temporary association devoted to the single, if ambitious, goal of slaying death: 'felawes, we thre been al ones' (VI.696). Their means of forging identity is the medium of language that the tale has just discounted in its admonition against swearing: 'Togidres han thise thre hir trouthes plight / To lyve and dyen ech of hem for oother, / As though he were his owene ybore brother' (VI.702–4). In their mutual pledge, the terms of relation remain uncertain. Their simulation of kinship depends on living and dying because of each other as well as in behalf of each other: 'ech of hem for oother.' Later, when one suggests to the other the murder of the third, this betrayal is presented as a 'freendes torn' (VI.815), echoing perhaps the merchant's 'freendes' in the Shipman's Tale. Like the original pledge, this convenant is reached through mock fidelity – 'I wol thee nat biwreye' (VI.823) – and through contract – 'thus acorded been thise shrewes tweye' (VI.835) – but its objective changes: 'Thanne may we bothe oure lustes all fulfille, / And pleye at dees right at oure owene wille' (VI.833–4).

Establishing voluntary forms of fellowship typically requires a statement of aims – cult veneration, memorialization, the furtherance of mutual welfare or common interests. The aim sought by the fellowship of rioters hovers uncertainly between the literal and figurative senses of its objective: 'we wol sleen this false traytour Deeth' (VI.699). The conceit of slaying death derives from Hosea 13: 14: 'ero mors tua, o mors.' Patristic and medieval commentators associated the biblical passage with Christ's redemption of mankind.[50] The tale itself refers three times (VI.501, 766, 902) to Christ's buying mankind again with his blood. The Pardoner, as Shoaf remarks, poses the redemption as literal because of his own bodily deformation and obsession with carnality.[51] But equally important in the tale is the idea that death literalized is the endpoint of transactions. The old man is a figure of living death: 'Lo how I vanysshe, flessh, and blood, and skyn!' (VI.732). Yet he cannot effect the transaction that would release him from life. He calls out in vain to the earth, his mother, to exchange riches for a burial cloth: 'with yow wolde I chaunge my cheste / That in my chambre longe tyme hath be, / Ye, for an heyre clowt to wrappe me!' (VI.734–6). Similarly, the eight bushels of florins, which stand in for death and temporarily cause the rioters to forget their sworn objective, do not circulate. The worst of the rioters sees the treasure in explicitly Boethian terms, without understanding their meaning. The treasure, he rightly says, is a gift of Fortune (VI.779), sent to secure their 'heigh felicitee' (VI.787); it has been given for them to spend as 'lightly as it comth' (VI.781) on mirth and merriment. The plan devised by the rioters to carry the treasure off by night is an effort to outwit mutability and changes in Fortune. The murder that ends their story reveals, however, that possession of the literal amounts to possession by death.

The Pardoner's Tale, then, explores agency and associational forms taken to their extremes. The rioters act only on their appetites; the fellowship they create transforms mutual interest to mutual destruction. Situated in social crisis, without institutional structures, the tale discloses what radical selfhood discovers when it confronts its own motives. The rioters do not experience false consciousness because they are all too quickly the victims of it, which is to say, the victims of each other. Chaucer thus shows that the elements of contract, improvisation, and temporality that make up late medieval modernity produce their own catastrophes. That he should represent them in an allegory contained within a dramatic performance suggests, too, that they cannot be sustained. A purely contractual world is, in some sense, historically unimaginable for him, as it is, in other ways, for Boccaccio. In the tales recounted by the Clerk and Franklin, he turns to a more plausible form of modernity, in which contract and exchange exert pressure on traditional hierarchies and redefine the meaning of human connections. Both tales have their most powerful intertexts in Boccaccio.

5

'The sclaundre of Walter':
The Clerk's Tale and the Problem
of Hermeneutics

The Clerk's Tale is a paradoxical but important case of Chaucerian modernity. Told by one of the most withdrawn Canterbury pilgrims, the story of Griselda is seemingly removed from all historical context, above all from the ceaseless brokering of appetite and desire we see in the fabliaux. It is an allegory of patience illustrating the medieval commonplace that true nobility resides in character and virtue rather than lineage, a theme that Chaucer also takes up in his didactic balade 'Gentilesse.' Yet it is precisely this exemplarity that connects the tale to the world of history, culture, and politics. Chaucer's medieval and Renaissance readers found in the tale themes and language suitable for a variety of cultural work.

In his *Temple of Glass*, John Lydgate records 'Grisildis innocence, / And al hir mekenes, & hir pacience' (75–6).[1] The language of the tale's Envoy reappears with new significance in his Christmas mumming at Hertford castle. There wives answer their husbands' complaint of mistreatment by citing the Wife of Bath (168) and affirming their intent 'to clappen as a mylle' (cf. Clerk's Tale IV. 1200).[2] Chaucer's claim, 'Griselde is deed, and eek hire pacience, / And bothe atones buryed in Ytaille' (IV.1177–8) is reformulated so that the patience is not Griselde's specifically but the wives' generally: 'þer pacyence was buryed long agoo / Gresyldes story recordeþe pleinly soo' (175–6). An anonymous *Remedy for Sedition*, extolling the obedience owed the king by the commons, cites Chaucer's reproval of the 'stormy peple! Unsad and evere untrewe' (IV.995) who switch allegiance from Griselde in the tale; and William Forrest's rhyme-royal biography of Catherine of Aragon (1558) styles its subject as a second Griselde and Henry VIII as a figure even crueler than Walter.[3]

Textual evidence also reveals important features of the tale's reception and adaptation. Apart from its inclusion in complete manuscripts of the *Canterbury Tales*, the story was popular in fifteenth-century excerpts and anthologies.[4] Showing few traces of correction and supervision, the anthologies compiled roughly in the third quarter of the century give us a picture of how the tale was framed and represented to late medieval readers. Frequently, it came to them as an independent narrative named after its heroine.[5] Sometimes, it was classified generically as a romance and associated with the Knight's Tale and *Anelida and Arcite*.[6] Undoubtedly, it was seen as a philosophical and moral tale, just the sort of preaching the Host makes a point of instructing the Clerk to avoid in the Prologue.

Recent interpreters have situated the reception of the Tale in a period of social anxiety, in which the poem appeals to an audience more decentralized, more socially mobile and diverse than Chaucer's original circle of court functionaries yet still conservative, backward-looking, and now belated.[7] David Lawton observes that the portion of the Chaucer canon most cited by fifteenth-century poets is a group of 'uniformly serious works' and that 'Griselda's patience, the supreme public virtue of the fifteenth century, is exalted as a model of behavior rather than censured for submission to the monstrous Walter.'[8] Paul Strohm argues that where fourteenth-century audiences valued tales (like the Franklin's Tale) which destabilized genre and challenged the social values associated with it, fifteenth-century readers favored works (like the Clerk's Tale) which were stable in genre and traditional in their outlook on social values and relations.[9] Incorporating Strohm's points about genre and outlook, Seth Lerer reads the version of the Clerk's Tale preserved in one of the fifteenth-century anthologies (Phillipps 8299, now Huntington Library HM 140) as a text that has been removed from an autonomous literary sphere and made to function as 'a fable for apprentice readers' addressed as children who need to learn the lessons of patience, governance, and stability in the face of authority.[10]

One feature of these readings is their sense of an exact fit between the tale and its late medieval readers. From the outset, the Clerk's Tale is presumed to be the right story for an age and readership that made dullness not just an authorial pose of humility, as in Hoccleve and Lydgate, but a psychological strategy and even a social and public virtue. On this view, Chaucer's beleaguered readers in the fifteenth century did not impose a constructed meaning on the text; rather, they turned to a text that they understood directly, without interpretive mediation. Though they feel the loss of Chaucer at one level, at another they occupy a position before the need for hermeneutics. They are not estranged from Chaucer's poem; nothing is lost for them. They are able to respond to the tale without registering its difference from them – which is to say, without a sense of its historicity or their own. The modernity they find is presumably transparent and contemporary.

Historical reception points, however, to a larger constellation of issues, and these involve what I have called the problem of hermeneutics. In the Clerk's Tale, the work of interpretation, I shall argue, is not deferred in time and external to the narrative but already present in the text as a condition of its poetic meaning. Interpretation operates before, around, and within the tale, most notably in the literary tradition Chaucer inherits from Boccaccio and Petrarch and subsequent exploits to his own ends. Leonard Michael Koff points out that Chaucer also constructs a future literary audience and their projected values.[11] Furthermore, the hermeneutic problems in the tale, not just the overt seriousness and moralizing, carry a deep resonance for Chaucer's late medieval readers. Rather than a stable genre and correspondingly stable values, the Clerk's Tale offers a structure of debated readings, and these readings characterize the tale as a narrative of social challenge and resolution. Its modernity lies in renegotiating the commonplaces of value and authority.

In this chapter, I want to show how text and reception, formal meaning and historical application are intimately joined in a pervasive hermeneutic project. I shall look first at the literary tradition of the Griselda story, emphasizing Petrarch's formulation of the interpretive issues. I shall then turn to Boccaccio's *Decameron* not as a direct influence for Chaucer but as a hermeneutic scandal that the subsequent tradition seeks to efface. Finally, I shall examine Chaucer's response to the readings that emerge in Boccaccio and Petrarch. Aesthetically Chaucer finds a middle ground between Boccaccio's hermeneutic multiplicity and Petrarch's closure, and historically his mediation of these readings produces a context of understanding in which Griselda's example of patience finds a rationale and application.

'Pia historia Griseidis'

The literary heritage of the Clerk's Tale, defined in its main outlines by J. Burke Severs, has three constant and interrelated features.[12] The Griselda story is primarily a narrative, the narrative is coterminous with hermeneutics, and the hermeneutics are contested. However much Griselda becomes a figure standing topically for patience, wifely submission, or political obedience, her exemplarity depends essentially on narrative, on what Robin Kirkpatrick calls the 'strong image of temporal sequence' recounting the increments of her testing and the constancy of her patience.[13] The importance attached to narrative as a sequence of action can be seen, for example, in a fifteenth-century manuscript at Montpellier recording the 'pia historia Griseidis' (Bibliothèque de l'École de Médicine 432). In this manuscript, the story has escaped the generic confusion of history and fable introduced by Petrarch (*Epistolae seniles* 17.4) and announces itself as history. The rubrics include the divisions familiar from the Clerk's Tale but offer a much closer articulation of the main parts of the story, marking steps in a sequence of action. They begin by labelling the description of the marquis, the interview with his followers, his response to them, the introduction of Griselda, and her marriage to Valterius; in the middle of the story, they mark the first two trials ('experienciae') of Griselda, the contrived second marriage, and the expulsion of Griselda ('Tertia experiencia'); at the end, they indicate the arrival of the supposed new wife and finally Griselda's restoration and the disclosure of the children's identity.[14] Boccaccio's authorship and Petrarch's translation are present in the makeup of the manuscript, but the narrative holds the central place, much like the detached versions of the Clerk's Tale in the fifteenth-century English manuscripts.

The poetic lesson contained in the rubrics applies directly to Chaucer's art. Though the *Canterbury Tales* establish a fully realized dramatic framework for the story, Chaucer's tale is basically a narrative. In his reading of the Clerk's Tale, Lerer suggests that the literary qualities and aesthetic complication depend strongly on the Prologue and Envoy; when they are absent, as in the anthology versions, the tale, Lerer argues, gives itself up to uninflected moral exemplification and becomes fit material for the literature of instruction.[15] It is a debatable point, however, whether complex literary representation depends solely on a dramatic framework anywhere in the *Canterbury Tales*.[16] Rather, poetic meaning in the *Tales* derives chiefly from Chaucer's narrative art and from the power of the story. For the Clerk's Tale, John M. Manly and Edith Rickert suggest it may even be possible to detect a stage of composition that precedes the *Canterbury Tales*, a version thus standing solely and unambiguously as narrative.[17]

If the story of Griselda is fundamentally a narrative text, it is one that nonetheless comes already marked by interpretation. As Anne Middleton and Charlotte C. Morse note, the beginnings of the Griselda story are simultaneously the beginnings of its interpretive and literary history.[18] Despite its origin and analogues in folklore, the history of the tale properly speaking starts with Boccaccio who sets the narrative within the multiple interpretive frames of the *Decameron*. In his Latin translation of the story, Petrarch dramatizes interpretation and reception as a warrant for translation. Though he admits to only a cursory reading of the *Decameron*, attending chiefly to the opening and ending of the collection, he nonetheless recognizes its mixture of amusing and serious material: 'Inter multa sane iocosa et levia, quaedam pia et gravia deprehendi.'[19] He responds specifically to Griselda's story because of its strangeness and dissimilarity with the stories preceding it: 'multis precedencium longe dissimilem' (Severs, p. 291). It is this dissimilar – in a precise sense, monstrous – story that he memorizes to recount for his friends in conversation and later to translate for the benefit of others. In his *Livre de la Vertu du Sacrement du Mariage*, Philippe de Mézières fashions Petrarch's translation as a 'miroir des dames marieés' in which Griselda's constancy and obedience to her twin husbands – Gautier and Christ, 'son espous immortel' – earn her a place among the nine worthy women recorded by ancient historians as heroic counterparts to the nine chivalric worthy. In comparison with their martial exploits, Griselda's valor, he says, consists in conquering herself and overcoming (*efforsant*) nature:

> Mais qui vaudra bien peser à la balance, qui rent à chascun le pois de sa valour, la grant vertu du corage invincible de la noble marquise de Saluce, fille d'un povre laboureur, en vaincant et surmontant soy meisme et en efforsant nature, qui est une chose de plus grant merite que n'est de vaincre autrui ....[20]

> But whoever wishes to weigh the balance which tells each one the weight of his virtue [should think of] the great virtue of the invincible heart of the noble marquise of Saluzzo, daughter of a poor laborer, in conquering and mastering herself and overcoming nature, which is a thing of greater merit than conquering someone else ....

As Kevin Brownlee points out, Philippe recovers the literal sense that Petrarch had suppressed in favor of a figural meaning, and his work consequently addresses two audiences – married women and every good Christian.[21]

The compiler of the *Menagier de Paris*, who inserted Philippe's translation into his work of domestic instruction, eliminates the pseudo-historical furnishings but still locates the story within a framework of direct reception by a specific reader: 'une leçon generale vous sera par moy escripte et a vous baillee' ('a general lesson will be written by me for you and handed over to you').[22] The Griselda story teaches his young wife what is necessary to acquire God's love, the salvation of one's soul, a husband's love, and peace in marriage in this world. As the husband enumerates these items in the plan of his book, they are arranged as a distributive proportion with corresponding terms: God's love is to a husband's love as salvation is to domestic peace. The spiritual goal of the Christian soul is analogous in the domestic sphere to a husband's peace: 'salvacon de l'ame et la paix du mary.' In this interpretive scheme, the wifely humility and obedience exemplified by Griselda are the efficient cause, not the final cause. The anonymous French version (*Le Livre Griseldis*) on which Chaucer relied for help in translating Petrarch directs the tale not only to wives but to other women as a model of conduct. The story is written, the translator tells us, 'a l'exemplaire des femmes mariees et toutes autres' (Severs, p. 257). There is, in short, no point at which the Griselda story is a narrative without hermeneutics.

The contested hermeneutics of the Griselda story begin with the interpretive categories Boccaccio sets out. As I want to show below, Boccaccio invents a sophisticated provocation to literary understanding. Petrarch responds to Boccaccio's story and its interpretive complexity in ways that promise, then forestall debate over meaning. He establishes what becomes the departure point for subsequent interpretation by rejecting direct imitation of Griselda as a wife and treating her instead as an example of female constancy ('ad imitandam saltem femine constanciam' [Severs, p. 288]). The aim of this allegorical shift is overtly hermeneutic. Petrarch does not intend merely to represent a virtue; rather, he wants to affect the reader's understanding: 'ut nobis nostra fragilitas notis ac domesticis indicijs innotescat' ('that our weakness should be made plain to ourselves by obvious and familiar proofs' [Severs, p. 288]). Self-conscious reading by a general reader thus displaces a prior, literal interpretation prescribing conduct for women ('matronas nostri temporis').

In his second letter about the Griselda story (*Seniles* 17.4), Petrarch orchestrates but again cancels interpretive debate. The initial dispute is about the genre and truth value of the story – whether it is *historia* or *fabula*. In her analysis, Middleton argues that for Petrarch there is no functional difference between history and fable.[23] But Petrarch has, I think, chosen a less radical course than annulling a venerable distinction from the rhetorical tradition he invokes elsewhere. He operates within a Ciceronian taxonomy of discourse that is signalled by debating whether the story is *historia* or *fabula*.[24] In suggesting that Griselda's patience is comparable to a class of extraordinary feats performed by well-known classical figures, he treats Griselda's story as a form of *argumentum*. Her tale belongs to a narrative discourse standing between documented history (*res gesta*) and sheer invention (*fabula*); it occupies the domain of the logically probable, where meaning is open to deliberation and contested understanding.

The possibility of such debate is the topic of the two narratives of reading that serve as the other focus of the letter. Petrarch recounts that a Paduan reader of the story is so overcome by its pathos that he bursts into tears and cannot continue. Later, a Veronese reader, hearing of the first reader's response, asks for the story and reads it through without displaying emotion. He readily admits to its pathetic appeal, but he rejects the tale as mere fable because no equal to Griselda can be found. Petrarch declines to answer his skeptical reader at this point, fearing to provoke dissension amidst friendly discussion. His letter is, however, a tacit refutation, listing men and women of antiquity who have performed comparably extraordinary feats. It is also a demonstration of the privileged position of his authorial intent, for the alternate responses he allows his circle of readers amount to silence and inadequacy.

As these narratives of reading suggest, the hermeneutics dramatized in Petrarch's letters are at base a strategy of displacement, moving our attention from a troubling story toward a spiritual application. The French versions following Petrarch's translation return the story to domestic instruction, the 'miroir des dames mariées' that Petrarch rejects but Philippe recommends. The literal application is no less debated, however, than the figural. Philippe ends his prologue with the exegetical figure of separating the wheat from the chaff, but like the Nun's Priest he provides no guidance for which is wheat and which chaff. The husband in the *Menagier* gives up on topical allegorical correspondences. Recognizing the social constraints imposed on him by his wife's superior lineage, he comments that the story cannot apply exactly: 'je ne suis mie marquis ne ne vous ay prise bergiere' (p. 73). He apologizes for its excess: 'Et me excuse se l'istoire parle de trop grant cruaulté, a mon adviz plus que de raison.' Yet he insists both on Petrarch's superior authority and his own pedagogical aims: 'je ... seulement pour vous endoctriner l'ay mise cy' (p. 72). In staging and withdrawing their readings, these responses reflect an effort to domesticate Boccaccio's story, in both senses of the term. They direct the story to the sphere of private relations between husband and wife. At the same time, they carry out the project, famously re-enacted at the end of the Clerk's Tale, of dissipating the disruptive force of poetic representation into narratives of reception. So successful has the aesthetic strategy been that the original ground of hermeneutic dispute, drawn carefully in Boccaccio, has dropped out of our field of vision and Petrarch's displacement has modelled our reading of the story. Nonetheless, the hermeneutic problems Boccaccio first put in place reveal much about the story, and they reflect the poetic multiplicity that Chaucer reinscribes in his translation of Petrarch.

Gualtieri's 'matta bestialità'

Boccaccio frames Griselda's story with an intricate, multi-levelled structure of interpretation. Panfilo, elected king for the final day of storytelling, establishes a unifying theme for the tales. Dioneo, who narrates Griselda's story, offers interpretive commentary at the beginning and end of his recitation. When he finishes, the women in the *brigata* take up debate, 'chi d'una parte e chi d'altra tirando, chi biasimando una cosa e chi un'altra intorno ad essa lodandone' ('some taking one side and some another, some finding fault with one of its details and some commending another'). Their comments provide a structural balance for Panfilo's instructions, while recasting his theme in a multiplicity of moral and aesthetic judgments. They offer as well a point of origin in the vernacular of feminine discourse for the learned conversations of the historical-imaginary 'Petrarchan Academy' that David Wallace has defined as 'a small, consciously exclusive, masculine group of initiates dedicated to the pursuit of Latin culture.'[25] These frames create a chiasmic structure of interpretation around the story, and within this structure interpretation operates as an element of the narrative itself, working through formal speeches and the reports of what people are saying and thinking. We have, then, a narrative encompassed by interpretation repeatedly dramatizing the theme and problems of its meaning.[26] As it does so, the ground of debate shifts, but Boccaccio's artistic and conceptual focus remains strikingly consistent.

Panfilo decides that the final day of storytelling will be devoted to tales that demonstrate generosity or magnificence – or, more significantly, tales about people who show these qualities: 'di chi liberalmente o vero magnificamente alcuna cosa operasse intorno a' fatti d'amore o d'altra cosa' (p. 675) (the acts of 'those who have performed liberal or munificent deeds, whether in the cause of love or otherwise' [p. 733]). By setting a narrative theme, he restores 'la legge usata' that Emilia had temporarily suspended on the previous day, and he announces that the stories have the moral purpose of instilling the desire to act virtuously.

As Neifile remarks at the start of the tenth day, the theme involves a preeminent virtue: 'come il sole è di tutto il cielo bellezza ed ornamento, è chiarezza e lume di ciascuna altra vertù' ('even as the sun embellishes and graces the whole of the heavens, [magnificence] is the light and splendour of every other virtue' [p. 680]). The two categories Panfilo specifies – generosity and magnificence – derive from Aristotle's discussion of moral virtues in Book 2 of the *Nicomachean Ethics* (1107b8–21), and they provide an initial, if subsequently contested, framework for interpreting the tale.

Aristotle discusses generosity and magnificence under the rubric of getting and spending money; their sphere of action is 'external goods.'[27] In his analytical scheme, generosity and magnificence differ primarily in scale and secondarily in scope: the former has to do with smaller, the latter with larger, sums of money. A magnificent man is thus always generous, but a generous man does not rise to the level of the magnificent. In a later discussion (Book 4.i, 1119b22), Aristotle extends the meaning of generosity to include property generally. He points out that generosity and magnificence have a public dimension, but magnificence, unlike ordinary transactions of giving and spending, is concerned only with expenditures; furthermore, it entails connoisseurship, a large outlay done in good taste (1122a17). Under the terms Panfilo establishes, Griselda's story will concern matters of property and actions that regulate external goods and not patience *per se*, which is the mean in the sphere of anger. Equally important, by invoking Aristotle, Panfilo's categories establish a criterion of judgment for the tale. Aristotle points out that generosity and magnificence operate in accord with the disposition of the giver, not the objects of his generosity. At issue is character, and disposition, the natural inclination of character, is what measures the ethical qualities of action – whether it is generous, prodigal, or miserly; magnificent, vulgar, or petty.

In the prefatory and closing remarks that bracket his story, Dioneo as narrator introduces a competing hermeneutics that complicates and challenges Panfilo's frame. Dioneo shifts the heuristic categories from moral virtues to the matter of disposition. He begins by saying, 'vo' ragionar d'un marchese non cosa magnifica ma una matta bestialità' ('I want to tell you of a marquis, whose actions...were remarkable not so much for their munificence as for their senseless brutality' [p. 758]). This shift brings character emphatically to the fore. By calling Gualtieri's action brutishness, Dioneo directly signals a textual and philosophical background. His phrase 'matta bestialità' echoes the passage in *Inferno* 11 where Vergil explains the plan of Hell and refers Dante specifically to the *Ethics* which treats 'le tre disposizion che 'l ciel non vole, / incontenenza, malizia e la matta / bestialitade' (11.81–3).[28]

Dioneo's claim that Gualtieri acts out of brutishness is, however, significantly misapplied. Aristotle says that brutishness rarely occurs; when it does, it occurs mostly among barbarians, and among Greeks the causes for it are sickness and loss, or the prevalence of vice (1145a33). Paraphrasing Aristotle, Aquinas explains, 'sicut virtus divina raro in bonis invenitur, ita bestialitas raro in malis' ('as divine virtue is rarely found among the good, so brutishness is rarely found among the vicious' [Spiazzi, p. 353; Litzinger, p. 410]). Brutishness exists in the realm of the subhuman, beyond judgments of virtue and vice. It is illustrated by the compounding of atrocity and carnality, such as ripping open the bellies of pregnant women to devour the fetuses or the practice of cannibalism among barbarians (Antiqua Translatio, section 967; Spiazzi, p. 368). The exemplary brutish figure is Phalaris, the notoriously cruel tyrant of Sicily whom Aristotle credits with such extreme acts as devouring children or using them for sexual pleasure (1149a14). Despite the model of tyrannical rule afforded by Phalaris, Dioneo's application of brutishness to Gualtieri fails the test of subhuman extremity. Such usage, as Aquinas notes in his discussion of the passage in Aristotle (Antiqua Translatio, sections 976–7), must be meant *metaphorice* rather than *simpliciter* (Spiazzi, p. 370).[29] Dioneo's claim is, instead, a hermeneutic response; rejecting the ethical framework of Panfilo's categories, Dioneo seeks to register, by his partial and defective analogy, the alarm that Gualtieri's actions provoke. Like Boccaccio in the rubrics, Dioneo responds as a reader – in this case, a reader even before the telling of his own story.[30]

Dioneo is a licensed figure of dissonance.[31] At the end of the previous day (9.10), he had described his function as radically contrastive; he plays the black crow to the ladies' white doves, the apparent fool to wise men. Here he introduces a story that refuses hermeneutic containment at several levels. His challenge to Panfilo's framework of moral virtues is only the most obvious example. As a narrator, Dioneo intensifies the hermeneutic problems of the story, frustrating expectations by granting Gualtieri precisely the happiness he seeks: 'gran peccato fu che a costui ben n'avvenisse' ('it was a great pity that the fellow should have drawn any profit from his conduct' [p. 758]). As his tale rejects Panfilo's strictures, he in turn rejects his tale. At the end of his recitation, Dioneo draws attention to the disparity between precepts and outcome by invoking again the shadowy contraries of god-like virtue and brutishness: 'anche nelle povere case piovono dal cielo de' divini spiriti, come nelle reali di quegli che sarien più degni di guardar porci che d'avere sopra uomini signoria' ('celestial spirits may sometimes descend even into the houses of the poor, whilst there are those in royal palaces who would be better employed as swineherds than as rulers of men' [p. 768]). He then imagines a different ending to the story he has told, in which Griselda, turned out only in the shift Gualtieri allows her, trades her sexual favors for a better dress. Up to this point, the story has moved through the epicycles of fortune that generate a sequence of provisional endings – comic in Griselda's marriage, tragic in her suffering, then comic again in her restitution. Dioneo's fabliau alternative cancels the tale's hard-won comic resolution; indeed, it is a parodic reworking of moral categories, in which generosity and magnificence are replaced by crude commerce and rough justice. Furthermore, Dioneo cancels out a potential, allegorizing reading of his story which is made possible by labelling Gualtieri brutish. Brutishness is conventionally defined by contrast to divine virtue.[32] Gualtieri's brutishness thus implies Griselda's superhuman virtue and potentially carries the story from matters of practical virtue and human character into the realm of the sublime. Dioneo's hypothetical ending, fashioning Griselda as a vengeful and shrewd sexual entrepreneur, forestalls this possibility, rejecting the sublime for the carnivalesque. Seen in this context, Petrarch's exemplary reading of the story is not only a displacement of meaning but a rescue of sorts.

The framing devices I have been describing in Boccaccio not only dramatize the story as a hermeneutic problem; they also furnish a means for analyzing the tale that drives it toward a problematic understanding. One critical tradition sees the tale as a story of humility triumphant, lending a final rising moral action to the *Decameron* as a whole.[33] Giuseppe Mazzotta has argued that Dioneo's story is built on the allegory of marriage and that Boccaccio's artistic motive is to reveal the distance between idealized allegorical meaning and human experience (p. 126). The explanation I want to propose locates the interpretation within the human sphere and practical judgments. Panfilo calls for stories about persons who act generously or magnificently. His focus is on the agent. The rubric introducing the story, which Jonathan Usher characterizes as Boccaccio's readerly response, portrays Gualtieri as an agent who will choose a wife 'a suo modo' – on his own and in a way appropriate to him. For all their disruptive potential, Dioneo's remarks about character are directed toward agents capable of the virtue of magnificence, even as they fail to achieve it. If the conceptual focus is on agents and Gualtieri is the chief agent, it follows necessarily, albeit paradoxically, that the moral index of the tale must be defined by his disposition.

This focus on paradoxical moral agency is a key feature of the narrative itself and represents Boccaccio's commitment to a literary world. Gualtieri's aim, expressed from the outset, is to achieve an appropriate match of temperaments that will guarantee his peace of mind. When his men approach him with their request that he marry, he resists on the grounds of incompatibility:

> 'Amici miei, voi mi strignete a quello che io del tutto aveva disposto di non far mai, considerando quanto grave cosa sia a poter trovare chi co' suoi costumi ben si convenga, e quanto del contrario sia grande la copia, e come dura vita sia quella di colui che a donna non bene a sé conveniente s'abbatte.'
>
> (p. 759)

> 'My friends, you are pressing me to do something that I had always set my mind firmly against, seeing how difficult it is to find a person who will easily adapt to one's own way of living, how many thousands there are who will do precisely the opposite, and what a miserable life is in store for the man who stumbles upon a woman ill-suited to his own temperament.'
>
> (p. 814)

As the vocabulary makes clear, the emphasis falls on Gualtieri's disposition. He says what he is inclined (*disposto*) not to do, asserts the need to find someone with habits (*suoi costumi*) appropriate to this inclination (*ben si convenga*), and warns of the perils of marrying someone ill-suited to one's habits of character (*non bene a sé conveniente*). Griselda is first described as a character satisfying his disposition: 'Erano a Gualtieri buona pezza piaciuti i costumi d'una povera giovanetta che d'una villa vicina a casa sua era, a parendogli bella assai, estimò che con costei dovesse potere aver vita assai consolata' ('Now, for some little time, Gualtieri had been casting an appreciative eye on the manners of a poor girl from a neighbouring village, and thinking her very beautiful, he considered that a life with her would have much to commend it' [p. 759]). Even Griselda's acceptance of his repudiation echoes Gualtieri's concern with the apt correspondence to his disposition: 'Signor mio, io conobbi sempre la mia bassa condizione alla vostra nobiltà in alcun modo non convenirsi' ('My lord, I have always known that my lowly condition was totally at odds with your nobility' [p. 764]). In the moral scheme debated by Panfilo and Dioneo, Gualtieri remains a moral agent acting virtuously.

A similar claim of moral action informs Gualtieri's exposition of his goals in the final speech that balances his earlier discussion with his men. Gualtieri addresses Griselda to explain the purpose of her suffering and speaks to the others to refute their contentions that he has been cruel, unjust, and brutish. Breaking the frame of the narrative, he also addresses the charge ('matta bestialità') that Dioneo has lodged even before telling the story. Gualtieri says he has acted with clear ends in mind ('ciò che io faceva ad anteveduto fine operava' [p. 767]): 'volendoti insegnar d'esser moglie ed a loro di saperla e tôrre e tenere, ed a me partorire perpetua quiete mentre teco a vivere avessi' ('I wished to show you how to be a wife, to teach these people how to choose and keep a wife, and to guarantee my own peace and quiet for as long as we were living beneath the same roof' [p. 767]). As in his earlier speech, Gualtieri is motivated by rational ends, clearly articulated in a patriarchal hierarchy in which teaching Griselda and the people is a secondary good and securing his peace is the higher good. Griselda's patience and humility are subordinate and complementary, as Petrarch's French translators surmised. In the hermeneutic logic of the story, her virtues are the means to his ends. Ironically, it is Gualtieri who grasps Aristotle's moral teaching that our activities aim at some good and that the good every person desires is happiness, expressed in this instance as peace and contentment. It is Gualtieri, too, who understands that such a good must be judged not absolutely in itself but in respect to the agent and his disposition.

The hermeneutic framework established for the final tale of the *Decameron* produces, then, a monstrous story – not in the way James Sledd described Chaucer's Griselde as monstrous in her abjection but in the perversion of the ethical structure that contains moral virtues like generosity and magnificence.[34] True to his disposition and fully conscious of his ends, Gualtieri is a grotesque of Aristotelian moral virtue; he is a prudent agent who understands the workings but not the spirit of the Mean and thereby deforms it. If Dioneo's narratorial comments reject this monstrous hermeneutic and seek to move our understanding of the story onto different grounds, such commentary is only a gesture of containment, not rebuttal. In its full dimensions, Griselda's story remains radically problematic because it destabilizes virtue from within, using the logic of moral virtue and character as the instrument of a troubled understanding. As Mazzotta remarks, Dioneo's tale 'suggests that nothing is definitive and final in this narrative universe' (p. 130).

One might add that the corollary of narrative indeterminacy is a universe of debated interpretation.

Boccaccian multiplicity and Petrarchan closure

In framing Griselda's story by interpretation, Boccaccio and Petrarch move in different directions and to opposite ends. Boccaccio's hermeneutics work to establish a domain of independent literary representation in which competing interpretations reflect the story's profound moral and aesthetic complexity. By contrast, Petrarch's hermeneutics force closure by alienating our understanding from our experience of the story. Where we anticipate the lesson of domestic obedience that subsequent French writers reflexively drew, Petrarch closes off meaning by defining a prior, authorial intent that overmasters us by turning the story on his readers: he has rewritten Boccaccio's story so that we recognize our weakness. Chaucer's version of the story stands between these two hermeneutic strategies. Grounded like its predecessors in dramatized interpretation, the Clerk's Tale absorbs and reorders the claims of Boccaccian multiplicity and Petrarchan closure.

Petrarch's hermeneutics are present from the start of the tale, in the Clerk's answer to the Host's instructions to '[t]elle us som myrie tale' (IV.9). His response is an ambitious claim concealed under Griselda-like obedience. Telling 'a tale which that I / Lerned at Padowe of a worthy clerk' (IV.26–7), the Clerk enrolls in the Petrarchan Academy, presenting himself as one of those cultivated friends for whose benefit Petrarch memorized and recited Boccaccio's story. Similarly, the ending of his tale dutifully preserves the substance of Petrarch's *moralitas*: Griselde is not a wifely model to imitate but an example of patience and constancy in the face of adversity. Between these points, the textual layout of the tale, as the Ellesmere, Hengwrt, and other manuscripts indicate, augments the Clerk's narrative with Petrarch's own glosses.[35] Petrarch's regulation of the text extends from his immediate circle of friends to his *legentes* and to their readers as well.

But if Chaucer begins and seems to end with the closure imposed by Petrarch's authorial intent, he moves as well toward the complexity signalled by Boccaccio's contested hermeneutics. The Host correctly, if unwillingly, intuits that the story is a 'sophyme' (IV.5), a tale that by its very nature embodies problematic meaning and the resources of human understanding, chief among them logic.[36] Although Petrarch's *moralitas* is present, it is defective and only temporary. The Clerk grasps the pattern of analogy between domestic and spiritual obedience in

Petrarch. Each person, he says, should suffer 'in his degree' (IV.1145) and the example of a patient mortal woman should teach us all to receive what God sends us. But as Kirkpatrick observes, 'the responsibility for the analogy seems to be transferred firmly to Petrarch' (p. 235). The element of self-knowledge that Petrarch announces as his final end ('nostre fragile humanité' in the anonymous French translation) also drops out, and we are left with the pious application: 'Lat us thanne lyve in vertuous suffraunce' (IV.1162). This moment of interpretive certainty gives way, in turn, as the Clerk pushes beyond the limit of Petrarch's text (IV.1162) to recontextualize Griselde in the female hermeneutics of the Wife of Bath and the archwives. Petrarchan closure is the ironic foil to Boccaccian multiplicity. This tension hovers over Chaucer's retelling of the story and gives his version its distinctive qualities.

Like Boccaccio and Petrarch, Chaucer locates interpretive problems early in his story. Boccaccio gives rhetorical prominence to Gualtieri's first speech to his retainers and thereby portrays him as a character prudently aware of the difficulties of finding someone appropriate to his disposition. Petrarch grants the retainers their own speech of supplication in a fine display of how one speaks to rulers. Martin McLaughlin argues that Petrarch describes Valterius as an ideal ruler, but Petrarch carefully omits Boccaccio's suggestion that the marquis acts as a prudent, rational agent.[37] Every trace of Gualtieri's speech on the need for a wife with a complementary disposition disappears, along with his clearly stated aim of acting to achieve a domestic peace that mirrors tranquil relations with his men. Instead, Petrarch's Valterius quickly resigns his *omnimoda libertas* and stakes his belief on the prudence and good faith of his subjects: 'Ceterum subiectorum michi voluntatibus me sponte subicio, et prudencie vestre fisus et fideo' ('I willingly submit to the wishes of my subjects, trusting in your prudence and devotion' [Severs, p. 258]). Trust in God rather than his own power of judgment will be the means to his ends: 'ipse [Deus] michi inveniet quod quieti mee sit expediens ac saluti' ('He will find for me that which shall be expedient for my peace and safety' [Severs, p. 258]).

Chaucer's treatment of this opening scene shifts the narrative elements to disclose a new array of motives and a different vision of political relations. In Petrarch, Valterius's aversion to marriage is the most prominent of his subjects' complaints: 'quodque in primis egre populi ferebant' (Severs, p. 256). Chaucer narrows the range of complaint to Walter's absorption in 'his lust present' (IV.80): 'Oonly that point his peple bar so soore' (IV.85). Petrarch identifies Valterius as the progenitor and exemplar of a line of noble rulers ('unus primusque omnium et maximus'); the crisis provoked by his reluctance to marry is a crisis of origins, and the outcome is consequently a civic foundation myth. Like Boccaccio, Chaucer places Walter within an established lineage, with 'his worthy eldres hym bifore' (IV.65). The crisis is consequently the threat of dynastic interruption:

> 'For if it so bifelle, as God forbede,
> That thurgh youre deeth youre lyne sholde slake,
> And that a straunge successour sholde take
> Youre heritage, O wo were us alyve!'
>
> (IV.136–9)

In Petrarch, the noble wife whom Valterius's subjects propose to choose for him offers the best hope ('spes optima') in a future yet to unfold. In Chaucer, her nobility signifies a known value because she will confer '[h]onour to God and yow' (IV.133).

The changes in the Clerk's Tale imply a political vision in Chaucer that is more heterogeneous and nuanced than Petrarch's absolutism.[38] Valterius deals with his subjects, while Walter negotiates the complex relations that bind him to his lords and his 'commune' (IV.70). As Chaucer uses the term, 'commune' means a third estate distinct from nobility and clergy.[39] Though recent critics have described Walter's rule as feudal or autocratic, Judith Ferster rightly observes: 'What is remarkable about the body politic of Walter's realm is not that there is hierarchy or tension and suspicion among the various groups, but that influence travels up as well as down the hierarchy.'[40] Rather than sheer absolutism, Chaucer's constellation of ruler, greater and lesser nobles, and *commune* portrays a moment of political transition and complication between traditional and emerging forces.[41] The spokesman who addresses Valterius gives voice to the silent wishes ('tacitas voluntates') of an obedient people ('qui nullum tuum imperium recusarent' [Severs, p. 256]). In the corresponding lines, Chaucer suggests a dual, if unequal, authority. The spokesman seeks audience 'to shewen oure requeste,' while Walter retains the prerogative 'to doon right as [he] leste' (IV.104–5). The passage suggests the kind of distributive justice Aristotle locates in monarchy and finds analogous to the relations between a husband and wife (Antiqua Translatio, sections 1199, 1209), with the provision that differential rights now extend over several classes of subordinates.

The relations suggested by this differentiation in authority find expression, too, in the lexicon of political anxiety. Valterius leaves his subjects with 'molesta solicitudine' because he is unmarried: he is a 'firste stok,' as Chaucer phrases it in 'Gentilesse' (line 1), but without the prospect of further branches. The equivalent term for the people's anxiety in the Clerk's Tale – 'bisy drede' (IV.134) – resonates against other uses. The dual bond uniting Walter to his nobility and citizens is affection and fear. Walter is 'Biloved and drad' (IV.69), and though he promises to marry so as to relieve popular fears, the people remain anxious: 'For yet alwey the peple somwhat dredde, / Lest that the markys no wyf wolde wedde' (IV.181–2). Even as the promised day approaches, the people nurture dread 'whan they were in privetee' (IV.249), wondering, in lines that Chaucer adds, 'Why wole he thus hymself and us bigile?' (IV.252). The *commune*'s concern for Walter and itself – panegyric 'wo' turned to statecraft – reflects a system of stratified political power. Whereas Petrarch, like Boccaccio, sees a coincidence of interests in which the marquis does not want to be left without a successor and the people without a governor, Chaucer portrays a system of subtle reciprocity in which the end of Walter's line and the introduction of a 'straunge successour' would cancel one of the proportional elements in a larger political equation. Continuity of lineage underwrites the stability of complex political and social relations with a network of differentiated authority rather than absolutism.

In the middle sections of the Clerk's Tale, which focus on Griselde, the problem of hermeneutics coincides with politics. Griselde represents the site of interpretive and political contest. Like Emily in the Knight's Tale, she is the object at once of desire and knowledge. In effect, desire becomes identical with hermeneutics. This conflation is most apparent in Walter's appreciation of Griselde, an innovation that Petrarch introduces and Chaucer recontextualizes. In Boccaccio, Griselda attracts Gualtieri's attention with the appearance of her good habits and beauty (p. 759), but Petrarch makes her the occasion of Valterius's penetrating insight:

> In hanc virgunculam Valterius, sepe illac transiens, quandoque oculos non iuvenili lascivia sed senili gravitate defixerat, et virtutem eximiam supra sexum supraque etatem, quam vulgi oculis conditionis obscuritas abscondebat, acri penetrarat intuitu.
>
> (Severs, p. 260)

> Walter, passing often by that way, had sometimes cast his eyes upon this little maid, not with the lust of youth, but with the sober thoughts of an older man; and his swift intuition had perceived in

her a virtue, beyond her sex and age, which the obscurity of her condition concealed from the eyes of the common throng.

Valterius's wandering, the symbolic extension of his search for prey in hunting and hawking, finds a point of attention and arrest in Griselda. There his gaze transforms from sensual passion to judgment, from youth to maturity. As Carolyn Dinshaw points out, Griselda is associated with a text to be read and interpreted by men.[42] Petrarch describes Valterius's gaze as insight, an intellectual virtue (*Ethics* 1139b18) that allows Valterius to penetrate the opaque surface of Griselda's appearance and grasp her hidden and inherent virtue. Insight also distinguishes his perception from the common understanding that her social condition obscures. Valterius's insight thus demonstrates prudence: 'quodque eximiam virtutem tanta sub inopia latitantem tam perspicaciter deprehendisset, vulgo prudentissimus habebatur' ('because he had so shrewdly discovered the remarkable virtue hidden under so much poverty, he was commonly held to be a very prudent man' [Severs, p. 266]). In Valterius and Griselda, we find as well a congruence of excess. Valterius goes beyond the wisdom of his age, while Griselda's unusual qualities ('virtutem eximiam') place her beyond the norms of her sex and age. By stressing excess, Petrarch establishes a basis for exemplarity and gestures toward recuperating the sublimity that Boccaccio tries to forestall in Dioneo's narration.

Chaucer's version of this passage (IV.232–45) follows the details of Petrarch's narrative outline but sets the scene in a different framework of understanding. Walter's gaze is not an intellectual virtue *per se*. Rather, Chaucer defines it by a series of literary contrasts. It is the lover's gaze in the *Roman de la rose* or Troilus's roving inspection of the Trojan women, now chastened and redirected from 'wantown lookyng of folye' (IV.236) to moral reflection: 'in sad wyse / Upon hir chiere he wolde hym ofte avyse, / Commendynge in his herte hir wommanhede' (IV.237–9). Walter's encounters with Griselde are a reversal of the collapsed *chanson d'aventure* that ends in rape in the Wife of Bath's Tale. His insight seeks to penetrate Griselde's 'rype and sad corage' (IV.220), to know her as a creature utterly different from his desires; and as Ferster remarks, to know her as other is also to know her as she is known by others.[43] Chaucer thus stages Walter's decision to marry Griselde as a reform of courtly conventions and particularly of the circular, solipsistic desire that serves as its primary model. As desire becomes the equivalent to hermeneutics, the tale banishes passion for knowledge.[44]

Walter's gaze is the constant element in a shifting array of interpretive positions, which express the strangeness of what he finds stable and seek to locate it within its proper social forms. Though Petrarch claims a dual descent for Valterius's lineage ('nec minus moribus quam sanguine nobilis' [Severs, p. 252]), it is Griselde's natural virtue that makes fully concrete and present the mystifying ideology of *gentilesse* in the story. She calls the question on the proposition, widely celebrated by the Dolce Stilnuovo, examined by Dante in the *Convivio*, and illustrated by the Wife of Bath in her tale, that nobility of character is more important than noble descent.[45] But if 'unto vertu longeth dignitee / And noght the revers' ('Gentilesse' 5–6), virtue devoid of lineage is still a powerfully confusing sight when it actually arrives. Chaucer follows Petrarch by reinscribing Griselde in the hereditary lineage she singularly disproves. Her integration is a consummate hermeneutic maneuver. She seems 'by liklynesse' (IV.396) to have been 'norissed in an emperoures halle' (IV.399), and those who have known her cannot now, on present evidence, believe she is really Janicula's daughter. In Ellesmere, Hengwrt, and other manuscripts, the marginal gloss emphasizes the point: 'Atque apud omnes supra fidem cara et venerabilis facta est vix quod hijs ipsis qui illius originem nouerant persuaderi posset Ianicule natam esse tantus vite tantus morum decor ea verborum grauitas atque dulcedo quibus omnium animos nexu sibi magni amoris astrinxerat' (Manly and Rickert, 3: 506). Griselde is, says Chaucer in a deft addition, 'another creature' in their estimate (IV.406), embodied virtue estranged from its origin and now at odds with the very ideology thought to promote character over lineage as the sign of true nobility. It is the strangeness of her virtue that produces Griselde's reputation and keeps her the object of continuing observation as 'men and wommen, as wel yonge as olde, / Goon to Saluce upon hire to biholde' (IV.419–20). Once she has been properly displayed, common people see openly what was reserved to Walter's exceptional insight. Griselde's strangeness in turn underwrites Walter's reputation as a 'prudent man' (IV.427), a point reinforced by the marginal gloss: 'Quodque eximiam virtutem tanta sub inopia latitantem tam perspicaciter deprendisset vulgo prudentissimus habebatur' (Manly and Rickert, 3: 506).

As Walter begins to test Griselde, these readings of his character produce another hermeneutic problem. He remains perversely steadfast in his purposes and searches vainly for 'variance' (IV.710) in Griselde's response to her losses. His scrutiny depends, of course, on disguising his own difference in feeling and appearance. Meanwhile, the 'sclaundre of Walter' replaces his reputation for prudence: 'where as his peple therbifore / Hadde loved hym wel, the sclaundre of his diffame / Made hem that they hym hatede therfore' (IV.729–31).[46] When Griselde is turned out, '[t]he folk hire folwe, wepynge in hir weye' (IV.897). But the forged papal edicts, purporting to restore peace between the marquis and his subjects, deceive the 'rude peple' (IV.750) who are subsequently beguiled by the sight of Walter's new bride. Chaucer accepts Petrarch's point that Walter is wrongly rehabilitated as a prudent man (IV.986) by the false documents, but he goes on to expose the popular wish that Griselde's virtue has suppressed and deferred. Not only is the new bride fairer and younger, but 'fairer fruyt bitwene hem sholde falle, / And moore plesant, for hire heigh lynage' (IV.990–1). If the new bride introduces 'noveltee' (IV.1004) into the city, she is a familiar aristocratic figure whose social standing the people recognize, even as they perceive no fault in Griselde's conduct (IV.1018). (With nobility apparently restored, virtue can evidently be separated again from lineage.) Chaucer's innovation is to emphasize the paradox of encountering natural virtue. Amidst wavering popular allegiance, Walter's perverse steadfastness is one of the few stable positions. Besides him, only the 'sadde folk in that citee' (IV.1002) reject the 'stormy peple! Unsad and evere untrewe' (IV.995). Chaucer adds the stanza of their repudiation, and Ellesmere and other manuscripts designate it by the notation 'Auctor' (Manly and Rickert, 3: 508).

Chaucer further accentuates the hermeneutic problems of the tale by reintroducing a tension present in Boccaccio but largely contained by Petrarch. Giulio Savelli notes that both Boccaccio and Dioneo assume authorial and interpretive functions at various points in the story.[47] Chaucer's equivalent is to add a series of comments by the Clerk that punctuates the course of Walter's testing and represents what Derek Pearsall sees as Chaucer's most systematic and audacious departure from Petrarch.[48] Petrarch describes Valterius's obsession with proving his wife as 'mirabilis quedam quam laudabilis...cupiditas' (Severs, p. 268). Chaucer's text cites the passage from Petrarch in a marginal gloss (Manly and Rickert 3: 506–7), but the Clerk amplifies the point rhetorically. He does not see the testing as 'subtil wit': 'But as for me, I seye that yvele it sit / To assaye a wyf whan that it is no nede, / And putten hire in angwyssh and in drede' (IV.459–62). When Griselde's son is taken from her, the Clerk stops short of saying Walter is brutish, but he charges him with moral vice in going beyond the mean: 'O nedelees was she tempted in assay! / But wedded men ne knowe no mesure, / Whan that they fynde a pacient creature' (IV.621–3). After Griselde returns to her father's house, the Clerk comes close to sounding like the Wife of Bath comparing Griselde to Job and lamenting clerks' habitual neglect of women's virtue (IV.932–8).

Chaucer brings a narrative resolution to his story that again renegoti-
ates the hermeneutic positions of his sources. Petrarch largely cancels
the final speech Gualtieri makes in the *Decameron*; he consequently
disrupts the structural symmetry of the first and last speeches and
nullifies Gualtieri's claims to instruct both wife and vassals and to
establish peace in his household. In Boccaccio the decisive point occurs
when Griselda banishes Gualtieri's doubts:

> Gualtieri, al qual pareva pienamente aver veduto quantunque disi-
> derava della pazienza della sua donna, veggendo che di niente la
> novità delle cose la cambiava, ed essendo certo, ciò per mentecattag-
> gine non avvenire, per ciò che savia molto la conoscea, gli parve
> tempo di doverla trarre dell'amaritudine la quale estimava che ella
> sotto il forte viso nascosa tenesse. . . .
>
> (p. 767)

> Gualtieri felt that he had now seen all he wishes to see of the patience
> of his lady, for he perceived that no event, however singular, pro-
> duced the slightest change in her demeanour, and he was certain that
> this was not because of her obtuseness, as he knew her to be very
> intelligent. He therefore considered that the time had come for him
> to free her from the rancour that he judged her to be hiding beneath
> her tranquil outward expression.

For Gualtieri, Griselda proves her patience and her intelligence; and she
disproves, by her generous reception of the new bride, the lingering
suspicion that she has been dissembling. She has, in other words, no
domain of interiority that Walter has not penetrated. Petrarch changes
the issue, however, from Griselda's proof to Walter's knowing. The
moment of decision occurs when Valterius declares, 'Satis . . . mea Griseldis, cognita et spectata mihi fides est tua' ('It is enough . . . my Grisildis! Your fidelity to me is made known and proved' [Severs, p. 286]). In
other words, Petrarch stages a moment of self-recognition in which
Valterius knows that he knows enough. Nor is Valterius suspicious of
Griselda's intelligence or honesty. She has proved herself as a wife to his
satisfaction, as his phrasing makes apparent: 'nec sub celo aliquem esse
puto qui tanta coniugalis amoris experimenta perceperit' ('nor do *I think*
that under heaven there is another woman who has undergone such
trials of her conjugal love' [my emphasis]). When he reveals the intention of his testing, he simultaneously confesses his own flaw: 'Sciant qui
contrarium crediderunt me curiosum atque experientem esse, non

impium; probasse coniugium, non dampnasse; occultasse filios, non mactasse' ('Let all know, who thought the contrary, that I am curious and given to experiments, but am not impious; I have tested my wife, not condemned her; I have hidden my children, not destroyed them'). Valterius's self-recognition corresponds in kind to the self-recognition Petrarch seeks for his readers; like the circle of cultivated readers, he learns his fragility.

The Clerk's Tale reformulates Petrarch's emphases in ways that lend further nuance to their meaning. Chaucer renders the decisive line in Petrarch with complete accuracy: 'This is ynogh, Grisilde myn' (IV.1051). As Jill Mann has shown, *ynogh* has a broad semantic range in Middle English, and Chaucer has extended Petrarch's use of the term to punctuate the structural divisions of his narrative.[49] The word is introduced here in a close echo of Griselde's wish that God send Walter and his new bride prosperity and '[p]lesance ynogh unto youre lyves ende' (IV.1036). Walter's intention is an accurate rendering, too, of Petrarch's *fides*: 'Now knowe I, dere wyf, thy stedfastnesse' (IV.1056). The term signifies more than loyalty, however. As Chaucer indicates in his balade to King Richard, steadfastness implies union, reciprocity, and virtue acting through proper social hierarchy; the compelling image is domestic: 'wed thy folk agein to stedfastnesse' (28).[50] Likewise, the passage that corresponds to Valterius's second address to his people deals with different issues:

> 'And folk that ootherweys han seyd of me,
> I warne hem wel that I have doon this deede
> For no malice, ne for no crueltee,
> But for t'assaye in thee thy wommanheede,
> And nat to sleen my children – God forbeede! –
> But for to keepe hem pryvely and stille,
> Til I thy purpos knewe and al thy wille.'
>
> (IV.1072–8)

Walter's curiosity is only implicit, and the charge he refutes is not impiety, as in Petrarch, but malice and cruelty – that is to say, moral instead of spiritual failings. Rather than test his wife by proofs of conjugal love ('coniugalis amoris experimenta'), as Valterius phrases it, Walter seeks something much closer to Gualtieri's purpose – to know her purpose and will, just as he has earlier seen the people's 'trewe entente' (IV.127, 148). Walter, like Gualtieri, wants to dispel the worry that there may be a disparity between his wife's visible actions and her private motives. That he himself has cultivated a similar disparity throughout the tests, as Kathryn Lynch points out (pp. 53–5), complicates his project and compromises his own standing, but it does not shift the focus of the story.

The ending of the Clerk's Tale takes shape, then, from the hermeneutic problems that bear on the narrative in its literary tradition and intertextual relations. Interpretations of intent and character converge in a cultural and political transformation debated successively through Boccaccio, Petrarch, and Chaucer. The integration of Griselde into the social order, for all her investitures and reversals of fortune, is secured finally when Janicula is brought to court.[51] Boccaccio says after the final test that Gualtieri takes the old man from his 'lavorìo' and installs him honorably as his father-in-law. Petrarch makes the delay part of Valterius's strategy: he has deferred taking Janicula in so as not to have him obstruct his plans for testing Griselde. Chaucer has him brought to live 'in pees and reste' (IV.1132). Meanwhile, Griselde's daughter is suitably married to a lord of high social standing, proving thereby that she has the cultural value that originally led Walter's subjects to propose a noble wife who would confer honor on him. Boccaccio says nothing of the son, but Petrarch and Chaucer make succession an issue.[52] Valterius leaves his son as his successor and lives happily with his wife and heirs. Chaucer writes an additional passage in which the son, enjoying the same 'reste and pees' (IV.1136) as Janicula, is 'fortunat' in marriage, without having to prove his wife. The males of three generations, now connected by a shared and unified heritage, live under the conditions of 'concord' and 'reste' that define Walter's marriage (IV.1129). In other words, Chaucer's Walter enjoys the complementarity of temperament and the domestic peace that Boccaccio's Gualtieri originally sees respectively as means and ends.

In this transformation, Chaucer's ending consolidates and absorbs the competing explanations of natural virtue and lineage. Griselde's qualities, operating alike in the domestic and political spheres, do not stand apart and independent from hierarchy and lineage. The strangeness she presents to those who would understand her is consciously and conspicuously brought into courtly life. Chaucer brilliantly expresses the point in a phrase that evidently confused fifteenth-century scribes but has fascinated modern critics: 'Whan she translated was in swich richesse' (IV.385).[53] Her 'translation,' like the removal and installation of relics, a bishop, or a literary text, is the movement of a given value to a new locale. In this movement, what renders Griselde knowable and displays her qualities is dress; and the rituals of investiture and devestiture accordingly punctuate her movement into, out of, and then back into courtly culture. The most interesting detail occurs in the first investiture, in which Griselde is clothed not just in a garment with the appropriate social badges but in clothes that have been measured for her beforehand (IV.256–9). In the symbolism of this act, natural virtue finds its proper form in an antecedent hierarchy that signifies descent and lineage. Griselde's children, heirs to her virtues and to Walter's, have themselves been raised in such a hierarchy, and the qualities apparent on their return to Saluzzo legitimate both natural virtue and lineage. In a sense, the final test of Griselde, which prompts Walter to realize that he knows enough, is for her to recognize the legacy of her natural virtue in the two young aristocrats who stand before her as her successors. Her instinctive response to them is the pendant to Walter's 'greet insight' (IV.242) about her. Like the Man of Law's Tale, the Clerk's Tale gives us a narrative that explains how new elements are brought into established political structures, how the margin (Janicula's 'throop' no less than the geographical limits of a Christianized Roman empire for Custance) is absorbed into the center. In this respect, we can discover a rationale as well for Chaucer's rejection of Petrarch's idea that Valterius stands at the start of a noble lineage. Chaucer locates Walter further up the family tree with 'his worthy eldres hym bifore' (IV.65) because he wants to demonstrate the power of grafting rather than the point of origins.

It is this idea of integration within hereditary hierarchy that may allow us to explain fully why the Clerk's Tale proved so popular in the century after Chaucer's death, why it retained a sense of modernity from one medieval audience to another. However compelling it may be as a figure for personal, spiritual, domestic, and political obedience, Griselde's patience is not self-sufficient in Chaucer's poem, though Petrarch makes it so in his version of the story. Her patience requires belief of some sort that Walter endeavors to act prudently and wisely, that his testing is not merely pathological but motivated by responsible concerns for personal and public interests, that the excess of curiosity is governed finally by calculation and judgment. It requires readers to believe, with Griselde in virtually her last words, that Walter is a 'benyngne fader' (IV.1097) who has preserved his line and so the social and cultural forms dependent on it. This belief is where, moreover, the problem of hermeneutics rejoins the problem of historical interpretation. Modern critics suggest that for fourteenth-century readers the Clerk's Tale bears a historical meaning because it serves as an analogue to monarchic excess and authoritarianism under Richard II's rule.[54] For fifteenth-century readers the tale bears a different historical meaning, which grows out of its hermeneutic problems. The Clerk's Tale is a narrative in which political authority lives up to the ideological commonplace of natural virtue. Griselde's noble qualities find their proper place and form in noble lineage. The tale is resolutely conservative in maintaining hierarchic rule, but it portrays an established hierarchy acting on the reasonable claims that the *commune* makes of its ruler, and it is optimistic in its belief that natural nobility can be not only recognized but accommodated into structures of power. The Clerk's Tale is not just a conduct book, extolling the value of obedience for a troubled age; it incorporates the political fantasy of Chaucer's new audience of country and mercantile gentry. It expresses what lies behind abjection – namely, the deep wish for a place within benevolent, purposive, rational authority. For these readers, Griselde's patience is a means that must imagine and endorse Walter's ends and accept the scandal of his moral agency.

6
Rewriting Menedon's Story: *Decameron* 10.5 and the Franklin's Tale

Despite its pseudo-antique setting among '[t]hise olde gentil Britouns' (V.709), the Franklin's Tale seems to be Chaucer's most modern narrative. Its celebration of mutual love and reciprocity within marriage finds confirmation at the end of the tale as each of the male characters demonstrates his 'fredom' by resigning a claim over his fellow. George Lyman Kittredge famously opined of the resolution, 'A better has never been devised or imagined.'[1] Love and freedom, as Kittridge's confident pronouncement indicates, exactly match our expectations of the values that should attend marriage and social relations. If we look to the literary context and sources of Chaucer's story, however, a different sense of modernity emerges, one that depends more on poetic revision and cultural translation than on moral themes and timeless values. In the Franklin's Tale, Chaucer adapts his source from Boccaccio and resituates it in a different social sphere. This dual process – at once aesthetic and historical – joins him still closer to Boccaccio, for in the *Canterbury Tales* and the *Decameron* the two writers share the common project of revising a story from Boccaccio's earlier writings. Their revisions follow the protocols enunciated in medieval literary theory for rewriting an antecedent text, but they do not produce merely a formal reconfiguration of the basic narrative. Boccaccio's revision moves the tale from a feudal, aristocratic milieu to an urban, civic locale, and it shows how new bonds of solidarity, expressed through the metaphor of charity, can replace traditional class identity. Chaucer's tale looks back nostalgically to a mythologized feudal world, while the defining terms of social relations in his story belong to an emergent mercantile culture. The modernity both writers portray and enact in their revisions is a historical modernity of changing social relations within traditional structures.

Sources and intertexts

Nearly a century ago, Pio Rajna pointed out that the tale recounted by Menedon in the *Questioni d'amore* of Book 4 of the *Filocolo* was closer to Chaucer's poem than the version appearing in *Decameron* 10.5.[2] In the English-speaking world, J.S.P. Tatlock was the most forceful advocate of Rajna's view, institutionalizing it in the chapter on the Franklin's Tale that he wrote with Germaine Dempster for the *Sources and Analogues of Chaucer's 'Canterbury Tales'*.[3] I have argued elsewhere that the sequence of thirteen *Questioni d'amore* in the *Filocolo*, in which Menedon tells the fourth story, provides the immediate context for Chaucer's borrowing and that Chaucer could well have read the story in a manuscript of the *Questioni* circulating independently from the *Filocolo* as a separate collection.[4] If the *Decameron* is arguably not Chaucer's immediate source, it nonetheless reveals the intertextual relations between Boccaccio and Chaucer. Both writers engage Menedon's story as an immediate source and as a narrative structure that remains open to further imaginative and expressive possibilities, to successive reconceptions. The similarities and differences in their revisions have much to teach us about how these possibilities are embodied in different historical moments and visions of a modern world.

For Chaucer, the project of rewriting Menedon's story means working on familiar terrain. The *Questioni* are staged in the pastoral setting of a *locus amoenus* not unlike the *Roman de la rose*. The stories are framed by the pseudo-scholasticism of love casuistry, so that each narrative is followed by an answer, objection, and response to the objection. The debate surrounding the question posed by each story affirms orthodox views without the sharp edge of irony or the decentering potential of improvisational wit and shrewd calculation. By contrast the task for Boccaccio is profoundly overdetermined. Composed several decades after the *Filocolo*, the *Decameron* here confronts and transforms its aristocratic past. Menedon's story is the most elaborate of the *Questioni* contained in the exuberant courtly romance of Florio and Biancifiore that Boccaccio wrote in the 1330s in the milieu of the Angevin court in Naples. With his return to Florence in the early 1340s, Boccaccio finds a different audience and social environment. The readers and inspiration for the *Decameron*, as distinct from the closeted women who comprise the fictional audience of its frametale, are merchants and mercantile oligarchs whose economic base and political outlook are urban and civic. One might object that Vittore Branca endows these men with heroic qualities as bringers of culture and knights errant in a disenchanted world, but the *Decameron* encodes the ideology they appropriated by privileging character over lineage and espousing charity to cement personal, domestic, associational and social bonds. In short, Boccaccio rewrites his earlier story into a different history from the one that informed the *Filocolo*.[5]

Moreover, within the *Decameron*, Boccaccio revises the *Filocolo* in several conspicuous ways. Generosity, the theme of Menedon's story but not the other *Questioni*, becomes the topic for the final day of storytelling, and here the meaning of magnificence and generosity is renegotiated from a traditional to an emergent social formation.[6] In the tale of Messer Gentile de' Carisendi (*Decameron* 10.4), Boccaccio reprises a story of devotion bordering on necrophilia from the last of the *Questioni*.[7] When the pregnant Madonna Catalina dies after rejecting his advances, Messer Gentile opens her tomb, caresses and revives her, and later contrives the elaborate occasion for the 'migliori cittadini di questa terra' (10.4.20) at which he returns her and her infant son to the husband. Emilia tells her story in *Decameron* 10.5 with the announced aim of refuting the women of the *brigata*, who hold that Messer Gentile demonstrated the highest ideal – aristocratic generosity – by returning the revived wife to the husband who had theoretically renounced his claim on her.[8] Emilia's tale is consciously, even coyly derivative from its source. Menedon prefaces his story in the *Questioni* with the warning that he proposes an extended treatment of his theme – 'una novella, che non fia forse brieve' ('a story, which may perhaps not be short'). Emilia tells a 'novelletta,' a diminutive and belated story that subtly reconceives its predecessor.

Boccaccio and Chaucer go beyond simply redeploying the elements of their source text in a new permutation, which is the practical goal of poetic invention, and they do more than devise a new narrative frame for the story. I want to argue that their aims are aesthetic but that they are not merely aesthetic or exclusively formal. In the tale of Messer Gentile, Boccaccio had introduced elements such as the 'Persian custom' of generosity to lend new perspective on a story told earlier in the *Questioni*, and he found his characters among contemporary Bolognese figures and families. In Emilia's tale, the frustrated lover, Ansaldo, is also a figure from contemporary history. In the *Canterbury Tales*, Chaucer avoids Boccaccio's conscious topical identifications, but he draws on occupational types and estates satire to ground art in social reality. In the Clerk's Tale

and the Merchant's Tale, his protagonists even give us contrasting portraits of Lombard noblemen. For Menedon's story, then, the historical
complement to poetic invention is to situate the tale in radically different
social and cultural contexts. In a later section, I intend to discuss the
social visions that Boccaccio and Chaucer reimagine for the story. To
appreciate how they shift elements of the story and elicit different meanings, we must look first, however, at the master narrative of Menedon's
story.

Menedon's story

The story that Boccaccio and Chaucer chose to rewrite is circular and
finally comic, beginning with a social world in equilibrium and restoring that equilibrium at the end. The principal elements of its narrative
structure are linked so as to produce a rhythm of false and then actual
closure.[9] The tale begins with a stable social vision expressed through a
traditional network of familial and associational relations. In the *Questioni*, a rich and noble gentleman loves his noble wife perfectly. For
the Oriental tales that provide the earliest analogues to Menedon's
story, the centerpiece and symbol of this order is a marriage arranged
for a woman who subsequently becomes the focus of action.[10] An
unanticipated threat to domestic and social order appears in the form
of another man's desire for the woman. In the fictional world of the
Questioni, this threat is at once a nostalgic echo of chivalric romance
and a refined version of the conventional sexual triad underlying the
fabliau. In the Oriental tales, it often carries the additional menace of
rape and physical violence to the woman.

The woman uses her wits to find a provisional resolution to the threat.
In the *Questioni* and subsequent versions, the wife sets an impossible
task, confident that she can frustrate and so over time discourage her
suitor. As Don Juan Manuel shows in *Conde Lucanor*, one of several
medieval analogues to Boccaccio's tale, the task can also be a search
for the answer to a question that brings the suitor back to an authentic
understanding of himself.[11] In the Oriental versions, the woman evades
the threat by promising to return at a later time, after her marriage
but before its consummation, to satisfy the unsought lover. In a sense,
the impossible task we see in medieval Western versions falls to her,
for she must contrive to balance loyalty to her word with fidelity to her
spouse. Her promise in these instances is not an empty pledge or
abstraction, and it is certainly not a ploy because she foresees consequences to not honoring her word, such as divine punishment and the

loss of redemption. As narrative devices, the task and the promise set up the predicament of the tale by validating and sanctioning the initial threat. In the logic of the tale, we cannot later dismiss the promise as a false predicament, though Fiammetta, the arbiter of the *Questioni*, makes precisely this claim, as do many modern interpreters of Boccaccio and Chaucer.

The crisis of the tale stems directly from the provisional resolution. In fact, the resolution presents a perverse fulfillment of the literalism and unexamined ambitions (to exert control over nature, to outwit a powerful antagonist) that allow the woman to stave off the immediate threat. In Menedon's story, the seemingly impossible task of creating a May garden in January is accomplished; in the Oriental analogues, the heroine's marriage brings the promise due. The threat deflected to the margin of the story thus returns to dominate the central set of allegiances. The story's resolution effects closure by saving the appearance of the heroine's oath, while restoring the stable social structure that unregulated desire has threatened. The key feature of this resolution is a sequence of iterated renunciations, each working to constrain the one that follows it. Told by his wife of her promise, the husband consents to her keeping her word. When he learns of this act, the suitor repeats it in turn, whether in admiration or rivalry.[12] In the Oriental analogues, the sequence involves three men of different social standing, one of them frequently a thief. The virtue ostensibly illustrated in their renunciations is generosity, but the real cultural work of renunciation is to establish solidarity among the various men who resign their claims.

The narrative structure underlying Menedon's story is the defining feature of the tale, and it offers us a consistent framework for analyzing Boccaccio's and Chaucer's revisions. In most critical readings of the Franklin's Tale, though, other issues have shaped discussion. Most interpretations have depended on some assessment of the Franklin's character; our concern here is with the social world he imagines in his story. In addition, two folk motifs have held a privileged position in critical discussion. The 'rash promise' made to forestall the suitor's threat is usually taken as both the starting point and chief element of narrative action.[13] Similarly, the question ending the story – 'who acted most generously?' – seems to hold the key to solving the predicament.[14] This emphasis on motifs obscures, however, a still more important textual feature. No version of the story gives us these motifs in isolation. Rather, aesthetic meaning depends on the sequence of action that furnishes the story its imaginative power and narrative logic. Moreover, we have no version that corresponds to a primitive folk story. In the

Oriental tales, our earliest witnesses, the story is often embedded in a larger narrative and told by a woman. The aim of her storytelling is to solve a mystery, usually the theft of treasure or a jewel, by forcing characters in the frame tale to choose among possible answers to the final question. The choices reveal their moral dispositions and thereby expose the criminal. However important the motifs may be, the crucial feature of the narrative is the artful linkage among the parts.

As Boccaccio and Chaucer rewrite Menedon's story, then, they work simultaneously with a determinate narrative structure and a range of local detail that their source text can only partially convey. The genius of invention lies predominantly in resituating the tale. For it is in the way both writers give specificity and embodiment to the narrative schema that their retellings assume a distinctive quality and locate themselves with respect to both literary tradition and history. Some of the changes are immediately apparent and widely discussed in the scholarship – Ansaldo's conversion in the *Decameron*, Dorigen's complaint and the substitution of the clerk for the magician in the Franklin's Tale. But there are more subtle changes in the text, and these frame the large-scale interpolations. As they ring changes in the details, Boccaccio and Chaucer redirect Menedon's story from the aristocratic milieu and love casuistry of the *Questioni* to a radically different understanding of personal, marital, and social relations. They move from a courtly world to a domain of mixed and competing practices that reflect an urban setting and a mercantile culture.

Reimagining the social sphere

The social world originally envisioned in Menedon's story derives its equilibrium from the surrounding frame as well as the setting described in the opening of the tale. In the *Filocolo*, Boccaccio ostensibly saves the noble story of Florio and Biancifiore from the 'fabulosi parlari degli ignoranti' (1.1.25). The company of men and women who exchange stories about love in the *Questioni* is composed of Fiammetta's circle and Florio's band of companions, who are invited into the garden to share the amusement because of their evident and transparent standing ('ne' sembianti gentili e di grande essere'). Though ostensibly Neapolitans and Spaniards, these figures are part of a homogeneous, undifferentiated caste of young aristocrats. Their shared interlude reflects a nostalgia for an aestheticized courtly life free from external contingencies and practical concerns.[15] Fiammetta guarantees the internal stability of their impromptu community by promising that as queen and arbiter she will give 'lievi resposte' ('trifling answers') to the questions they pose – 'senza cercare le profundità delle proposte questioni' ('without exploring the depths of the questions proposed' [4.18.6]). The internal contradictions of their social and fictional worlds are deferred, while the narrators of the *Questioni* gaze into an adult, married world of sexuality with some measure of distance and even naïveté. They see in Menedon's story an idealization of courtly tropes set in a fictional pagan past but acting through the social codes of contemporary life.[16] The husband of the tale is rich and noble, and his ideal love – 'perfettissimo amore' – for a beautiful woman leads him to marriage. The opening of the narrative arranges these expected tropes in a concise formula: 'un ricchissimo e nobile cavaliere...di perfettissimo amore amando una donna nobile della terra, per isposa la prese' ('a very rich and noble gentleman...loving a lady of the city with a perfect love, took her for his wife').

Boccaccio and Chaucer transform the initial social vision in several important ways. In the *Decameron* the husband, Gilberto, is no longer the ideal figure of stable, inherited aristocracy but a civic personality – 'un gran ricco uomo...assai piacevole e di buona aria' ('a most agreeable and good-natured man, exceedingly wealthy'). He exists within the urban social sphere of Udine rather than a feudal world. Meanwhile, the idealization of the *Questioni* transfers to the importuning aristocratic lover. Ansaldo is 'un nobile e gran barone...uomo d'alto affare e per arme e per cortesia conosciuto per tutto' ('a great and noble lord...a man of high repute, famous throughout the land for his feats of arms and deeds of courtesy'). The unnamed husband of the *Questioni* loves his wife perfectly; in the *Decameron*, it is Ansaldo who loves her 'sommamente' and 'ferventemente.' Ansaldo's desire and its courtly base are a vestige of the milieu that Boccaccio abandons in moving from the *Filocolo* to the *Decameron*.

In the Franklin's Tale, Chaucer independently exploits some of the possibilities that Boccaccio saw in revising the story. The husband's wealth, which is correlated with his nobility in the *Filocolo* and made his chief trait in the *Decameron*, emerges as a defining economic theme in the Franklin's Tale. Arveragus's service 'in his beste wise' (V.731) is expressed as 'labour' (732) and a 'greet emprise' (732) that leads to 'blisse' (744, 802) and 'prosperitee' (799). Though these last two terms have a theological meaning elsewhere in Chaucer's works, here they signify the result of material benefits.[17] Chaucer thus rewrites the formula of idealization. Where a rich and noble man loved a woman perfectly and consequently took her as a wife, here a knight of no special degree undertakes the speculative enterprise of courtly love, proves his 'worthynesse' (738), and secures a wife of 'so heigh kynrede' (735). Hereditary privilege and social value are not a condition of degree but a commodity to be acquired by the knight-adventurer shrewd and determined enough to take on the entrepreneurial risks: 'To seke in armes worshipe and honour' (811). Arveragus works, in other words, specifically to possess the 'worshipe and honour' (962) that Aurelius enjoys by descent.

The most drastic revision that Chaucer makes to the social world of the *Questioni* is, of course, the marriage agreement negotiated by Arveragus and Dorigen and celebrated at some length by the Franklin (761–98). In both of Boccaccio's versions, marriage conforms to patriarchy and church doctrine, which treated a wife as a *socia* (hence an equal), while insisting that she submit to governance by her husband, just as the unruly body is governed by the rational head (hence a subordinate). Dorigen and Arveragus devise a different arrangement that preserves the appearance of male sovereignty and conventional marriage but allows equality and reciprocity in fact. Arveragus freely resigns 'maistrie' (747), and Dorigen consequently pledges 'trouthe' (759). Their agreement, we should remember, is a means and not an end. Its aim is to promote worldly happiness – 'to lede the moore in blisse hir lyves' (744) and '[t]o lyve in ese' (788) – rather than further salvation, the ostensible goal of Christian marriage. It is precisely this 'sovereyn blisse' (1552) that is restored at the end of the tale.

Arveragus and Dorigen further modify Menedon's formula so that love and marriage are concurrent and not consecutive. Arveragus is a '[s]ervant in love, and lord in mariage' (793). Their marriage reconceives the division of public and domestic spheres that Boccaccio accepts. In medieval marriage doctrine, the public and the domestic are separate but analogous zones, regulated by the same metaphor of governance even as they correlate outside and inside, male and female space, masculine and feminine authority.[18] Chaucer's characters imagine a different set of categories, dividing the public and private spheres. What occurs in the domestic sphere of marriage is determined not by external doctrine brought into the marriage but by the contract negotiated between them and known only to themselves. They thereby create a form of subjectivity out of the isolation and concealment that stand at the heart of their marriage. They are joined in reciprocity, mutuality, and subterfuge. Leonard Michael Koff points out that their arrangement produces not interdependence so much as autonomy.[19] The mechanism binding these autonomous agents is 'accord,' the freedom of the interiorized, mercantile subject to negotiate and act in his best interests.

Chaucer uses this term to bracket the marriage agreement and the Franklin's excursus on marriage (741, 791). In the Friar's Tale and the Shipman's Tale, he gives a vision of what such arrangements look like when *trouthe* and sworn allegiance operate for appetite and individual interests, unmediated by charity.[20] As Branca explains for Boccaccio, the 'ragion di mercatura' imposes a logic of social life and personal conduct that offers a prospect of extraordinary freedom at the final cost of utter isolation and horror.[21]

Threat, desire, and compact

The construction of the social worlds in Boccaccio and Chaucer goes a long way toward explaining the exact nature of the threat posed by the lover's desire. The lady of the *Questioni* suffers Tarolfo's attention in silence, as he follows an Ovidian strategy of attrition and penetration that she seeks to outwit.[22] She strives to contain within herself the meaning of his public display in haunting her house, jousting, and fighting in tournaments and his private approach to her through messengers and intermediaries: 'Le quali cose la donna tutte celatamente sostenea' ('The lady bore all these things quietly'). Her fear is that rumor of the courtship will come to her husband's notice and that he may consequently assume she is complicit in it. She checks her first impulse to divulge Ansaldo's love, however, and her second thoughts ('miglior consiglio') show what is really at stake: 'Io potrei, s'io il dicessi, commettere tra costoro cosa che io mai non viverei lieta' ('I might, if I told him, start something between them that would never let me live happily again'). The threat she discovers on reflection is that rivalry may escalate into vendetta; the two noblemen in conflict can overturn family and civic order, with terrible consequences for her. Besides inciting violence and slaughter, she will legitimate misogyny, much as Helen does in the medieval Troy story or Criseyde in *Troilus and Criseyde*.

When Boccaccio reconceives this element in the *Decameron*, the scale of the threat is notably reduced. Dianora shows no fear of wider upheaval; she is simply weary of Ansaldo's solicitations. In the Franklin's Tale, by contrast, something larger is at risk. Aurelius's sudden declaration of love, couched in the language of courtly complaint that Absolon, Damian, and others in the *Canterbury Tales* have already discredited, threatens Dorigen's pledge to Arveragus. The language of this scene directly echoes the terms of their marriage agreement in which Dorigen pledges, 'I wol be youre humble trewe wyf' (758). The issue is not just marital fidelity but the entire structure of 'accord' and reciprocity that

Arveragus and Dorigen have negotiated for themselves as the private domain of their marriage. *Trouthe* underlies their relations, and it means both marital fidelity and the obligation to stand by a promise. Dorigen's 'fynal answere,' her intention once she has seen Aurelius's 'entente,' encompasses the public and private facets of her marriage: 'Ne shal I nevere been untrewe wyf / In word ne werk, as fer as I have wit; / I wol been his to whom that I am knyt' (984–6).[23] She is joined to Arveragus as the words of the marriage ceremony prescribe, and she is bound in a private relation where full faith in the literal word secures social ties.

Deferral and the counterfactual

The stratagem by which all the women defer the menace of desire reflects different possibilities in reconceiving and resituating the story. The wife in the *Questioni* exercises a kind of improvisational guile and succeeds in bluffing Tarolfo. She devises a 'sottile malizia,' a devious trick that invites Tarolfo into an erotic trial and sets impossible conditions for winning. Boccaccio makes it clear that the impossibility of the task is an index of her intentions. Tarolfo recognizes the task as impossible and knows immediately why the lady has asked for it: 'egli conoscesse bene perché la donna questo gli domandava' ('he understood perfectly why the lady had requested it'). Boccaccio also leaves unexplained a potential contradiction that comprises her bluff to Tarolfo. Concealing her fear of disclosure, she threatens Tarolfo with telling her husband of his attentions, if he does not observe the terms of her challenge either to produce the wondrous garden or to desist altogether.[24] She turns fear against Tarolfo, though Boccaccio never explains why the threat that constrains her earlier is not felt as such now. The verb she uses for Tarolfo's attentions – *stimolare* – conveys the dual meaning of irritation and incitement, and it returns significantly later in the story.

In the *Decameron*, Boccaccio explores another range of nuances in Dianora's ploy. She, too, devises 'una nuova e al suo giudicio impossibil domanda' ('something for her that was both bizarre and, as she thought, impossible'), but Boccaccio amplifies the disingenuous promise into a simulation of complicity with Ansaldo. The lady of the *Questioni* had sworn by her gods and a lady's loyalty to satisfy Tarolfo's every desire but without suggesting in any way that she might possibly share his wishes. When Dianora summons Ansaldo's go-between, she raises different expectations. His gifts, she says, do not induce her to love him, but if she can be certain of his love, she will love him and fulfill his desires: 'E se io potessi esser certa che egli cotanto m'amasse quanto tu di', senza fallo io mi recherei a amar lui e a far quello che egli volesse' ('If only I could be certain, however, that he loved me as much as you claim, I should undoubtedly bring myself to love him and do his bidding'). Within the impossible task Dianora places the bait of love itself as well as the promise of physical submission to the lover's desire. Meanwhile, the aim she attaches to the task is an ironic version of her own fidelity to Gilberto. The test is for Ansaldo to prove his faith ('far fede') to her by satisfying her demand. If he declines the test but persists in his attentions, she threatens in turn to provoke precisely the interfamilial, civic violence that the lady of the *Questioni* recognized as the larger, unspoken danger: 'se più mi stimolasse, come io infino a qui del tutto al mio marito e a' miei parenti tenuto ho nascoso, così, dolendomene loro, di levarlomi da dosso m'ingegnerei' ('For if he should provoke me any further, I shall no longer keep this matter a secret as I have until now, but I shall seek to rid myself of his attentions by complaining to my husband and kinsfolk'). Boccaccio's revision thus voices not just the silence of an antecedent text but the repressed fear of his own original.

What Boccaccio explores in Dianora's faithful dissembling gives a useful perspective on Dorigen's rash promise to Aurelius. The key element in Chaucer's restaging of the scene from the *Questioni* is that Dorigen makes her pledge 'in pley' (V.988). The distinction between earnest and game, that most venerable of authorized Chaucerian antinomies (I.3186), collapses, as we shall see, because in a social and personal world constructed solely on the strength of promise every pledge, serious or playful, has to be taken literally, at face value. The world of the marketplace may run on credit, but it cannot accept false coinage. Whatever Dorigen says about her intent and however much medieval ethics may have privileged intent over the literal language of promises, Dorigen wrongly assumes that she can quibble with language, just as Dianora can dissemble with it.[25] Like Dianora, she pledges love and not just submission in her counterfactual promise: 'Thanne wol I love yow best of any man' (V.997). Unlike Dianora, she has no other realm outside language, for the domestic has been subsumed into the private and the private has turned the public into a shadow and disguise of meaning. Besides the narrative situation, the social context of late-medieval oath-making, as Richard Firth Green points out, works to constrain Dorigen to her promise.[26]

We see in Dorigen's failed effort to separate reality from play a reduction toward the literal that becomes a feature of both authors' revisions, as their tales move from provisional resolution into crisis. The imaginative world of the *Questioni* is progressively depopulated and disenchanted. Tarolfo departs with a company of friends to seek the advice ('consiglio') of someone who can help him accomplish the impossible task; like Filocolo in the master narrative, he carries his social world with him. Ansaldo travels alone to find 'aiuto o consiglio.' Aurelius, like Troilus, withdraws to melancholy and fruitless prayer to the pagan gods for two years. The mediators each lover finds represent a similar reduction. Tarolfo encounters Tebano on the plain of Pharsalia, which is still stained by Roman blood and menaced by the 'furiosi spiriti' of those slain in the battle over empire between Caesar and Pompey. Tebano is a laborer and tradesman in herbal remedies, and his squalid appearance occasions a dispute over true identity and worth, which is also a debate about appearance and reality. As he tells Tarolfo, 'Tu e molti altri il sapere e le virtù degli uomini giudicate secondo i vestimenti' ('You and many others judge the knowledge and power of men according to their clothes'). In the *Decameron*, the magician comes directly to Ansaldo, without any narrative preparation, offering his services for a price. In the Franklin's Tale, Aurelius and his brother journey toward Orléans, famous for the science of 'diverse apparences' (1140); the only magical element occurs when they are met, inexplicably, by a clerk who knows the cause of their journey. The treasure required by these mediators to meet the impossible demand moves progressively toward a cash nexus. Tarolfo promises half his holdings, which consist of land and property: 'Io signoreggio ne' miei paesi più castella, e con esse molti tesori, i quali tutti per mezzo partirei con chi tal piacere mi facesse' ('I am lord over many castles in my land and much treasure because of them, all of which I will divide in half with whoever does me this favor'). Ansaldo promises a 'grandissima quantità di moneta' ('a huge sum of money'). The clerk drives a hard bargain with Aurelius and extorts payment of a thousand pounds.

The most notable feature of this insistent demystification is the transformation that each magician effects. In Menedon's story, Boccaccio develops the magical elements at length. Tebano prepares an elaborate ritual invoking Hecate, Ceres, and the powers of the night. He journeys throughout the known world in a dragon-drawn chariot to secure the herbs and liquids he needs. When he returns on the third day, the smell of the herbs causes the dragons to slough off their scales and rejuvenate. The brew he concocts makes a dried branch from an olive tree flower and bear fruit. He places sticks in the ground he has selected beforehand, pours the liquid on them, and watches as they turn verdant and ripe.

The description of Tebano's magic draws consciously on the passage in Ovid's *Metamorphoses*, where Medea uses her powers to reverse the aging of Jason's father, Aeson (7.179–293). Victoria Kirkham has argued that the adaptation of Ovid is really Boccaccio's central interest in the story.[27] In the *Decameron*, the episode disappears completely, and Boccaccio merely reports that the magician used his art to create the garden.

Chaucer's adaptation in the Franklin's Tale is no less literal but a good deal more elaborated than the *Decameron*. Aurelius's brother recalls the power of 'thise subtile tregetoures' to produce wondrous effects (1141–51). In his house, the magician presents a spectacle of hunting, tournaments, and even the image of Aurelius dancing with Dorigen. What makes Chaucer's treatment of these wondrous events distinctive is the acknowledgment that they are 'magyk natureel' (1125). Unlike Boccaccio's Ovidian imitation in the *Questioni*, Chaucer's wonders have nothing to do with transforming the natural order. They are marvels, operating within the realm of natural laws. The clerk knows how to manipulate natural law, but he does nothing to suspend, much less supplant it. It is not insignificant that when he claps his hands and dispels the 'revel' of hunting, jousting, and dance, Aurelius and his brother find themselves 'in his studie, ther as his bookes be' (1207). His wonders restage the literary conventions of romance and courtly lyric. Later, when he makes the rocks seem to disappear from the Breton coast, he uses another text, '[h]is tables Tolletanes' (1273), to calculate the positions of the stars, moon, and planets. Chaucer's use of 'magyk natureel' has links to the *House of Fame* (1266), the Physician in the *Canterbury Tales* (I.416), and above all the Squire's Tale. A conscious rewriting of Tebano's astral journey, natural magic serves two poetic functions. It rejects the extravagant invocation of the supernatural in favor of a natural world whose laws are finally literal and reductive. At the same time, it defines the aim of magic in the tale as insubstantial – 'to maken illusioun, / By swich an apparence or jogelrye' (1264–5).[28] This difference from Boccaccio's version will furnish a new rationale for the sequence of resignations that ends the tale.

The crisis of literalism

The crisis occasioned by fulfilling the impossible task produces a sense of increasing isolation as we move from one text to another. Tarolfo presents the garden to the lady on a solemn feast day for the city. She visits it the following morning, accompanied by many people, and the garden is a source of curiosity and amazement to those in the region. In the *Decameron*, Boccaccio cancels many of these social and public dimensions. Though Dianora later visits the garden in the company of many other women of the city, Ansaldo first sends a selection of beautiful fruits and flowers secretly ('occultamente') to her as proof of his love. He holds her, in other words, to the literalism of her hypothetical pledge to love him and do his bidding, if she can be certain of his love: 'se io potessi esser certa che egli cotanto m'amasse quanto tu di'.' The fruits and flowers are a memorial sign of her sworn promise ('con saramento fermata'), hence of the paradoxical obligation of a 'leal donna' to keep her part of the bargain. Aurelius searches out Dorigen in the public space of the temple, but he waits for a private moment to convey word of his marvel and to renew his lover's supplication: 'But of my deeth thogh that ye have no routhe, / Avyseth yow er that ye breke youre trouthe' (1319–20). Tarolfo and Ansaldo make their case by an enthymeme, reminding the lady of her promise, stipulating that they have completed their task, but leaving unexpressed their demand that the lady now honor her part of the bargain. Aurelius rehearses the full argument and makes the confrontation scene a test of Dorigen. He tells her, 'Dooth as yow list; have youre biheste in mynde, / For, quyk or deed, right there ye shal me fynde' (1335–6).

The women react to this remarkable disclosure in ways that reflect the differences among the underlying social formations of the tales. The lady in the *Questioni* recognizes that she is a pawn in a chivalric contest. She tells Tarolfo, 'guadagnato avete l'amore mio' ('you have gained my love'), and her husband not only confirms but echoes her words, 'egli l'ha ragionevolmente e con grande affanno guadagnato' ('he has earned it reasonably and with great labor'). The favor ('grazia') that the lady asks of Tarolfo – delaying his pleasure until her husband is out of town hunting or on some other business – is also part of the tale's aristocratic vision. Tarolfo and the lady will ostensibly use the same device as courtly lovers like Tristan and Isolt, Launcelot and Guinevere, or even Paolo and Francesca. Meanwhile, she withdraws to her chamber, 'piena di noiosa malinconia' ('full of dejection'). Her melancholy only grows as she finds herself constrained by her predicament. Her fear is the dread of misunderstanding that originally motivated her 'sottile malizia': 'dubitando non il marito malvagia la tenesse' ('fearing that her husband might think her wicked'). Dianora likewise repents her promise, but Boccaccio complicates her response. She not only admires the garden, but the garden enchants her with the result that she returns home more ambivalent and even more sorrowful.

Against this background, Chaucer's insertion of Dorigen's lament is an instance of narrative amplification that reflects a major authorial rethinking of the source text. As David Wallace observes, 'The most radical differences between the two narratives stem from Chaucer's decision to bring his female protagonist to prominence.'[29] Dorigen is 'astoned' (1339), secure in her belief that the 'inpossible' is guaranteed by the very laws of nature that, unknown to her, have aided Aurelius. Arveragus's absence, which is the ostensible cause of delay when the lady of Menedon's story asks Tarolfo for a 'grazia,' provides the fictional and thematic space for her lament. The lament has attracted various readings in the critical literature. Whatever the reception, though, it is clear that the roster of classical wives and maidens who chose death before dishonor sorts oddly with Dorigen. She may share their resolve to accept death rather than defilement, but unlike them she is a victim of her own blindness, her blithe assumption that reality can be separated from play in a world of relationships founded on language. Moreover, for all her claims to share the predicaments of exemplary figures from the classical past, Dorigen is profoundly isolated. She speaks to a moral universe of remote analogues who do not share the source of her pathos. She sees Fortune as the cause of her predicament, but it is Fate that haunts the others. Her situation is thus closer to the figures of Ovid's *Heroides*, bound to each other by the abstract resemblance of their situations yet isolated in the artificiality of their utterances.

Boccaccio and Chaucer devise notably different narrative resolutions as they rewrite the ending of Menedon's story. In the *Questioni*, the husband forces the wife's disclosure by the same means – 'continui stimoli' – that Tarolfo earlier uses in his courtship. His decision to send her 'copertamente' and 'liberamente' to keep her promise is the result of deliberation ('il cavaliere lungamente pensò'). His deliberation answers the wife's fear that he might suspect her of betrayal. He acts from a consideration of intent – 'conoscendo nel pensiero la purità della donna' – that cannot enter the decision in the Franklin's Tale. The wife's intent in the *Questioni* has a status outside of language and negotiation; it is the external referent against which the internal logic of promises and understandings can be measured, though promises retain their coercive power. The husband makes this disparity clear in his final instruction. Acting to forestall melancholy and suicide and thus demonstrating the perfect love that begins Menedon's story, he warns her of the dangers of language: 'un'altra volta ti guarderai di sì fatte impromesse, non tanto ti paia il domandato dono impossibile ad avere' ('beware of these kinds of promises next time, even if you think the gift you ask for is impossible to have').

The scene between Gilberto and Dianora follows the main outlines of its model in the *Questioni*, but Boccaccio makes changes that play significantly off the source text. Dianora's sadness cannot be hidden, and it breaks out, despite her efforts to contain it ('nol potendol ben dentro nascondere'). She is constrained ('constretta') rather than 'stimolata' to reveal the cause. Gilberto is first angry and only then begins to resemble the deliberative husband of Menedon's story. Boccaccio's phrasing shows itself as a conscious rewriting of the earlier text: 'poi, considerata la pura intenzion della donna, con miglior consiglio cacciata via l'ira' ('bearing in mind the purity of his wife's intentions, he put aside his anger'). Boccaccio goes on, however, to amplify the husband's remonstrance. Gilberto says that Dianora was wrong to hide the lover's entreaties, to bargain her chastity ('pattovire sotto alcuna condizione con alcuno la sua castità'), to underestimate the power of words to enlarge upon meaning, and to disregard what is possible to lovers. Like the husband in the *Questioni*, he can separate intent from the literalism of the promise. Even as he chastises her for concealment and bargaining, he tells Dianora, 'io conosco la purità dello animo tuo' ('I know you were acting from the purest of motives'). In this formulation, Boccaccio effects a separation of the social from the personal. Gilberto relieves Dianora from the obligation of her personal bond to Ansaldo, holding suspended her obligation to him: she may give her body one time but not her heart. The other condition that Boccaccio adds is a gesture back to the *Questioni*. Gilberto mentions that he is also motivated by fear of the magician, should Ansaldo feel he is being made a fool ('se tu il beffassi'). His remark is an oblique and displaced reference to Tarolfo's fear throughout Menedon's story that Tebano may be making a fool of him before he produces the wondrous garden.

In the Franklin's Tale, Chaucer reworks the elements of the scene to a different effect. On his return, Arveragus finds Dorigen prepared to reveal the cause of her sorrow with little prompting. Unlike Gilberto, he reacts 'with glad chiere' (1467), asking, 'Is ther oght elles, Dorigen, but this?' (1469). Arveragus's immediate reaction is to instruct her to keep her word. He approaches her predicament as an example illustrating the first principle of his moral philosophy: 'Trouthe is the hyeste thyng that man may kepe' (1479). Lee Patterson points out that *trouthe* is an internal condition and sense of integrity equivalent to identity.[30] It is only when he breaks into tears and resumes the mastery he has earlier foregone, ordering Dorigen to keep silence about 'this aventure' (1483) on pain of death, that we see the other dimension of Arveragus's response. Like Gilberto, Arveragus has another motive. For him, the motive is shame – that is, the translation of the private into the social and public arena. Arveragus's wish is that dishonor, like the real terms of his marriage, remain an item of agreement between him and his wife. The Franklin's intervention at this point, which has no counterpart in Boccaccio, highlights Arveragus's predicament: 'Paraventure an heep of yow, ywis, / Wol holden hym a lewed man in this / That he wol putte hys wyf in jupartie' (1493–5). The point of the comment is not that Dorigen is in actual peril but that Arveragus has risked her as a figure of the private world they have constructed.

New resolutions

In all three versions of the story, the resolution depends on the force of narrative performance. The tale is brought consciously inside its own fictional realm. The husband of the *Questioni* prevails on his wife to tell him the cause of her melancholy, and she gives a full account: 'dal principio infino alla fine gli narrò.' When she goes to Tarolfo, she relates the complete story: 'Narrò allora la donna interamente a Tarolfo come la cosa era tutta per ordine.' Returning home, she tells her husband what has happened 'per ordine.' Meanwhile, Tarolfo relates the events to Tebano, who tests Tarolfo's fidelity to his promise. In the *Decameron*, Dianora reveals her secret completely to Gilberto: 'ordinatamente gli aperse ogni cosa.' Later, when she returns home, she recounts her interview to Gilberto. Dorigen also gives Arveragus a complete account, though the Franklin chooses to omit it in his presentation: 'It nedeth nat reherce it yow namoore' (1466). When Aurelius releases her from the promise, she returns home to Arveragus, bearing the complete tale: 'hoom unto hir housbonde is she fare, / And tolde hym al, as ye han herd me sayd' (1546–7). Aurelius subsequently repeats the story to the clerk, and Chaucer suggests the parallelism of his narration to Dorigen's by using the same terms: '[he] tolde hym al, as ye han herd bifoore; / It nedeth nat to yow reherce it moore' (1593–4).

Boccaccio breaks with this pattern at one crucial point. Tarolfo learns of the husband's 'gran liberalità' and realizes the censure he courts ('gravissima riprensione') through the lady's story. By contrast, Ansaldo reacts directly to Dianora's explanation of why she has come. He responds not just by recognizing his culpability but by converting desire to charity: 'dalla liberalità di Gilberto commosso il suo fervore in compassione cominciò a cambiare' ('because he was deeply moved by

Gilberto's liberality, his ardour gradually turned to compassion'). In this moment, he sees Dianora as a sister, and Emilia ends the story by saying that desire ('concupiscibile amore') has been converted to charity ('onesta carità'). By suppressing the wife's narration in this scene, Boccaccio achieves a dramatic focus on Ansaldo's character. In part, this focus serves to advance Emilia's rival claim against the preceding story, where Messer Gentile abandons his desire, regards Catalina as a sister and her infant as his godchild, and lives as a close friend of her husband and kinsmen: 'messer Gentile sempre amico visse di Niccoluccio e de' suoi parenti e di quei della donna' ('as for Messer Gentile, for the rest of his life he remained a close friend of Niccoluccio as well as of the families of both Niccoluccio and his wife'). The stability of a complete aristocratic world is restored. Something more – and different – is involved in Emilia's story. Ansaldo responds feelingly, while Tarolfo calculates. Both characters express wonder at the situation, but Tarolfo turns inward, reflecting on his situation before releasing the wife from her promise. In the Franklin's Tale, Chaucer exploits the same possibilities of dramatic focus. Aurelius responds to the situation, moved by 'greet compassioun' (1515) and 'routhe' (1520). He sets his lust aside in the interest of Arveragus's 'gentillesse' (1527) and Dorigen's 'distresse' (1528). Both Ansaldo and Aurelius show a capacity for identification largely undeveloped in Tarolfo.

Much as Boccaccio and Chaucer introduce a dramatic focus, they also write a new set of relations into the end of Menedon's story. Tarolfo's moral insight is phrased in social rather than ethical terms. The husband has shown him generosity, and for him to press his claim on the wife would be a 'villania.' He sends apologies to the husband for his 'follia,' along with the promise to desist in the future. As Fiammetta remarks to Menedon, the husband has been generous with his honor and Tarolfo with his desire ('libidinoso volere'). The fundamental structure of relations has not changed, however; it remains an aristocratic transaction, as the two potential rivals return to the original equilibrium. Even when Tebano resigns his claim to half Tarolfo's property, he acts to endorse the existing social arrangement, for his announced purpose is not to act 'meno che cortese' ('less than courteous').

As they revise their source, Boccaccio and Chaucer show how social relations can be transformed in the story's resolution. Dianora complains that Gilberto has more concern for the pain of Ansaldo's uncontrolled love ('disordinato amore') than his own honor or his wife's. But it is exactly this empathy that sparks Ansaldo's self-recognition and compassion. He rejects the possibility of dishonoring a man who shows compassion for his love. Gilberto and Ansaldo are bound ethically as lovers. At the same time, the conversion of desire to charity reformulates social and civic relations into family bonds. As Dianora's spiritual brother, Ansaldo is Gilberto's brother-in-law and his brother in a Christian community. Virtuous friendship supersedes their roles as erotic rivals and civic actors: 'strettissima e leale amistà lui e messer Ansaldo congiunse' ('Gilberto and Messer Ansaldo became the closest of loyal friends'). Charity establishes not only friendship but new grounds of social parity: virtuous friendship is possible only among equals.[31] When the magician resigns his claim to payment, the terms likewise echo and reformulate the ending of Menedon's story. He says that Gilberto is generous with his honor and Ansaldo with his love and that he will be generous with his gift. Whereas Tebano had set out fine-grained distinctions that expressed a similarity in kind as a difference in degree (*liberalità-villania-cortesia*), the magician expounds a single value joining all three men in a way that reaches across their objective social roles.

In Chaucer's revision, these issues come immediately to the fore. Just as Tarolfo hesitates to commit 'villania,' Aurelius fears to do 'a cherlyssh wrecchednesse' (1523). He acts for the greater good – '[c]onsiderynge the beste on every syde' (1521) – and his motive is to preserve 'franchise and alle gentillesse' (1524). In other words, nobility of character drives his generous act, and Aurelius makes a point of demonstrating that virtue extends across social and occupational roles: 'Thus kan a squier doon a gentil dede / As wel as kan a knyght, withouten drede' (1543–4). When the clerk in turn resigns his claim, all three characters are joined by a common value, as in the *Decameron*. Their identity is reinforced by the fact that, in Chaucer's version, nothing has actually occurred in their transactions. Arveragus's wife remains chaste, and they resume their 'sovereyn blisse.' Aurelius is absolved of his nominal debt. The magician forgoes payment for an act of nature, not his art.

Still, Chaucer turns part of Boccaccio's revision back into its original form. He phrases the moral virtue of generosity in social rather than ethical or spiritual terms. As the clerk remarks, the two nobles have acted 'gentilly til oother' (1608). He proposes the same act for himself: 'But God forbede, for his blisful myght, / But if a clerk koude doon a gentil dede / As wel as any of yow, it is no drede' (1610–12). In this passage, Chaucer is at once more conservative and more radical than Boccaccio. Social terms (*gentillesse*) encode ethical concerns, yet those terms remain accessible to characters profoundly different in their social conditions. Saving the appearance of traditional hierarchy, Chaucer subverts it from within by making the case for natural virtue over inheritance and lineage. It is not by accident that the final question applies to the three men with new urgency and significance. The question debated at the end of Menedon's story ('Dubitasi ora quale di costoro fosse maggiore liberalità') concerns an action. Chaucer follows in the direction specified for the tenth day of the *Decameron*: 'si ragiona di chi liberalmente o vero magnificamente alcuna cosa operasse' ('the discussion turns upon those who have performed liberal or munificent deeds'). The Franklin's question is about the defining quality of the moral agents: 'Which was the mooste fre' (1622). The equilibrium restored at the end of the tale argues for the triumph of character over lineage in its male protagonists.

For Boccaccio and Chaucer, rewriting Menedon's story means reconceiving the foundations of their fictional worlds and their modernity as well as transposing the aesthetic elements of their source. Both writers take the *Questioni* as a stable social realm but find in it possibilities for dynamic change. In their revisions, social relations are both given by traditional structures and renegotiated within them. The private and domestic spheres of their tales register the internal tensions of a feudal social vision and the conflicts of moving toward relations governed by promises and contracts, the foundations of mercantile culture. The solidarity of class values gives way in some measure to other claims on allegiance such as charity and character. As they explore these possibilities, Boccaccio and Chaucer also renegotiate the boundaries between reality and imagination. The personnel of the *Decameron* mingle fictional with contemporary figures; Arveragus and Dorigen construct an internal world in such a way that they cannot distinguish earnest from game. In its relation to literary tradition and to a changing social and cultural context, the revisionary project shared by Chaucer and Boccaccio writers finally claims a dual historicity.

Notes

Preface

1 Important formulations about medieval English authorship appear in J.A. Burrow, *Medieval Writers and Their Work: Middle English Literature and its Background 1100–1500* (New York: Oxford University Press, 1982); Janet Coleman, *Medieval Readers and Writers, 1350–1400* (New York: Columbia University Press, 1981); and Alastair J. Minnis, *Medieval Theory of Authorship: Scholastic Literary Attitudes in the Later Middle Ages*, 2nd edn (Philadelphia: University of Pennsylvania Press, 1988).

2 A.C. Spearing, '*Troilus and Criseyde*: The Illusion of Allusion,' *Exemplaria* 2 (1990): 263–77, rightly cautions about the complexity of interpreting textual references.

3 Kathryn Kerby-Fulton and Steven Justice, 'Langlandian Reading Circles,' *New Medieval Literatures* 1 (1989): 59–83, argue that Chaucer and Langland address the same class of readers in government.

4 Stephen Justice, *Writing and Rebellion: England in 1381* (Berkeley and Los Angeles: University of California Press, 1994), pp. 213–31.

Introduction

1 See Douglas Kelly, *The Arts of Poetry and Prose*, Typologie des sources du moyen âge occidental, fasc. 59 (Turnholt: Brepols, 1991), pp. 64–8. Geoffrey of Vinsauf advises writers not to follow the tracks of the words (*vestigia verborum*) but to be silent where the text speaks and to speak where the text is silent; see his *Documentum de modo et arte dictandi et versificandi*, in *Les arts poétiques du XIIe et du XIIIe siècle*, ed. Edmond Faral (Paris: Champion, 1924), p. 309. Ernest Gallo, *The 'Poetria Nova' and its Sources in Early Rhetorical Doctrine* (The Hague: Mouton, 1971), p. 224, credits Geoffrey with being 'the first to give theoretical expression to the medieval method of reworking one's sources.' Geoffrey draws on Statius's instructions at the end of the *Thebaid* to follow the *Aeneid* from afar.

2 For genre as a feature of Chaucer's intertextuality, see Barbara Nolan, *Chaucer and the Tradition of the 'Roman Antique'* (Cambridge: Cambridge University Press, 1992); and Barry Windeatt, 'Classical and Medieval Elements in Chaucer's *Troilus*,' in *The European Tragedy of Troilus*, ed. Piero Boitani (Oxford: Clarendon Press, 1989), pp. 111–31.

3 T.D. Kendrick, *British Antiquity* (London: Methuen & Co., 1950), pp. 13–14.

4 Ranulph Higden, *Polychronicon Ranulphi Higden Monaci Cestrensis* (with translations by John Trevisa and an anonymous writer), ed. Churchill Babington (vols. 1–2) and Joseph R. Lumby (vols. 3–9), 9 vols. Rolls Series (London: Longmans, Green, and Co., 1865–86); Gower, *Confessio Amantis* 5: 747–1959 on the various cultic beliefs contained in the poets' fables.

5 Morton W. Bloomfield, 'Chaucer's Sense of History,' *Journal of English and Germanic Philology* 51 (1952): 301–13; rpt. in *Essays and Explorations: Studies in Ideas, Language, and Literature* (Cambridge, MA: Harvard University Press, 1970), pp. 13–26.

6 See Erwin Panofsky, *Renaissance and Renascences in Western Art* (Stockholm: Almqvist and Wiksell, 1960), p. 7.

7 Alastair J. Minnis, *Chaucer and Pagan Antiquity* (Cambridge: D.S. Brewer; Totowa, NJ: Rowman & Littlefield, 1982), p. 24.

8 Alastair J. Minnis, 'From Medieval to Renaissance? Chaucer's Position on Past Gentility,' *Proceedings of the British Academy* 72 (1986): 245.

9 Janet Coleman, *Ancient and Medieval Memories: Studies in the Reconstruction of the Past* (Cambridge: Cambridge University Press, 1992), p. 558. For early medieval history, see Matthew Innes, 'Introduction: Using the Past, Interpreting the Present, Influencing the Future,' in *The Uses of the Past in the Early Middle Ages*, ed. Yitzhak Hen and Matthew Innes (Cambridge: Cambridge University Press, 2000), pp. 1–8.

10 Virtuous pagans represent one exception on a moral plane, as in the figure of Trajan for Dante and Langland or the righteous pagan judge buried under St. Paul's in *Saint Erkenwald*.

11 A.C. Spearing, 'Classical Antiquity in Chaucer's Chivalric Romances,' in *Chivalry, Knighthood, and War in the Middle Ages*, ed. Susan J. Ridyard (Sewanee, TN: University of the South Press, 1999), p. 54.

12 I am grateful to Rita Copeland for this last point. Chaucer's contemporary Thomas Walsingham reacted to this curricular dimension by resorting to the tradition of Fulgentian allegory about the pagan gods ('omnes res poeticas apprehendisse profundius'); see *Thomae Walsingham de archana deorum*, ed. Robert A. van Kluyve (Durham, NC: Duke University Press, 1968), p. 3.

13 Thomas Walsingham, *Historia Anglicana*, ed. Henry T. Riley, 2 vols., Rolls Series (London: Longman, Green, Longman, Roberts, and Green, 1863–64), 2: 173–4.

14 David Anderson, 'Theban History in Chaucer's *Troilus*,' *Studies in the Age of Chaucer* 4 (1982): 109–33; and Lee Patterson, *Chaucer and the Subject of History* (Madison: University of Wisconsin Press, 1991), pp. 47–83, 130–6.

15 *OED* cites William Dunbar's 'Ane Ballat of Our Lady': 'Hodiern, modern, sempitern, / Angelicall regyne' (2.5–6); see William Dunbar, *The Poems of William Dunbar*, ed. James Kinsley (Oxford: Clarendon, 1979), p. 4.

16 Alessandro Ghisalberti, 'I Moderni,' in *Lo Spazio letterario del Medioevo*, ed. Guglielmo Cavallo, Claudio Leonardi, and Enrico Menestò, 5 vols. (Rome: Salerno Editrice, 1992–97), 1: 605–31.

17 See Robert Markus, *The End of Christian Antiquity* (Cambridge: Cambridge University Press, 1990) and Irena Backus, *The Reception of the Church Fathers in the West* (Leiden: Brill, 1996). I am grateful to Mark Vessey and Anthony Cutler for their advice on the origins of Christian antiquity.

18 Walter Map, *De nugis curialium: Courtiers' Trifles*, ed. M.R. James, rev. C.N.L. Brooke and R.A.B. Mynors (Oxford: Clarendon, 1983), pp. 2–3.

19 Jean Froissart, *Chroniques*, in *Oeuvres de Froissart*, ed. M. Le baron Kervyn de Lettenhove, 23 vols. (Bruxelles: V. Devaux, 1867–77), 16: 161; *Chronicles*, ed. and trans. Geoffrey Brereton (Harmondsworth: Penguin, 1978), p. 442.

20 See Richard Firth Green, *A Crisis of Truth: Literature and Law in Ricardian England* (Philadelphia: University of Pennsylvania Press, 1999).

21 Charles Muscatine, *Poetry and Crisis in the Age of Chaucer* (Notre Dame, IN: University of Notre Dame Press, 1972), pp. 14–15.

22 David Aers, 'A Whisper in the Ear of Early Modernists; or, Reflections on Literary Critics Writing the "History of the Subject,"' in *Culture and History 1350–1600: Essays on English Communities, Identities and Writing*, ed. David Aers (London: Harvester, 1992), pp. 179–86.

23 Lee Patterson, 'The Place of the Modern in the Late Middle Ages,' in *The Challenge of Periodization: Old Paradigms and New Perspectives*, ed. Lawrence Besserman (New York: Garland, 1996), pp. 61, 55; rpt. from 'Perpetual Motion: Alchemy and the Technology of the Self,' *Studies in the Age of Chaucer* 15 (1993): 25–57.

24 Lee Patterson, *Chaucer and the Subject of History*, pp. 265 and 313.

25 David Wallace, *Chaucerian Polity: Absolutist Lineages and Associational Forms in Medieval England and Italy* (Stanford, CA: Stanford University Press, 1997), p. 262; and Carolyn Dinshaw, *Chaucer's Sexual Poetics* (Madison: University of Wisconsin Press, 1989), pp. 154–5.

26 Brunetto Latini, *Li Livres dou Tresor de Brunetto Latini*, ed. Francis J. Carmody (Berkeley: University of California Press, 1948), p. 178. Cf. *Trésor* II.25, II.37 for the deviations from the mean of sociability.

27 John M. Ganim, 'The Experience of Modernity in Late Medieval Literature: Urbanism, Experience and Rhetoric in Some Early Descriptions of London,' in *The Performance of Middle English Culture: Essays on Chaucer and the Drama in Honor of Martin Stevens*, ed. James J. Paxson, Lawrence M. Clopper, and Sylvia Tomasch (Cambridge: D.S. Brewer, 1998), p. 77.

28 David Wallace, 'Chaucer and the Absent City,' in *Chaucer's England: Literature in Historical Context*, ed. Barbara A. Hanawalt (Minneapolis: University of Minnesota Press, 1992), p. 84.

29 Alastair J. Minnis, *Chaucer and Pagan Antiquity*, pp. 24–5.

30 David Wallace, 'Chaucer's Continental Inheritance: The Early Poems and *Troilus and Criseyde*,' in *The Cambridge Chaucer Companion*, ed. Piero Boitani and Jill Mann (Cambridge: Cambridge University Press, 1986), p. 31.

31 A.C. Spearing, 'Classical Antiquity in Chaucer's Chivalric Romances,' p. 61.

32 In his Introduction to *Chaucer's French Contemporaries: The Poetry/Poetics of Self and Tradition* (New York: AMS Press, 1999), p. xxv, R. Barton Palmer finds the relationship 'a matter of poetry prompting other poems.' James I. Wimsatt, *Chaucer and His French Contemporaries: Natural Music in the Fourteenth Century* (Toronto: University of Toronto Press, 1991), p. 121, argues for locating French influence on Chaucer in the period post-1356. John M. Bowers, 'Chaucer after Retters: The Wartime Origins of English Literature,' in *Inscribing the Hundred Years' War in French and English Culture*, ed. Denise N. Baker (Albany: State University of New York Press, 2000), pp. 91–125, offers a view that aligns Chaucer's literary relations with shifting military and diplomatic pressures between England and France.

33 Derek Pearsall, *The Life of Geoffrey Chaucer: A Critical Biography* (Oxford: Blackwell, 1992), pp. 118–20, proposes that Boccaccio represented less of a threat to Chaucer than Dante or Petrarch.

34 J.A.W. Bennett, 'Chaucer, Dante and Boccaccio,' in *Chaucer and the Italian Tre-cento*, ed. Piero Boitani (Cambridge: Cambridge University Press, 1983), pp. 90–2.

35 See Robert A. Pratt, 'Chaucer and the Visconti Libraries,' *ELH* 6 (1939): 191–9; and William E. Coleman, 'Chaucer, the *Teseida* and the Visconti Library at Pavia: A Hypothesis,' *Medium Ævum* 51 (1982): 92–101.

36 For the former view, see David Wallace, *Chaucer and the Early Writings of Boccaccio* (Cambridge: D.S. Brewer, 1985), pp. 39–60; for the latter, see Robert R. Edwards, 'Source, Context, and Cultural Translation in the *Franklin's Tale*,' *Modern Philology* 94 (1996): 141–62.

37 John Dryden, 'Preface to the Fables,' in *Essays of John Dryden*, ed. W.P. Ker, 2 vols. (1900; rpt. New York: Russell & Russell, 1961), 2: 268.

38 Helen Cooper, *The Canterbury Tales*, Oxford Guides to Chaucer (Oxford: Oxford University Press, 1989), p. 9; and N.S. Thompson, *Chaucer, Boccaccio, and the Debate of Love: A Comparative Study of 'The Decameron' and 'The Canterbury Tales'* (Oxford: Clarendon Press, 1996), pp. 1–4.

39 Peter G. Beidler, 'Just Say Yes, Chaucer Knew the *Decameron*: or, Bringing the *Shipman's Tale* out of Limbo,' in *The 'Decameron' and the 'Canterbury Tales': New Essays on an Old Question*, ed. Leonard Michael Koff and Brenda Deen Schildgen (Madison, NJ: Fairleigh Dickinson University Press, 2000), pp. 25–46; and Donald McGrady, 'Chaucer and the *Decameron* Reconsidered,' *Chaucer Review* 12 (1977–78): 1–26.

40 David Wallace, *Chaucer and the Early Writings of Boccaccio*.

41 A.C. Spearing, 'Lydgate's Canterbury Tale: *The Siege of Thebes* and Fifteenth-Century Chaucerianism,' in *Fifteenth-Century Studies: Recent Essays*, ed. Robert F. Yeager (Hamden, CT: Archon, 1984), p. 355; rpt. in Spearing's *From Medieval to Renaissance* (Cambridge: Cambridge University Press, 1985), p. 86 with some changes.

42 See James H. McGregor, *The Shades of Aeneas: The Imitation of Vergil and the History of Paganism in Boccaccio's 'Filostrato,' 'Filocolo,' and 'Teseida'* (Athens: University of Georgia Press, 1991), pp. 1–7, which emphasizes Christian allegory.

43 Vittore Branca, *Boccaccio: The Man and His Works*, trans. Richard Monges and Dennis J. McAuliffe (New York: New York University Press, 1976), pp. 276–307; *Boccaccio medievale e nuovi studi sul Decameron*, rev. and corr. edn (Florence: Sansoni, 1996), pp. 134–64.

44 See Michael Leonard Koff's Introduction to *The 'Decameron' and the 'Canterbury Tales': New Essays on an Old Question*, p. 12.

45 N.S. Thompson, 'Local Histories: Characteristic Worlds in the *Decameron* and the *Canterbury Tales*,' in *The 'Decameron' and the 'Canterbury Tales': New Essays on an Old Question*, p. 86.

46 Erich Auerbach, *Mimesis: The Representation of Reality in Western Literature*, trans. Willard Trask (Garden City, NY: Doubleday Anchor, 1957), pp. 177–203.

47 David Wallace, *Chaucerian Polity*, p. 10.

Chapter 1

1 For background, see John Lydgate, *The Siege of Thebes*, ed. Robert R. Edwards, TEAMS: Middle English Texts Series (Kalamazoo, MI: Medieval Institute Publications, 2001), pp. 1–11.

2 Though the lines from the *Thebaid* do not appear in all manuscript sources, they are preserved in the most authoritative witnesses – the Ellesmere and Hengwrt manuscripts for the *Canterbury Tales* and Fairfax 16 and Bodley 638 for *Anelida*.

3 Paul M. Clogan, 'Chaucer's Use of the "Thebaid,"' *English Miscellany* 18 (1967): 28.

4 Boyd Ashby Wise, *The Influence of Statius upon Chaucer* (1911; rpt. New York: Phaeton, 1967), pp. 45–8.

5 Paul M. Clogan, 'Chaucer and the *Thebaid* Scholia,' *Studies in Philology* 61 (1964): 611–14; cf. Francis P. Magoun, Jr., 'Chaucer's Summary of Statius' Thebaid II–XII,' *Traditio* 11 (1955): 409–20.

6 David Anderson, *Before the Knight's Tale: Imitation of Classical Epic in Boccaccio's 'Teseida'* (Philadelphia: University of Pennsylvania Press, 1988), p. x.

7 Conrad of Hirsau, *Dialogus super Auctores* 1489–99, in R.B.C. Huygens, ed., *Accessus ad Auctores, Bernard d'Utrecht, Conrad d'Hirsau: 'Dialogus super Auctores'*, rev. edn (Leiden: Brill, 1970), pp. 119–20.

8 David Vessey, *Statius and the Thebaid* (Cambridge: Cambridge University Press, 1973) offers the most optimistic reading of Statius's poem; cf. Paul Échinard-Garin, 'La douceur de Stace dans la *Thébaïde*,' *Bulletin de l'Association Guillaume Budé* (1992): 31–46.

9 Frederick M. Ahl, 'Statius' "Thebaid": A Reconsideration,' *Aufstieg und Niedergang der römischen Welt* 2.32.5 (1986): 2817. Cf. John Kevin Newman, *The Classical Epic Tradition* (Madison: University of Wisconsin Press, 1986), pp. 234–43; William J. Dominik, *The Mythic Voice of Statius: Power and Politics in the 'Thebaid'*, Mnemosyne Supplement 136 (Leiden: Brill, 1994); and Winthrop Wetherbee, ' "Per te poeta fui, per te cristiano": Dante, Statius, and the Narrator of Chaucer's *Troilus*,' in *Vernacular Poetics in the Middle Ages*, ed. Lois Ebin, Studies in Medieval Culture 16 (Kalamazoo, MI: Medieval Institute Publications, 1984), pp. 153–76.

10 See the discussion of differing historical uses of this frame in Anderson, *Before the Knight's Tale*, pp. 13–23.

11 Dante, *De vulgari eloquentia*, ed. and trans. Stephen Botterill (Cambridge: Cambridge University Press, 1996), pp. 52–3. Warman Welliver, *Dante in Hell: The 'De vulgari eloquentia'* (Ravenna: Longo, 1981), p. 198, notes that Dante uses *venus* only in this passage; cf. *De vulgari eloquentia* 2.4.8.

12 See *Amores* 1.9, 1.1, 2.1, 2.18; *Ars amatoria* 1.36, 2.741, 2.746. For discussion of Ovid's genre theory, see Patrick Cheney, *Marlowe's Counterfeit Profession: Ovid, Spenser, Counter-Nationhood* (Toronto: University of Toronto Press, 1998), pp. 3–27.

13 For commentary, see Patrick Boyde, 'Style and Structure in "Doglia mi reca,"' *Dante's Style in His Lyric Poetry* (Cambridge: Cambridge University Press, 1971), pp. 317–31; text in *Dante's Lyric Poetry*, ed. and trans. Kenelm Foster and Patrick Boyde, 2 vols. (Oxford: Clarendon Press, 1967), 1: 182–93.

14 Piero Boitani, *Chaucer and Boccaccio*, Medium Ævum Monographs, n.s. 8 (Oxford: Society for the Study of Mediæval Languages and Literatures, 1977), p. 12. James H. McGregor, *The Image of Antiquity in Boccaccio's 'Filocolo,' 'Filostrato,' and 'Teseida'* (New York: Peter Lang, 1991) argues that Boccaccio portrays ancient religious belief and cultic practice accurately.

15 Barbara Nolan, *Chaucer and the Tradition of the 'Roman antique'* (Cambridge: Cambridge University Press, 1992), pp. 155–97.

16 For the Troy story as chronicle history, see C. David Benson, *The History of Troy in Middle English Literature: Guido delle Colonne's 'Historia destructionis Troiae' in Medieval England* (Woodbridge, Suffolk: Brewer, 1980), pp. 3–41.

17 Alberto Limentani, ed. *Teseida*, p. 890, notes the echo of Turnus's death in Creonte.

18 James H. McGregor, *The Shades of Aeneas: The Imitation of Vergil and the History of Paganism in Boccaccio's 'Filostrato,' 'Filocolo,' and 'Teseida'* (Athens: University of Georgia Press, 1991), pp. 44–103, stresses Teseo's failures at self-control, as against Vergil's Aeneas. Aeneas notably fails at the end of Vergil's poem, and he was seen as a traitor to Troy in medieval literary traditions.

19 Robert W. Hanning, ' "The Struggle between Noble Designs and Chaos": The Literary Tradition of Chaucer's Knight's Tale,' *The Literary Review* 23 (1980): 528. Susanna Morton Braund, 'Ending Epic: Statius, Theseus, and a Merciful Release,' *Proceedings of the Cambridge Philological Society* n.s. 42 (1996–97): 12–13, contends that Statius makes Theseus a Roman figure.

20 Colin Burrow, *Epic Romance: Homer to Milton* (Oxford: Clarendon, 1993), pp. 38–51, examines *pietas* as an ambiguous and fragmented term.

21 See Helen Cooper, *The Structure of The Canterbury Tales* (London: Duckworth, 1983), pp. 94–100; and Cooper, *The Canterbury Tales*, p. 74, on the structural balance of parts shown by the divisions in the Ellesmere and Hengwrt manuscripts.

22 I am grateful to Patrick Cheney for pointing out the significance of this addition to the poem and for suggesting its difference from other places where Chaucer seems to cancel feminine subjectivity.

23 See P.M. Kean, *Chaucer and the Making of English Poetry*, shortened edn (London: Routledge & Kegan Paul, 1982), pp. 122–3; Alfred David, *The Strumpet Muse: Art and Morals in Chaucer's Poetry* (Bloomington: Indiana University Press, 1976), p. 85; and J.A. Burrow, 'Chaucer's *Knight's Tale* and the Three Ages of Man,' in *Essays on Medieval Literature* (Oxford: Clarendon Press, 1984), pp. 27–48.

24 Anne Middleton, 'War by Other Means: Chivalry and Marriage in Chaucer,' *Studies in the Age of Chaucer*, Proceedings 1 (1984): 129, argues that Saturn plays the role of Old Counsellor, which Gower enacts in his poems of advice to rulers.

25 Winthrop Wetherbee, 'Romance and Epic in Chaucer's Knight's Tale,' *Exemplaria* 2 (1990): 305, 315–16.

26 'Romance and Epic in Chaucer's Knight's Tale,' p. 318.

27 Elizabeth Salter, *Fourteenth-Century English Poetry: Contexts and Readings*, ed. Derek Pearsall and Nicolette Zeeman (Oxford: Oxford University Press, 1983), p. 163.

28 *Before the Knight's Tale*, pp. 57–65.

29 *Chaucer and Boccaccio*, p. 141.

30 Warren Ginsberg, *The Cast of Character: The Representation of Personality in Ancient and Medieval Literature* (Toronto: University of Toronto Press, 1983), p. 112, observes that in the *Teseida* Arcita and Palemone remain refined in their love and friendship so long as there is no prospect of actually gaining Emilia.

31 Susan Crane, 'Medieval Romance and Feminine Difference in *The Knight's Tale*,' *Studies in the Age of Chaucer* 12 (1990): 47–63; rpt. *Gender and Romance in Chaucer's 'Canterbury Tales'* (Princeton, NJ: Princeton University Press, 1994), pp. 165–203, sees Emily, like the genre of romance, as a source of resistance in the Knight's Tale; cf. Angela Jane Weisl, *Conquering the Reign of Femeny: Gender and Genre in Chaucer's Romance* (Woodbridge, Suffolk: Boydell & Brewer, 1995).

32 Boccaccio's description of Emilia tropes Dante's use of the veil to cover Beatrice's body in the *Vita Nuova*, ch. 3.

33 See V.A. Kolve, *Chaucer and the Imagery of Narrative: The First Five 'Canterbury Tales'* (Stanford, CA: Stanford University Press, 1984), pp. 85–157, on the iconography.

34 *The Riverside Chaucer*, p. 837, insists that 'dye' is not a sexual pun because the sexual meaning is not cited before the sixteenth century; see further Larry D. Benson, 'The "Queynte" Punnings of Chaucer's Critics,' *Studies in the Age of Chaucer* 1 Proceedings (1984): 23–47. In both Boccaccio and Chaucer Palamon enrolls himself in the *militia Veneris*, and so death in Venus's service may be figurative in more than one sense.

35 The couplet does not appear in the most authoritative manuscripts of the *Canterbury Tales*, but as Cooper observes (*The Canterbury Tales*, p. 62), there is no reason to doubt its authenticity.

36 *OED*, s.v. *merci* and *merciede*, citing *Piers Plowman*, A 3.21; *MED*, citing *Piers Plowman* A 1.41; cf. Damyan's cry of 'Mercy' in the Merchant's Tale (IV.1942).

37 See J.D. Burnley, *Chaucer's Language and the Philosophers' Tradition* (Cambridge: D.S. Brewer and Totowa, NJ: Rowman and Littlefield, 1979), pp. 25–7.

38 *Fourteenth-Century English Poetry: Contexts and Readings*, pp. 144–5.

39 *Chaucer and Boccaccio*, p. 19.

40 See Kean, pp. 129–33 for discussion of Palamon's and Arcite's incomplete assimilation of Boethius, especially on the role of Fortune.

41 Boitani, *Chaucer and Boccaccio*, pp. 121–2, proposes that Dante's and Boccaccio's Fortune becomes destiny through the intermediary of Chaucer's translation of *Consolatio* 6 pr4.48–50.

42 Kean, pp. 158–60, has a more positive reading of Egeus's speech.

43 The theme appears in writers such as Ambrose, *De Iacob et vita beata*, in *Sancti Ambrosii Opera*, ed. C. Schenkl, CSEL 32.3 (Vienna: Tempsky; Leipzig: Freytag, 1897), pp. 3–70; Jerome, *Epistula* 54, in *Sancti Evsebii Hieronymi Epistvlae*, ed. I. Hilberg, CSEL 54–56 (Vienna: Tempsky, 1910–18), 54: 472; and Isaac de Stella (1110/1120–ca.1169), *Sermo* 53, in *Sermons*, ed. A. Hoste, G. Salet, and G. Raciti, Sources Chrétiennes 130, 207, 339 (Paris: Éditions du Cerf, 1967–87), 3:6.

44 Augustine, *De natura et gratia*, ed. C.F. Vrba and J. Zychen, CSEL 60 (Vienna: Tempsky; Leipzig: Freytag, 1913), p. 278.

45 Bernard of Clairvaux, Sermo 42, *Sermones super Cantica Canticorum*, in *Bernardi Opera*, ed. J. Leclerq, C.H. Talbot, and H.M. Rochais, 8 vols. (Rome: Editiones Cistercienses, 1957–77), 1:38.

46 The relevant passage is Muscatine's famous description of the poem as 'a sort of poetic pageant' whose 'design expresses the nature of the noble life'; see *Chaucer and the French Tradition* (Berkeley: University of California Press, 1957), p. 181, with the important qualification that chaos always threatens order.

47 David Aers, *Chaucer* (Brighton, Sussex: Harvester Press, 1986), p. 24; cf. Aers, *Chaucer, Langland and the Creative Imagination* (London: Routledge & Kegan Paul, 1980). Challenges to Muscatine's position, which explains rather than endorses the ideology of the Knight's Tale, go back to Dale Underwood, 'The First of *The Canterbury Tales*,' *ELH* 26 (1959): 455–69.

48 *Chaucer and the Imagery of Narrative*, p. 145.

49 Lee Patterson, *Chaucer and the Subject of History* (Madison: University of Wisconsin Press, 1991), pp. 168, 227, 230.

50 F. Anne Payne, *Chaucer and Menippean Satire* (Madison: University of Wisconsin Press, 1981), pp. 207–88, argues that the poem abandons the hope of reconciling contradictions.

51 Salter, p. 178.

52 Robert B. Burlin, *Chaucerian Fiction* (Princeton: Princeton University Press, 1977), p. 105.

53 On Lydgate's absorption of Chaucer's troubled outlook on recursive history, see James Simpson, '"Dysemol daies and fatal houres": Lydgate's *Destruction of Thebes* and Chaucer's *Knight's Tale*,' in *The Long Fifteenth Century: Essays for Douglas Gray*, ed. Helen Cooper and Sally Mapstone (Oxford: Clarendon Press, 1997), pp. 15–33.

54 H. Marshall Leicester, Jr., *The Disenchanted Self: Representing the Subject in the 'Canterbury Tales'* (Berkeley and Los Angeles: University of California Press, 1990), p. 375.

Chapter 2

1 A.C. Spearing, 'A Ricardian "I": The Narrator of "Troilus and Criseyde,"' in *Essays on Ricardian Literature In Honour of J.A. Burrow*, ed. A.J. Minnis, Charlotte C. Morse, and Thorlac Turville-Petre (Oxford: Clarendon Press, 1997), p. 11; Spearing, 'Classical Antiquity in Chaucer's Chivalric Romances,' in *Chivalry, Knighthood, and War in the Middle Ages*, ed. Susan J. Ridyard (Sewanee, TN: University of the South Press, 1999), pp. 53–73; and John A. Burrow, *Ricardian Poetry: Chaucer, Gower, Langland and the 'Gawain' Poet* (London: Routledge and Kegan Paul, 1971), pp. 69–72.

2 Sanford B. Meech, *Design in Chaucer's Troilus* (Syracuse: Syracuse University Press, 1959); and Barry Windeatt, *Troilus and Criseyde*, Oxford Guides to Chaucer (Oxford: Clarendon Press, 1992), pp. 50–72; see also, Windeatt, ed., *Troilus and Criseyde: A New Edition of 'The Book of Troilus'* (New York: Longman, 1984).

3 C.S. Lewis, 'What Chaucer Really Did to *Il Filostrato*,' in *Chaucer Criticism*, ed. Richard Schoeck and Jerome Taylor, 2 vols. (Notre Dame, IN: Notre Dame University Press, 1961), 2: 16–33.

4 D.W. Robertson, Jr., *A Preface to Chaucer: Studies in Medieval Perspectives* (Princeton: Princeton University Press, 1962), and Chauncey Wood, *The Elements of Chaucer's 'Troilus'* (Durham, NC: Duke University Press, 1984) reject Lewis's contention that Chaucer revises Boccaccio so as to bring him into agreement with a doctrine of courtly love. See John V. Fleming, *Classical Imitation and Interpretation in Chaucer's 'Troilus'* (Lincoln: University of Nebraska Press, 1990) on moral readings in classical authors; and C. David

Benson, *Chaucer's 'Troilus and Criseyde'* (London: Unwin, 1990), p. 123, on views of secular love.

5   Giulia Natali, 'A Lyrical Version: Boccaccio's *Filostrato*,' in *The European Tragedy of Troilus*, ed. Piero Boitani (Oxford: Clarendon Press, 1989), pp. 52–3.

6   See H.M. Smyser, 'The Domestic Background of *Troilus and Criseyde*,' *Speculum* 31 (1956): 297–315; and Barry Windeatt, '"Love that Oughte Ben Secree" in Chaucer's *Troilus*,' *Chaucer Review* 14 (1979–80): 116–31.

7   Mark Lambert, 'Telling the Story in *Troilus and Criseyde*,' in *The Cambridge Chaucer Companion*, ed. Piero Boitani and Jill Mann (Cambridge: Cambridge University Press, 1986), p. 62; and Leonard Michael Koff, 'Ending a Poem Before Beginning it, or the "Cas" of Troilus,' in *Chaucer's 'Troilus and Criseyde': 'Subgit to alle Poesye'* – *Essays in Criticism*, ed. R.A. Shoaf (Binghamton, NY: Medieval & Renaissance Texts & Studies, 1992), p. 171.

8   George Lyman Kittredge, *Chaucer and His Poetry* (Cambridge, MA: Harvard University Press, 1915), pp. 108–45, especially pp. 112, 114, 117, 119, 120–1. See also John P. McCall, 'The Trojan Scene in Chaucer's "Troilus,"' *ELH* 29 (1962): 263–75; rpt. *Chaucer among the Gods: The Poetics of Classical Myth* (University Park, PA: Penn State Press, 1979), pp. 93–104, and Barbara Nolan, *Chaucer and the Tradition of the 'Roman Antique'* (Cambridge: Cambridge University Press, 1992), p. 224.

9   Stephen Barney, 'Troilus Bound,' *Speculum* 47 (1972): 445–58; and Martin Stevens, 'The Winds of Fortune in the *Troilus*,' *Chaucer Review* 13 (1978–79): 285–307.

10 Malcolm Andrew, 'The Fall of Troy in *Sir Gawain and the Green Knight* and *Troilus and Criseyde*,' in *The European Tragedy of Troilus*, p. 93, argues that Trojan 'bliss and blunder' carry forward into the Arthurian realm.

11 The sole exception is the *demande* at I.1347–54. The narrator accommodates the dramatic frame of the *Canterbury Tales* at the beginning (I.886–96) and end (I.3108) of the tale.

12 Morton W. Bloomfield, 'Distance and Predestination in *Troilus and Criseyde*,' in *Chaucer Criticism*, ed. Richard J. Schoeck and Jerome Taylor, 2 vols. (Notre Dame, IN: University of Notre Dame Press, 1961), 2: 196–210, here pp. 201, 197, 204. Kittredge, pp. 112, 114 makes absolute claims for determinism; Derek Brewer, 'Comedy and Tragedy in *Troilus and Criseyde*,' in *The European Tragedy of Troilus*, p. 96, finds the narrator in the poem but not the story.

13 Winthrop Wetherbee, *Chaucer and the Poets: An Essay on 'Troilus and Criseyde'* (Ithaca: Cornell University Press, 1984), p. 46, extending E. Talbot Donaldson, 'The Ending of Troilus,' in *Speaking of Chaucer* (New York: Norton, 1970), pp. 84–101; Donald R. Howard, 'The Philosophies in Chaucer's *Troilus*,' in *The Wisdom of Poetry: Essays in Early English Literature in Honor of Morton W. Bloomfield*, ed. Larry D. Benson and Siegfried Wenzel (Kalamazoo, MI: Medieval Institute Publications, 1982), p. 158.

14 Walter Clyde Curry, 'Destiny in *Troilus and Criseyde*,' in *Chaucer Criticism*, ed. Schoeck and Taylor, 2: 55; cf. Theodore A. Stroud, 'Boethius' Influence on Chaucer's *Troilus*,' in Schoeck and Taylor, 2: 122–35; and Howard Patch 'Troilus on Determinism,' in Schoeck and Taylor, 2: 71–85.

15 Lee Patterson, *Chaucer and the Subject of History* (Madison: University of Wisconsin Press, 1991), pp. 114–26.

16 Isidore of Seville, *Etymologiae* (1.37.11), in *Etymologiarum siue Originum libri xx*, ed. W.M. Lindsay, 2 vols. (Oxford: Clarendon, 1911), n.p. Isidore's discussion is followed by *Ars Laureshamensis: Expositio in Donatum maiorem*, ed. Bengt Löfstedt, CCCM 40A (Turnholt: Brepols, 1977), p. 228; Hugh of St. Victor, *De grammatica* [ch. 20], in *Hugonis de Sancto Victore Opera Propaedeutica: Practica geometriae, De grammatica, Epitome Dindimi in philosophiam*, ed. R. Bacon (Notre Dame, IN: University of Notre Dame Press, 1966), p. 152; Murethach (Muridac), *In Donati artem maiorem*, ed. Ludwig Holtz, CCCM 40 (Turnholt: Brepols, 1977), p. 241; Sedulius Scottus, *In Donati artem maiorem*, ed. Bengt Löfstedt, CCCM 40B (Turnholt: Brepols, 1977), p. 381.

17 Barry Windeatt, 'Classical and Medieval Elements in Chaucer's *Troilus*,' in *The European Tragedy of Troilus*, p. 118.

18 *Chaucer and the Subject of History*, p. 106.

19 For discussion of the chronicle tradition, see C. David Benson, *The History of Troy in Middle English Literature: Guido delle Colonne's 'Historia Destructionis Troiae' in Medieval England* (Woodbridge, Suffolk: D.S. Brewer, 1980), pp. 3–31; 134–8; and William H. Brown, Jr., 'A Separate Peace: Chaucer and the Troilus of Tradition,' *JEGP* 83 (1984): 492–508.

20 *Chaucer and the Tradition of the 'Roman Antique'*, p. 206.

21 John Lydgate, *Troy Book: Selections*, ed. Robert R. Edwards, TEAMS: Middle English Texts Series (Kalamazoo, MI: Medieval Institute Publications, 1998), pp. 4–7; Robert R. Edwards, 'Lydgate's *Troy Book* and the Confusions of Prudence,' in *The North Sea World in the Middle Ages*, ed. Thomas R. Liszka and Lorna E.M. Walker (Dublin: Four Courts Press, 2001), pp. 52–69.

22 Guido delle Colonne, *Historia destructionis Troiae*, ed. Nathaniel Edward Griffin (Cambridge, MA: Mediaeval Academy of America, 1936), p. 43. Subsequent citations of Guido will be internalized with reference to book number and the page in Griffin's edition.

23 In *Confessio Amantis*, Gower includes three episodes that represent alternatives to tragic history – the parliament that seeks Hesione's return (5.7269–73), Hector's prudential speech against Paris's mission (5.7334–70), and the prophecies of Cassandra and Helenus (5.7441–67).

24 Jill Mann, 'Chance and Destiny in *Troilus and Criseyde* and the *Knight's Tale*,' in *The Cambridge Chaucer Companion*, ed. Piero Boitani and Jill Mann (Cambridge: Cambridge University Press, 1986), pp. 75–92. Pierre Michaud-Quantin, *Études sur le vocabulaire philosophique du Moyen Age* (Rome: Edizioni dell'Ateneo, 1970), pp. 73–84, argues that in the concept of Fortune developed in the High Middle Ages, Boethian chance emerges as a supplement to Aristotle's four causes (formal, material, instrumental, and final) in the analysis of causality.

25 'Chance and Destiny in *Troilus and Criseyde* and the *Knight's Tale*,' p. 80.

26 Most critics take the speech as an indication of Troilus's character: Peter Elbow, *Oppositions in Chaucer* (Middletown, CT: Wesleyan University Press, 1973), pp. 49–72; Henry Ansgar Kelly, *Chaucerian Tragedy* (Cambridge: D.S. Brewer, 1997), pp. 113–14; Karl Reichl, 'Chaucer's *Troilus*: Philosophy and Language,' in *The European Tragedy of Troilus*, pp. 135–8; and Alastair J. Minnis, *Chaucer and Pagan Antiquity*, (Cambridge: D.S. Brewer; Totowa, NJ: Rowman & Littlefield, 1982), pp. 94–9.

27 Larry Scanlon, 'Sweet Persuasion: The Subject of Fortune in *Troilus and Criseyde*,' in *Chaucer's Troilus and Criseyde*, ed. Shoaf, pp. 211–23.

28 Benoît de Sainte-Maure, *Le Roman de Troie*, ed. Léopold Constans, SATF, 6 vols. (Paris: Firmin-Didot, 1904–12), 1: 192–6.

29 'The Winds of Fortune in the *Troilus*,' p. 297.

30 The marginal gloss in Bodleian Library, Ms. Rawlinson Poet. 163 at the line where Troilus first sees Criseyde (1.267) reads, 'How Troilus was supprysed of the loue of Cressede.'

31 The phrase 'cares colde' first appears as the opposite of 'joie' in this passage (1.264), recurs in the scenes of consummation and parting (3.1202, 3.1260, 4.1692), and finally signifies the dissolution of the love affair (5.1342, 5.1747).

32 British Library, Ms. Harley 2392 gloss: 'de potestate amoris.'

33 Gerald Morgan, 'Natural and Rational Love in Medieval Literature,' *Yearbook of English Studies* 7 (1977): 49.

34 F. Anne Payne, *Chaucer and Menippean Satire* (Madison: University of Wisconsin Press, 1981), p. 124.

35 *Chaucer and the Poets*, pp. 46–52.

36 Scholars assume that Chaucer knew Guinizelli's poem through *Convivio* 4.20, though Francesca echoes it in *Inferno* 5.100; for commentary see, *The Poetry of Guido Guinizelli*, ed. and trans. Robert R. Edwards (New York: Garland, 1987), pp. 108–16.

37 *The Riverside Chaucer* prints 'him,' which accords with the grammatical reference in Boccaccio; Windeatt, ed. *Troilus*, p. 249 notes, that all MSS read *hem* at 3.17. The plural probably results from attraction to the phrase 'thynges...alle' (3.14); a number of witnesses preserve the plural throughout the stanza, suggesting that Venus's power gives mortal creatures success or failure in love and sends them down to earth to love in many forms.

38 I omit the editorial comma in the second quotation in order to emphasize the grammatical and syntactic parallelism of the phrases. Windeatt, ed., *Troilus*, p. 339, notes the complex textual situation of these lines. The verb *knetteth* has the variants *endytyth, kennyth, endith*, and *endueth*. Moreover, in the manuscript generally accepted as the base (Corpus Christi College, Cambridge 61) and in others, the key phrase 'lawe of compaignie' reads 'lawe and compaignie.' In the succeeding line, Huntington Library HM 114 (formerly Phillipps 8252), probably through an eye-skip, reads the corollary phrase 'couples doth in vertue forto dwelle' as 'couples doth in lawe forto dwelle.'

39 Laurence Eldredge, 'Boethian Epistemology and Chaucer's *Troilus* in the Light of Fourteenth-Century Thought,' *Mediaevalia* 2 (1976): 62.

40 Gerald Morgan, 'Natural and Rational Love in Medieval Literature,' pp. 49–51, reiterated in 'The Freedom of the Lovers in *Troilus and Criseyde*,' in *Literature and Learning in Medieval and Renaissance England*, ed. John Scattergood (Dublin: Irish Academic Press, 1984), p. 62.

41 Robert apRoberts, 'Love in the *Filostrato*,' *Chaucer Review* 7 (1972–73): 1–26; and Robert Hanning, 'Come in out of the Code: Interpreting the Discourse of Desire in Boccaccio's *Filostrato* and Chaucer's *Troilus and Criseyde*,' in *Chaucer's 'Troilus and Criseyde'*, ed. Shoaf, pp. 120–37.

42 Derek Pearsall, 'Criseyde's Choices,' *Studies in the Age of Chaucer* Proceedings 2 (1986): 20.

43 On the psychological portraiture, see Donald R. Howard, 'Experience, Language, and Consciousness: *Troilus and Criseyde*, II.596–931,' in *Medieval Literature and Folklore Studies: Essays in Honor of Francis Lee Utley*, ed. Jerome A.

Mandel and Bruce Rosenberg (New Brunswick, NJ: Rutgers University Press, 1970), pp. 173–92; C. David Benson, *Chaucer's 'Troilus and Criseyde'* (London: Unwin Hyman, 1990), pp. 103–11 and 133–41; and Warren Ginsberg, *The Cast of Character: The Representation of Personality in Ancient and Medieval Literature* (Toronto: University of Toronto Press, 1983), pp. 102–7.

44 James I. Wimsatt, 'Guillaume de Machaut and Chaucer's *Troilus and Criseyde*,' *Medium Ævum* 45 (1976): 277–93.

45 John M. Fyler, 'The Fabrications of Pandarus,' *Modern Language Quarterly* 41 (1980): 115–30; rpt. in *Chaucer's 'Troilus and Criseyde'*, ed. Shoaf, pp. 107–19, here p. 108.

46 Wetherbee, *Chaucer and the Poets*, p. 157.

47 With 1.1065–71, cf. Geoffrey of Vinsauf, *Poetria nova* lines 43–59, in *Les arts poétiques du XIIe et du XIIIe siècle*, ed. Edmond Faral (Paris: Champion, 1924), pp. 198–9 and ultimately Dionysus of Halicarnassus's *On Composition*, ch. 6.

48 Dean S. Fansler, *Chaucer and the 'Roman de la Rose'* (New York: Columbia University Press, 1914), p. 209; *Riverside Chaucer*, p. 1046.

49 Carolyn Dinshaw, *Chaucer's Sexual Poetics* (Madison: University of Wisconsin Press, 1989), pp. 58–64.

50 Cf. Criseyde's corresponding remark on Troilus (2.167–8).

51 Wetherbee, *Chaucer and the Poets*, pp. 206–7.

52 The term recurs ironically when Criseyde rejects the idea of fleeing Troy (4.1529–31).

53 Ida L. Gordon, *The Double Sorrow of Troilus: A Study of Ambiguities in 'Troilus and Criseyde'* (Oxford: Clarendon, 1970), p. 97.

54 R.A. Shoaf, *Dante, Chaucer, and the Currency of the Word: Money, Images, and Reference in Late Medieval Poetry* (Norman, OK: Pilgrim Books, 1983), p. 122.

55 C. David Benson, 'True Troilus and False Cresseid: The Descent from Tragedy,' in *The European Tragedy of Troilus*, pp. 153–70.

56 Windeatt, ed., *Troilus*, p. 103, notes that Chaucer intensifies the sense of penetration and that Chaucer's verb *percede* generates a large number of variant readings: *procede, preceded, persedyn, perceyvid, departed, perceded, persed*.

57 Chaucer presents the same false argument in the *Book of the Duchess*; for discussion, see Robert R. Edwards, *The Dream of Chaucer: Representation and Reflection in the Early Narratives* (Durham, NC: Duke University Press, 1989), pp. 86–7.

58 Vittore Branca, ed., *Il Filostrato*, 2:849, notes the echo of *Purgatorio* 30.

59 Sarah Stanbury, 'The Lover's Gaze in *Troilus and Criseyde*,' in *Chaucer's 'Troilus and Criseyde'*, ed. Shoaf, pp. 229–32.

60 *Riverside Chaucer*, p. 1109; Windeatt, ed., *Troilus*, p. 109.

61 Windeatt, ed., *Troilus*, p. 323, argues for *biteth* over *streyneth* as the authentic reading.

62 The same terms describe Criseyde in the Greek camp, looking back on Troy and portraying Troilus's 'worthynesse' and good words (5.716–21).

63 Richard Firth Green, 'Troilus and the Game of Love,' *Chaucer Review* 13 (1978–79): 201–20.

64 Robert R. Edwards, 'The Desolate Palace and the Solitary City: Chaucer, Boccaccio, and Dante,' *Studies in Philology* 94 (1999): 394–416.

65 E. Talbot Donaldson, 'The Ending of "Troilus,"' p. 96.

66   John M. Steadman, *Disembodied Laughter: 'Troilus' and the Apotheosis Tradition – A Reexamination of Narrative and Thematic Contexts* (Berkeley and Los Angeles: University of California Press, 1972) discusses the tradition.

67   Elsewhere in the poem, the terms denote the activities of attention, perception, and practical deliberation. Lydgate takes them over in *Troy Book* and associates them most forcefully with prudence.

68   If Lucan's *Pharsalia* is indeed a direct source for Troilus's laugh, the contrast is even sharper, for Pompey's ghost looks back to laugh at the mutilation of his body (*Pharsalia* 9.11–14).

Chapter 3

1   A.C. Spearing, 'Classical Antiquity in Chaucer's Chivalric Romances,' in *Chivalry, Knighthood, and War in the Middle Ages*, ed. Susan J. Ridyard (Sewanee, TN: University of the South Press, 1999), p. 68, rightly calls the Knight's Tale 'exaggeratedly patriarchal.'

2   Gower asserts man's responsibility in the marginal gloss to this passage and he rejects Fortune as a cause: 'the man is overal / His oghne cause of wel and wo' (*Confessio Amantis* Prologue 546–7). He repeats the idea in discussing civil strife (*division*) and war: 'al this wo is cause of man' (Prologue 905).

3   Carolyn Dinshaw, *Chaucer's Sexual Poetics* (Madison: University of Wisconsin Press, 1989), pp. 65–72.

4   Even reader response approaches accept the terms of the Prologue; e.g., Peter L. Allen, 'Reading Chaucer's Good Women,' *Chaucer Review* 21 (1986–87): 417–34.

5   John Fyler, *Chaucer and Ovid* (New Haven, CT: Yale University Press, 1979), p. 113; cf. Lisa J. Kiser, *Telling Classical Tales: Chaucer and the 'Legend of Good Women'* (Ithaca, NY: Cornell University Press, 1983), and Donald W. Rowe, *Through Nature to Eternity: Chaucer's 'Legend of Good Women'* (Lincoln: University of Nebraska Press, 1988).

6   Florence Percival, *Chaucer's Legendary Good Women* (Cambridge: Cambridge University Press, 1998), p. 3.

7   Marilynn Desmond, *Reading Dido: Gender, Textuality, and the Medieval 'Aeneid'* (Minneapolis: University of Minnesota Press, 1994), p. 141.

8   Louis Brewer Hall, 'Chaucer and the Dido-and-Aeneas Story,' *Mediaeval Studies* 25 (1963): 150, notes that the Dido episode and the wars in Italy are the chief features of redactions of the *Aeneid* from late antiquity through the Middle Ages.

9   Fyler, *Chaucer and Ovid*, p. 35; *Riverside Chaucer*, p. 980.

10   Christopher Baswell, *Virgil in Medieval England: Figuring the 'Aeneid' from the Twelfth Century to Chaucer* (Cambridge: Cambridge University Press, 1995), p. 230, points out that the visual images described by the narrator are both ekphrastic and codicological.

11   The marginal glosses in Bodley 638 and Fairfax 16, the base manuscripts for the *House of Fame*, suggest that Chaucer's undermining of Vergil's textual authority is itself contested in scribal practice; though the glosses add occasional moralizations (HF 305, 358–9), for the most part they quote Vergil's text.

12   *Chaucer and Ovid*, pp. 36–9.
13   Fulgentius, *Virgiliana continentia* in *Opera*, ed. Rudolph Helm, rev. Jean Préaux (Stuttgart: Teubner, 1970), pp. 93–5; *The Commentary on the First Six Books of the 'Aeneid' of Vergil Commonly Attributed to Bernardus Silvestris*, ed. Julian Ward Jones and Elizabeth Frances Jones (Lincoln: University of Nebraska Press, 1977), pp. 3, 12, 23–5, 83, 95–6; *An 'Aeneid' Commentary of Mixed Type: The Glosses of MSS Harley 4946 and Ambrosianus G111 inf.*, ed. Julian Ward Jones, Jr. (Toronto: Pontifical Institute of Mediaeval Studies, 1996), pp. 73, 106.
14   Sheila Delany, *The Naked Text: Chaucer's 'Legend of Good Women'* (Berkeley and Los Angeles: University of California Press, 1994), pp. 178–81.
15   Florence Verducci, *Ovid's Toyshop of the Heart: Epistulae Heroidum* (Princeton: Princeton University Press, 1985), pp. 4–32; cf. Alastair J. Minnis, *The Shorter Poems*, Oxford Guides to Chaucer (Oxford: Clarendon, 1995), pp. 357–60.
16   E.K. Rand, *Ovid and His Influence* (New York: Cooper Square Publishers, 1963), p. 146.
17   Warren Ginsberg, *The Cast of Character: The Representation of Personality in Ancient and Medieval Literature* (Toronto: University of Toronto Press, 1983), p. 50.
18   Peter E. Knox, *Ovid, Heroides: Selected Epistles* (Cambridge: Cambridge University Press, 1995), pp. 14–25.
19   In Gower's *Confessio Amantis* (4.77–137), Dido's letter is the focal point.
20   Robert W. Frank, Jr., *Chaucer and 'The Legend of Good Women'* (Cambridge, MA: Harvard University Press, 1972), p. 65.
21   *Chaucer and 'The Legend of Good Women'*, p. 68.
22   Richard C. Monti, *The Dido Episode and the Aeneid*, Mnemosyne, Supplement 66 (Leiden: Brill, 1981), pp. 30–6, discusses the political implication of Dido's love in Vergil. Percival sees Dido as 'a composite portrait of Woman, or an abstraction "Womanness"' (p. 240).
23   Lee Patterson, *Chaucer and the Subject of History* (Madison: University of Wisconsin Press, 1994), pp. 238–9.
24   Baswell, pp. 260–1, contends that Dido's royal status is emphasized more in the *Legend* than in the *House of Fame* or in Vergil and Ovid.
25   Percival, pp. 223–4.
26   If Vincent of Beauvais's *Speculum Historiale* is Chaucer's source, the political implications would be apparent. The second half of Vincent's entry is devoted to Augustus's imperial role and Egypt's fate as a Roman province; see Vincent of Beauvais, *Speculum Historiale* 6.53, in *Speculum Maius*, 4 vols. (Douai: Belleri, 1674), 4: 190.
27   Delany, *The Naked Text*, p. 188; Frank, *Chaucer and 'The Legend of Good Women'*, p. 40.
28   Minnis, *The Shorter Poems*, pp. 354–7, makes the most recent case for Vincent as Chaucer's source.
29   For incisive discussion of appetite and desire, see David M. Halperin, 'Platonic *Erôs* and What Men Call Love,' *Ancient Philosophy* 5 (1985): 161–204.
30   Minnis, *The Shorter Poems*, pp. 367–9.
31   Guido delle Colonne, *Historia destructionis Troiae* [Bk. 2], ed. Nathaniel Edward Griffin, (Cambridge, MA: The Mediaeval Academy of America, 1936), p. 17.

32 In the *Thebaid*, Jason manages to quell the storm at the same time he stops the Lemnian women's attack; Statius phrases his gesture as a fulfillment of Venus's promise: 'poposcit foedera' (5.418–19).

33 Verducci argues that Hypsipyle's social virtues are a sham in Ovid (p. 65).

34 *Chaucer and the Subject of History*, pp. 239–42.

35 Frank, *Chaucer and 'The Legend of Good Women'*, pp. 116–17.

36 Ovid does not directly record this detail in the *Heroides*. Filippo Ceffi's translation of the *Heroides*, Boccaccio's *Genealogie deorum gentilium*, or a gloss on the *Heroides* are variously cited as possible sources; see Frank, *Chaucer and the 'Legend of Good Women'* and *The Riverside Chaucer*, p. 1073. Guido delle Colonne, *Historia destructionis Troiae* [Bk. 32], p. 251, also mentions Demophon's return.

37 Filippo Ceffi, *Epistole Eroiche di Ovidio Nasone*, ed. Sisto Riessinger, rev. edn Vincenzo Monti (Milan: Giuseppe Bernardoni, 1842), p. 9.

38 *Epistole Eroiche di Ovidio Nasone*, p. 11; quoted in Sanford B. Meech, 'Chaucer and an Italian Translation of the *Heroides*,' *PMLA* 45 (1930): 121.

39 The false claim of nobility that Guinizelli rejects in 'Al cor gentil' is 'Gentil per sclatta torno' ('I am made noble by birth' [4.33]). *Sclatta* is the consensus of modern editors. The earliest manuscripts preserving Guinizelli's lyrics contain the variants 'schiatta' and 'ischiatta'; for discussion see *The Poetry of Guido Guinizelli*, ed. and trans. Robert R. Edwards (New York: Garland, 1987), pp. 111–12.

40 Jerome, *Commentarii in Prophetas Minores* [*In Osee*, 1.2.16–17], ed. M. Adriaen, CCSL 76–76a (Turnholt: Brepols, 1969–70), p. 28, identifies Ninus as the first king of Asia. Bede, *De temporibus liber* [ch. 18], ed. Charles W. Jones in *Opera Didascalica*, CCSL 123c (Turnholt: Brepols, 1980), p. 603, situates Semiramis's building the walls in the second of mankind's six ages.

41 Isidore of Seville, *Etymologiarum siue Originum libri xx*, ed. W.M. Lindsay, 2 vols. (Oxford: Clarendon, 1911), n.p.

42 Salimbene de Adam, *Cronica*, ed. G. Scalia, CCCM 125 (Turnholt: Brepols, 1994), p. 92.

43 *Speculum virginum* [ch. 4], ed. Jutta Seyfarth, CCCM 5 (Turnholt: Brepols, 1990), p. 103.

44 In Gower, Thisbe blames Venus and Cupid for the 'unhapp' that befalls her and Piramus (*Confessio Amantis* 3.1462–81).

45 Gower's marginal gloss for the story (*Confessio Amantis* 7.5131–306) accentuates the political dimensions. Virginius is 'dux exercitus Romanorum,' while Apius is the 'Imperator' (2: 377).

46 Carole E. Newlands, *Playing with Time: Ovid and the 'Fasti'* (Ithaca: Cornell University Press, 1995), pp. 148–9, points out that Ovid shifts Livy's exemplary tale about the chastity of the Roman *matrona* and the foundation of Republican government to emphasize instead 'the sexual violence at the heart of Roman history' and the silencing of Lucretia so that eloquent men can appropriate her as a political symbol.

47 For the classical and medieval treatments of Lucrece, see Newlands, pp. 146–74; and Craig Bertolet, 'From Revenge to Reform: The Changing Face of "Lucrece" and Its Meaning in Gower's *Confessio Amantis*,' *Philological Quarterly* 70 (1991): 403–21.

48 Chaucer's description of play builds on *Fasti* 2.724–5.

49 *Fasti* 2.739–40 and Vatican Mythographer I, *Mythographus I* [ch. 73], in *Mythographi Vaticani I et II*, ed. Péter Kulcsár, CCSL 91c (Turnholt: Brepols, 1987), p. 32.

50 Augustine, *De civitate Dei*, ed. Bernard Dombart and A. Kalb, 2 vols., CCSL 47–8 (Turnholt: Brepols, 1955), 1: 20–1; cf. Disputatio 1 of pseudo-Augustine, *Contra philosophos uel Altercationes christianae philosophiae*, ed. Diethard Aschoff, CCSL 58A (Turnholt: Brepols, 1975), pp. 24–5.

51 Tertullian, *Ad martyras* [ch. 4], ed. E. Dekkers, CCSL 1 (Turnholt: Brepols, 1954), p. 6; cf. Tertullian, *De exhortatione castitatis* [13.3], ed. E. Kroymann, in *Tertulliani Opera*, 2 vols. CCSL 1–2 (Turnholt: Brepols, 1954), 2: 1034–5.

52 Jerome, *Adversus Jovinianum* 1.46, in *Jankyn's Book of Wikked Wyves*, ed. Ralph Hanna III and Traugott Lawler, vol. 1: The Primary Texts, The Chaucer Library (Athens: University of Georgia Press, 1997), pp. 172–73; Abelard, *Theologia christiana* [2.81], ed. Eligius M. Buytaert, CCCM 12 (Turnholt: Brepols, 1969), p. 167.

53 Ranulph Higden, *Polychronicon Ranulphi Higden Monaci Cestrensis* (with translations by John Trevisa and an anonymous writer), ed. Churchill Babington (vols. 1–2) and Joseph R. Lumby (vols. 3–9), 9 vols. Rolls Series (London: Longmans, Green, and Co., 1865–86), 3: 156–67.

54 The phrase is C. David Benson's, from his introduction to *Chaucer's Religious Tales*, ed. C. David Benson and Elizabeth Robertson (Cambridge: D.S. Brewer, 1990), p. 6.

55 Stephen Knight, 'Chaucer's Religious Canterbury Tales,' in *Medieval English Religious and Ethical Literature: Essays in Honour of G.H. Russell*, ed. Gregory Kratzmann and James Simpson (Cambridge: D.S. Brewer, 1986), p. 159.

56 Barbara Nolan, 'Chaucer's Tales of Transcendence: Rhyme Royal and Christian Prayer in the *Canterbury Tales*,' in *Chaucer's Religious Tales*, pp. 21–38.

Chapter 4

1 For a useful formulation of these issues, see John M. Ganim, 'Chaucer, Boccaccio, Confession, and Subjectivity,' in *The 'Decameron' and the 'Canterbury Tales': New Essays on an Old Question*, ed. Leonard Michael Koff and Brenda Deen Schildgen (Madison, NJ: Fairleigh Dickinson University Press, 2000), pp. 128–47.

2 Vittore Branca, *Boccaccio: The Man and His Works*, trans. Richard Monges and Dennis J. McAuliffe (New York: New York University Press, 1976), pp. 276–307; *Boccaccio medievale e nuovi studi sul Decameron*, rev. and corr. edn (Florence: Sansoni, 1996), pp. 134–64.

3 K.B. McFarlane, 'Bastard Feudalism,' *Bulletin of the Institute of Historical Research* 20 (1943–45): 161–81. McFarlane means by the term not feudalism modified but an essentially different structure of relations superficially similar to feudalism.

4 For applications and assessments of McFarlane's 'bastard feudalism,' see Paul Strohm, *Social Chaucer* (Cambridge, MA: Harvard University Press, 1989), pp. 15–21; and David Wallace, *Chaucerian Polity: Absolutist Lineages and Associational Forms in England and Italy* (Stanford, CA: Stanford University Press, 1997), pp. 62–4.

5 McFarlane, 'Bastard Feudalism,' p. 162.
6 *Chaucerian Polity*, p. 76.
7 *Social Chaucer*, p. 21.
8 Anne Middleton, 'War by Other Means: Marriage and Chivalry in Chaucer,' *Studies in the Age of Chaucer* Proceedings 1 (1984): 130.
9 Omer Jodogne, *Le Fabliau*, Typologie des sources du moyen âge occidental, fasc. 13 (Turnholt: Brepols, 1975), p. 23: *'un conte en verse où, sur un ton trivial, sont narrées une ou plusieurs aventures plaisantes ou exemplaires, l'un et l'autre ou l'un ou l'autre'* (italics original).
10 N.S. Thompson, *Chaucer, Boccaccio and the Debate of Love: A Comparative Study of 'The Decameron' and 'The Canterbury Tales'* (Oxford: Clarendon, 1996), p. 220.
11 Derek Pearsall, *The Canterbury Tales* (London: George Allen & Unwin, 1985), pp. 169–70.
12 Derek Brewer, 'The Fabliaux,' in *Companion to Chaucer Studies*, ed. Beryl Rowland, rev. edn (New York: Oxford University Press, 1979), p. 297.
13 R. Howard Bloch, *The Scandal of the Fabliaux* (Chicago: University of Chicago Press, 1986), pp. 72–100.
14 For the details about the clerk's social position and roles, see J.A.W. Bennett, *Chaucer at Oxford and Cambridge* (Toronto: University of Toronto Press, 1974), pp. 44–8.
15 Though social reality outruns the social models of the late Middle Ages, contemporary works like Gower's *Vox clamantis* and the Prologue to his *Confessio Amantis* invoke the social models of the estates as an item of political belief that can still muster consensus.
16 E. Talbot Donaldson, 'The Idiom of Popular Poetry in the Miller's Tale,' in *Speaking of Chaucer* (New York: Norton, 1970), pp. 13–29.
17 Robert E. Kaske, 'The *Canticum Canticorum* in the *Miller's Tale*,' *Studies in Philology* 59 (1962): 479–500.
18 Like Chaucer's play on 'pryvetee,' Boccaccio's 'Paradiso' in *Decameron* 3.4 is both the spiritual goal that the duped Frate Puccio seeks and the sensual pleasure that the lovers achieve.
19 Absolon's wish also tropes Arcite's wish in the Knight's Tale: 'That I may seen hire atte leeste weye, / I nam but deed' (I.1121–2). I am grateful to Victor Doyno for pointing out the connection to me long ago.
20 Pearsall, *The Canterbury Tales* p. 156.
21 Winthrop Wetherbee, *The Canterbury Tales* (Cambridge: Cambridge University Press, 1989), p. 59.
22 *The Canterbury Tales*, p. 174.
23 R.A. Shoaf, *Dante, Chaucer, and the Currency of the Word: Money, Images, and Reference in Late Medieval Poetry* (Norman, OK: Pilgrim Books 1983), pp. 167–72, distinguishes 'vertical' quiting (within each tale) from 'horizontal' quiting (between pairs of tales).
24 Aristotle, *Nicomachean Ethics* [5.3 (1130b30–31a29)], trans. J.A.K. Thompson, rev. Hugh Tredennick (Harmondsworth: Penguin, 1976), pp. 177–78.
25 Ellesmere: 'Vim Vi repellere'; John M. Manly and Edith Rickert, eds., *The Text of the Canterbury Tales*, 8 vols. (Chicago: University of Chicago Press, 1940), 3: 492.
26 *MED* s.v. *feith* 8a cites this passsage as an example of an oath or asseveration, but the sense of a sworn oath or pledge (6a), here applied in a social and economic context, is also available as a meaning.

27 *The Riverside Chaucer*, p. 851; Helen Cooper, *The Canterbury Tales*, Oxford Guides to Chaucer (Oxford: Oxford University Press, 1989), p. 109.

28 *MED* s.v. *esement* 3 cites the passage in the sense of compensation or redress, but the examples quoted under the primary sense of 'the comforts of life' (1) deal with the effects of conveniences such as food, shelter, drink, and entertainment.

29 See Alain de Libera, *Penser au moyen âge* (Paris: Seuil, 1991) on philosophy and intellectual elites.

30 Chaucer seems also to echo the Legend of Lucrece by mentioning that the miller's wife knows the 'estres' of her house (I.4295) in much the same way that he says Colatyn knows the 'estris' of his house (LGW 1715); in both cases, the interior space of a household is equated with sexuality.

31 *The Canterbury Tales*, p. 115.

32 Thomas A. Hahn, 'Money, Sexuality, Wordplay, and Context in the *Shipman's Tale*,' in *Chaucer in the Eighties*, ed. Julian N. Wasserman and Robert J. Blanch (Syracuse: Syracuse University Press, 1986), pp. 236–9.

33 Albert H. Silverman, 'Sex and Money in Chaucer's *Shipman's Tale*,' *Philological Quarterly* 32 (1953): 329–36.

34 Lee Patterson, *Chaucer and the Subject of History* (Madison: University of Wisconsin Press, 1991), p. 354. In the *Politics* 1.10–11 (1258a-b), Aristotle distinguishes wealth-getting as an aspect of household management and therefore natural from wealth-getting as an aspect of exchange (commerce, interest, service for hire) and therefore unnatural. Aristotle's view is that all economic activity outside the agricultural world (and needed by the household, *oikonomia*) is unnatural. I am grateful to Cosimo Perrotta for sharing a draft of his introductory essay to *From Starkey to A. Smith – The Hunger for Goods*, vol. 1 of *Consumption as Investment: The History of a Missing Idea*.

35 Jill Mann, 'Satisfaction and Payment in Middle English Literature,' *Studies in the Age of Chaucer* 5 (1983): 45–8, points out that *ynogh* is 'elusive of definition' in the Shipman's Tale; it is not what is required for present needs but what will cover contingency and maintain appearance, which is the currency of exchange in a shifting world.

36 Eustache Deschamps, *Le miroir de mariage*, ed. Gaston Reynaud, in *Oeuvres complètes de Eustache Deschamps*, ed. Le Marquis de Queux de Saint-Hilaire, SAFT, 11 vols. (Paris: Firmin Didot, 1878–1903), 9: 11.

37 *Dante, Chaucer, and the Currency of the Word*, p. 14.

38 Patterson, *Chaucer and the Subject of History*, p. 349. Mann, p. 48, notes that sexuality produces surplus: 'Sex has the same careless abundance, the same inexhaustible outpouring, as God's grace.'

39 *The Canterbury Tales*, pp. 283–4.

40 Bartlett Jere Whiting, *Proverbs, Sentences, and Proverbial Phrases, from English Writings Mainly Before 1500* (Cambridge, MA: Belknap Press of Harvard University Press, 1968), S185; cf. Merchant's Tale IV.1314–15 and Parson's Tale X.1068. *The Riverside Chaucer*, p. 965, suggests that Chaucer adds the phrase 'on the wal.'

41 *Biblia sacra iuxta Vulgatam versionem*, ed. Robert Weber, 2 vols. (Stuttgart: Württembergische Bibelanstalt, 1975), 1: 724–5.

42 For discussion of Chaucer's economic themes, see Eugene Vance, 'Chaucer's *House of Fame* and the Poetics of Inflation,' *Boundary 2* 7 (1979): 17–37.

43 Strohm, *Social Chaucer*, pp. 100–2, emphasizes the motives of singular profit and self-interest in the tale, while holding out the prospect of publicly sanctioned bonds.
44 *Chaucer and the Subject of History*, p. 356.
45 *Canterbury Tales*, p. 210.
46 Thompson, *Chaucer, Boccaccio and the Debate of Love*, pp. 208–9, discusses the outcome of Panfilo's tale as a form of domestic sentimentality in which the priest and Monna Belcolore continue their liaison after reaching accommodation over the earlier transactions. For Chaucer's suspension of moral judgment, see Murray Copland, 'The Shipman's Tale: Chaucer and Boccaccio,' *Medium Ævum* 35 (1966): 11–28; and V.J. Scattergood, 'The Originality of the *Shipman's Tale*,' *Chaucer Review* 11 (1976–77): 210–31.
47 Paul Strohm, ' "Lad with revel to Newegate": Chaucerian Narrative and Historical Meta-Narrative,' in *Art and Context in Late Medieval English Narrative: Essays in Honor of Robert Worth Frank, Jr.*, ed. Robert R. Edwards (Cambridge: D.S. Brewer, 1994), pp. 163–76.
48 See Alastair J. Minnis, 'Chaucer's Pardoner and the "Office of Preacher," ' in *Intellectuals and Writers in Fourteenth-Century Europe*, ed. Piero Boitani and Anna Torti, J.A.W. Bennett Symposium (Tübingen: Narr; Cambridge: D.S. Brewer, 1986), pp. 88–119, on theological debates over preaching.
49 Robert S. Sturges, *Chaucer's Pardoner and Gender Theory: Bodies of Discourse* (New York: St. Martin's Press, 2000), pp. 102–5, argues that the Pardoner emphasizes the materiality of the rioters' language.
50 Augustine, Sermo 265B, in *Sancti Augustini Sermones post Maurinos reperti*, ed. G. Morin, *Miscellanea Agostiniana: testi e studi*, 2 vols. (Rome: Tipografia poliglotta vaticana, 1930–31), p. 415; Jerome, *Commentarii in prophetas minores: In Osee* [3.13], ed. M. Adriaen, 2 vols., CCSL 76–76A (Turnholt: Brepols, 1969–70), p. 148–50; Leo the Great, Tract 59, in *Tractatus septem et nonaginta*, ed. A. Chavasse, 2 vols., CCSL 138–138A (Turnholt: Brepols, 1973), 2: 360; Gregory the Great, *Moralia in Iob* [12.11], ed. M. Adriaen, 3 vols. CCSL 143–143A-B (Turnholt: Brepols, 1979–81), 2: 673.
51 *Chaucer, Dante, and the Currency of the Word*, p. 221.

Chapter 5

1 *Lydgate's Temple of Glas*, ed. J. Schick, EETS, e.s. 60 (London: Kegan Paul, Trench, Trübner & Co., 1891), p. 3; cf. Venus's remark to her petitioner, 'Griseld[e] was assaied at[te] ful, / That turned aftir to hir encrese of Ioye' (405–6).
2 Text in Eleanor P. Hammond, 'Lydgate's Mumming at Hertford,' *Anglia* 22 (1899): 364–74.
3 Cited in Caroline F.E. Spurgeon, *Five Hundred Years of Chaucer Criticism and Allusion: 1357–1900*, 3 vols. (Cambridge: Cambridge University Press, 1925), 1: 181. For recent accounts of imitations of the Clerk's Tale and of Griselde's exemplarity, see Helen Cooper, *The Canterbury Tales*, Oxford Guides to Chaucer (Oxford: Oxford University Press, 1989), pp. 422–4; Anna P. Baldwin, 'From the *Clerk's Tale* to *The Winter's Tale*,' in *Chaucer Traditions: Studies in Honour of Derek Brewer*, ed. Ruth Morse and Barry Windeatt (Cambridge:

Cambridge University Press, 1990), pp. 199–212; and *La storia di Griselda in Europa*, ed. Raffaele Morabito (L'Aquila: Japadre, 1990).

4 M.C. Seymour, *A Catalogue of Chaucer Manuscripts, I: Works before the 'Canterbury Tales'* (Aldershot: Scolar Press, 1995), pp. 131–54. On the religious character of collections and selections, see Stephen Knight, 'Chaucer's Religious Canterbury Tales,' in *Medieval English Religious and Ethical Literature: Essays in Honour of G.H. Russell*, ed. Gregory Kratzmann and James Simpson (Cambridge: D.S. Brewer, 1986), p. 156.

5 In anthologies: British Library, Harley 1239; Longleat 257; Bodleian Library, Rawlinson C.86. In complete manuscripts of the *Canterbury Tales*: Bodleian Library, Rawlinson Poetry 223. Cambridge, Trinity College Library R.3.15 indicates 'hic gresild' for placing the Clerk's headlink and tale next in a mutilated copy of the *Canterbury Tales*; see John M. Manly and Edith Rickert, eds., *The Text of the 'Canterbury Tales'*, 8 vols. (Chicago: University of Chicago Press, 1940), 1: 529.

6 Manly and Rickert, 1: 377, on Naples, Royal Library 13.b.29; Derek Pearsall, *The Canterbury Tales* (London: George Allen & Unwin, 1985), p. 323, on Longleat 257.

7 Thomas J. Heffernan, 'Aspects of the Chaucerian Apocrypha: Animadversions on William Thynne's Edition of the *Plowman's Tale*,' in *Chaucer Traditions*, p. 166 n.13, observes that Chaucer's readers in wealthy country households in the fifteenth century both appropriate and create a new image of the poet.

8 David Lawton, 'Dullness and the Fifteenth Century,' *ELH* 54 (1978): 780.

9 Paul Strohm, 'Chaucer's Fifteenth-Century Audience and the Narrowing of the "Chaucer Tradition,"' *Studies in the Age of Chaucer* 4 (1982): 26.

10 Seth Lerer, *Chaucer and His Readers: Imagining the Author in Late-Medieval England* (Princeton: Princeton University Press, 1993), p. 113.

11 Leonard Michael Koff, 'Imagining Absence: Chaucer's Griselda *and* Walter *without* Petrarch,' in *The 'Decameron' and the 'Canterbury Tales': New Essays on an Old Question*, ed. Michael Leonard Koff and Brenda Deen Schildgen (Madison, NJ: Fairleigh Dickinson University Press, 2000), p. 280.

12 J. Burke Severs, *The Literary Relationship of Chaucer's 'Clerkes Tale'*, Yale Studies in English 96 (New Haven: Yale University Press, 1942).

13 Robin Kirkpatrick, 'The Griselda Story in Boccaccio, Petrarch, and Chaucer,' in *Chaucer and the Italian Trecento*, ed. Piero Boitani (Cambridge: Cambridge University Press, 1983), p. 232.

14 With only slight differences, the same rubrics appear in Munich, Bayerische Staatsbibliothek, MS. 78, which also contains *Seniles* 17.3; see Severs, pp. 50–1, with a supplementary list of manuscripts without Petrarch's letter in Vittore Branca, *Boccaccio medievale e nuovi studi sul Decameron*, 5th edn (Florence: Sansoni, 1981), p. 391n.

15 *Chaucer and His Readers*, p. 39; cf. pp. 88, 100.

16 See C. David Benson, *Chaucer's Drama of Style: Poetic Variety and Contrast in the Canterbury Tales* (Chapel Hill: University of North Carolina Press, 1986) for a critique of the 'dramatic principle' of the *Canterbury Tales*.

17 Manly and Rickert, 1: 286–7; Charlotte C. Morse, 'The Value of Editing the *Clerk's Tale* for the *Variorum* Chaucer,' in *Manuscripts and Texts: Editorial*

Problems in Later Middle English Literature, ed. Derek Pearsall (Cambridge: D.S. Brewer, 1987), pp. 127–9, rejects Manly and Rickert's claim.

18 Anne Middleton, 'The Clerk and His Tale: Some Literary Contexts,' *Studies in the Age of Chaucer* 2 (1980): 124; Charlotte C. Morse, 'The Exemplary Griselda,' *Studies in the Age of Chaucer* 7 (1985): 73.

19 Text in Severs, p. 290. For convenience, I shall cite the translations reprinted by Robert P. Miller, *Chaucer: Sources and Backgrounds* (New York: Oxford University Press, 1977), pp. 136–52. Glending Olson, 'Petrarch's View of the *Decameron*,' *MLN* 91 (1976): 69–79, argues that Petrarch's assessment is generally the one held by Boccaccio's contemporaries.

20 Elie Golenistcheff-Koutouzoff, *L'histoire de Griseldis en France au XIVe et au XVe Siècle* (Paris, 1933; rpt. Geneva: Slatkine, 1975), p. 154. In Golenistcheff-Koutouzoff's listing of manuscripts for Philippe's translation (pp. 34–7), the Griselda story appears with *Le Livre du Chevalier du Tour Landry pour l'enseignement des ses filles*.

21 Kevin Brownlee, 'Commentary and the Rhetoric of Exemplarity: Griseldis in Petrarch, Philippe de Mézières, and the *Estoire*,' *South Atlantic Quarterly* 91 (1992): 867–70.

22 *Le Menagier de Paris*, ed. Georgine E. Brereton and Janet M. Ferrier (Oxford: Clarendon Press, 1981), p. 3.

23 'The Clerk and His Tale: Some Literary Contexts,' p. 135.

24 For discussion of the Ciceronian distinctions among *historia*, *argumentum*, and *fabula* in the High Middle Ages, see Robert R. Edwards, *Ratio and Invention: A Study of Medieval Lyric and Narrative* (Nashville: Vanderbilt University Press, 1989), pp. 75–89.

25 David Wallace, '"Whan She Translated Was": A Chaucerian Critique of the Petrarchan Academy,' in *Literary Practice and Social Change in Britain, 1380–1530*, ed. Lee Patterson (Berkeley and Los Angeles: University of California Press, 1990), p. 160; rpt. in *Chaucerian Polity: Absolutist Lineages and Associational Forms in England and Italy* (Stanford, CA: Stanford University Press, 1997), p. 264.

26 On Boccaccio's attitude toward literary interpretation, see Susan Noakes, *Timely Reading: Between Exegesis and Interpretation* (Ithaca: Cornell University Press, 1988), pp. 68–97; and Francesco Bruni, 'Interpretation within the *Decameron*,' *Interpretation: Medieval and Modern*, ed. Piero Boitani and Anna Torti, J.A.W. Bennett Memorial Symposium, 8th ser. (Cambridge: D.S. Brewer, 1993), pp. 123–36.

27 St. Thomas Aquinas, *In decem libros Ethicorum Aristotelis ad Nicomachum Expositio*, ed. Raimundo M. Spiazzi (Turin: Marietti, 1949), p. 96; trans. C.I. Litzinger, *Commentary on Aristotle's 'Nicomachean Ethics'* (Chicago: Henry Regnery, 1964), p. 113. Since Aquinas's commentary uses the Antiqua Translatio of the *Ethics* by William of Moerbeke known to Boccaccio and Dante, I cite both Aristotle and Aquinas in Spiazzi's edition and Litzinger's translation. John Larner, 'Chaucer's Italy,' in *Chaucer and the Italian Trecento*, p. 24, notes that Boccaccio transcribed Aquinas's commentary on the *Ethics*.

28 Dante Alighieri, *The Divine Comedy*, trans. Charles S. Singleton, 3 vols. in 6 (Princeton: Princeton University Press, 1970–75), 1: 114. Alfred A. Triolo, '"Matta Bestialità" in Dante's "Inferno": Theory and Image,' *Traditio* 29 (1968): 247–92, argues that Dante's conception of brutality has to do with

violence rather than treachery. For discussion of Boccaccio's use of the phrase, see Charles Haines, 'Patient Griselda and *matta bestialitade*,' *Quaderni d'Italianistica* 6 (1985): 233–40.

29 In the *Ethics* 7.i (1145a33), Aristotle accepts a semantic definition of brutishness: 'We also use the word brutish to express reprobation of extremely vicious persons' (*Ethics*, trans. J.A.K. Thomson [Harmondsworth: Penguin, 1953, rpt. 1981], p. 226). The Antiqua Translatio portrays a rhetorical excess that matches an excess of vice: 'et propter malitiam autem hominum superexcedentes, sic superinfamamus' (Spiazzi, 351).

30 For Boccaccio as a reader in the rubrics, see Jonathan Usher, 'Le rubriche del *Decameron*,' *Medioevo romanzo* 10 (1985): 417n.

31 Itala Tania Rutter, 'The Function of Dioneo's Perspective in the Griselda Story,' *Comitatus* 5 (1974): 34.

32 Giuseppe Mazzotta, *The World at Play in Boccaccio's 'Decameron'* (Princeton: Princeton University Press, 1986), p. 125, notes that in his commentary on *Inferno* 11 (*Esposizioni sopra la Comedia*) Boccaccio refers to brutishness and divine wisdom (not divine virtue) as contraries.

33 Victoria Kirkham, 'The Last Tale in the *Decameron*,' *Mediaevalia* 12 (1989 for 1986): 203–23.

34 James Sledd, 'The *Clerk's Tale*: The Monsters and the Critics,' in *Chaucer Criticism*, ed. Richard Shoeck and Jerome Taylor, 2 vols. (Notre Dame, IN: University of Notre Dame Press, 1960), 1: 160–74.

35 Manly and Rickert, 3: 505–8. Germaine Dempster, 'Chaucer's Manuscript of Petrarch's Version of the Griselda Story,' *Modern Philology* 41 (1943–44): 6, argues that Hengwrt preserves the glosses from the parent copy Chaucer used and that Corpus Christi College, Cambridge MS 275 is the witness closest to Chaucer's text of Petrarch. See Thomas J. Farrell, 'The Style of the *Clerk's Tale* and the Function of Its Glosses,' *Studies in Philology* 86 (1989): 290, on the thematic and stylistic effects of the glosses.

36 James A. Weisheipl, O.P., 'Curriculum of the Faculty of Arts at Oxford in the early Fourteenth Century,' *Mediaeval Studies* 26 (1964): 178, notes that in fourteenth-century academic usage, *sophisma* 'signified a proposition which could be defended by logical arguments' and consequently that the term is not limited to a negative sense of *aenigmata* and *obscuritates*. John M. Ganim, 'Carnival Voices and the Envoy to the *Clerk's Tale*,' *Chaucer Review* 22 (1987–88): 117, argues that Chaucer's use of 'sophyme' is semantically related to 'study,' a term he takes to mean both intellectual inquiry and melancholy.

37 Martin McLaughlin, 'Petrarch's rewriting of the *Decameron*, X.10,' in *Renaissance and Other Studies: Essays Presented to Peter M. Brown*, ed. Eileen A. Millar (Glasgow: University of Glasgow, 1988), pp. 47–50.

38 Barbara Nolan, 'Chaucer's Tales of Transcendence: Rhyme Royal and Christian Prayer in the *Canterbury Tales*', in *Chaucer's Religious Tales*, ed. C. David Benson and Elizabeth Robertson (Cambridge: D.S. Brewer, 1990), pp. 27–32, argues for the conjunction of political and spiritual themes in the Clerk's Tale.

39 *MED*, s.v. commune, sense 2.

40 Judith Ferster, *Chaucer on Interpretation* (Cambridge: Cambridge University Press, 1985), p. 110.

41 Lynn Staley Johnson, 'The Prince and His People: A Study of the Two Covenants in the *Clerk's Tale*,' *Chaucer Review* 10 (1975–76): 17–29, sees the relations

as feudal; Lars Engle, 'Chaucer, Bakhtin, and Griselda,' *Exemplaria* 1 (1989): 429–59, sees only an autocratic state; Michaela Paasche Grudin, 'Chaucer's *Clerk's Tale* as Political Paradox,' *Studies in the Age of Chaucer* 11 (1989): 63–92, argues for an exploration of absolute monarchy.

42 Carolyn Dinshaw, *Chaucer's Sexual Poetics* (Madison: University of Wisconsin Press, 1989), p. 133.

43 *Chaucer on Interpretation,* pp. 94–109. This reciprocity, as Ferster notes, sets up not only Walter's oppression but also Griselde's collaboration in his oppression.

44 For discussion of the tale's epistemological concerns, see Kathryn L. Lynch, 'Despoiling Griselda: Chaucer's Walter and the Problem of Knowledge in *The Clerk's Tale,*' *Studies in the Age of Chaucer* 10 (1988): 41–70.

45 The opening of Guido Guinizelli's doctrinal canzone ('Al cor gentil rempaira sempre amore') reappears in *Troilus and Criseyde*, deriving from Dante's discussion in the *Convivio*, which is also the source for the hag's disquisition in the Wife of Bath's Tale; see J.S.P. Tatlock, 'Dante and Guinicelli in Chaucer's Troilus,' *Modern Language Notes* 35 (1920): 443. D'Arco Silvio Avalle, 'Due tesi sui limiti di amore,' in *Ai luoghi di delizia pieni: Saggio sulla lirica italiana del XIII secolo* (Milan: Ricciardi, 1977), pp. 17–55, argues that the thesis about virtue and lineage has two distinct formulations in Capellanus's *De amore*, one egalitarian and the other aristocratic.

46 The marginal gloss reads at this point: 'Ceperit sensim de Waltero decolor fama crebescere' (Manly and Rickert, 3: 507). The manuscript owned by Jean d'Angoulême (Paris, Bibliothèque Nationale, Fonds Anglais 39) adds the lines at this point: 'And thus he lost here loue euery deel / For though a man by hygh on fortunes wheel' (Manly and Rickert 6: 330).

47 Giulio Savelli, 'Struttura e valori nella novella di Griselda,' *Studi sul Boccaccio* 14 (1983–84): 278–301.

48 Derek Pearsall, *The Canterbury Tales* (London: George Allen & Unwin, 1985), p. 273.

49 Jill Mann, 'Satisfaction and Payment in Middle English Literature,' *Studies in the Age of Chaucer* 5 (1983): 17–48. Mann's discussion emphasizes that the definition of satisfaction generally involves a notion of the mean. See also her *Geoffrey Chaucer* (Hemel Hempstead: Harvester, 1991), pp. 146–64.

50 See *Riverside Chaucer*, pp. 1085–6, for the problems of dating 'Lak of Stedfastnesse.'

51 Norman Blake, 'Chaucer's Text and the Web of Words,' in *New Perspectives in Chaucer Criticism*, ed. Donald M. Rose (Norman, OK: Pilgrim Books, 1981), pp. 227–8, offers a different interpretation of these lines, based on Hengwrt. The accepted text reads: 'His wyues fader in his court he [Walter] kepeth' (1133). Hengwrt reads: 'His wyues fader and his court he kepeth.' Blake says of Hengwrt, 'This reading implies that Walter looked after his wife's father (though not necessarily by transferring him from the cottage to live at his own palace) and that he maintained his court (that is, his household, which symbolizes his estate and management) in dignified peace until he, Walter, died.'

52 Usher, pp. 410–17, usefully analyzes the discrepancy between the tale's chiasmic structure, which places the birth of Gualtieri's son at the center of the narrative, and the opening rubric, which obscures the narrative structure and emphasizes the importance of marriage bonds.

53   Manly and Rickert, 6: 286–7, record the following variants for *translated:
      transmuwed, transmuted, transnewid, transformed, transposed.* In Petrarch, the
      relevant phrase is 'insignatum gemmis et corona velut subito transforma-
      tam'; in the *Livre Griseldis,* 'ainsi ordonnee et paree de couronne et de
      pierrerie tres grandement, comme soudainement transmuee et changié'
      (Severs, pp. 306, 307).
54   Wallace, ' "Whan She Translated Was," ' pp. 208–13; Carol Falvo Heffernan,
      'Tyranny and *Commune Profit* in the *Clerk's Tale,' Chaucer Review* 17 (1982–
      83): 334–5.

Chapter 6

1   George Lyman Kittredge, 'Chaucer's Discussion of Marriage,' in *Chaucer Criti-
     cism,* ed. Richard Schoeck and Jerome Taylor, 2 vols. (Notre Dame, IN: Notre
     Dame University Press, 1960), 1: 145, 158.
2   Pio Rajna, 'L'Episodio delle questioni d'amore nel *Filocolo* del Boccaccio,'
     Romania 31 (1902): 28–81, esp. 40–3; and 'Le Origini della novella narrata
     del "Frankeleyn" nei Canterbury Tales del Chaucer,' *Romania* 32 (1903):
     204–67.
3   Germaine Dempster and J.S.P. Tatlock, 'The Franklin's Tale,' in *Sources and
     Analogues of Chaucer's 'Canterbury Tales',* ed. W.F. Bryan and Germaine Demp-
     ster (Chicago: University of Chicago Press, 1941), pp. 377–97. See also
     Tatlock's 'Boccaccio and the Plan of Chaucer's *Canterbury Tales,' Anglia* 37
     (1913): 69–117.
4   Robert R. Edwards, 'Source, Context, and Cultural Translation in the *Frank-
     lin's Tale,' Modern Philology* 94 (1996–97): 141–62.
5   From the manuscript evidence, we might surmise, further, that this reinscrip-
     tion is a continuing process, not a discrete event. Boccaccio's autograph
     manuscript of the *Decameron* (Berlin, Staatsbibliothek, MS. Hamilton 90)
     dates to the 1370s, after his decades of engagement in public life and his
     turn to Latin letters. Charles S. Singleton, ed. *Decameron* (Baltimore: The
     Johns Hopkins Press, 1974), offers a diplomatic transcription of Hamilton
     90. One of the lacunae in the manuscript is the portion of the tenth day up to
     Decameron 10.10, the story of Griselda.
6   In the *Nicomachean Ethics* (4.1–4; 1119b22–1125b25), Aristotle discusses gen-
     erosity and magnificence as moral virtues dealing with riches and other
     external goods; they differ in scale rather than in kind, so that a magnificent
     man acts on a public stage, dispensing large sums. Boccaccio copied the
     commentary on the *Ethics* written by St. Thomas Aquinas; see John Larner,
     'Chaucer's Italy,' in *Chaucer and the Italian Trecento,* ed. Piero Boitani (Cam-
     bridge: Cambridge University Press, 1983), p. 24. For discussion of how
     effectively the theme of generosity works in the final day, see Nadia D'Aronco
     Pauluzzo, 'La novella friulana del Boccaccio,' *La porta orientale* 26 (1956):
     436–44, and Francesco Guardini, 'Boccaccio dal *Filocolo* al *Decameron*: vari-
     azioni di poetica e di retorica dall'esame di due racconti,' *Carte italiane* 7
     (1985–86): 28–46. Guardini contends that generosity is a secondary concern
     in the *Decameron.* David Wallace, *Giovanni Boccaccio: Decameron* (Cambridge:
     Cambridge University Press, 1991), p. 99, argues, 'Boccaccio's tenth day

narratives show a sophisticated understanding of the political dimensions and limits of magnificence.'

7   Dennis Dutschke, 'Boccaccio: A Question of Love (A Comparative Study of *Filocolo* IV, 13 and *Decameron* X, 4),' *The Humanities Association Review* 26 (1975): 300–12, discusses the elements of Boccaccio's revision.

8   Joseph Markulin, 'Emilia and the Case for Openness in the *Decameron*,' *Stanford Italian Review* 3 (1983): 183–99, argues that the characterization of Emilia as 'baldanzosa' connects her with a narrative style that breaks down expected interpretations.

9   Mauda Bregoli-Russo, 'Boccaccio tra le fonti dell'*Orlando innamorato?*,' *Studi e problemi di critica testuale* 26.8 (1983): 21–7, offers a different analysis of narrative structure, which accommodates comparison with Boiardo's *Orlando Innamorato* but cuts out the opening and closing sections and reduces the releases from the promise to a proof of courtesy.

10 W.A. Clouston, 'The Damsel's Rash Promise: Indian Original and Some Asiatic and European Variants of Chaucer's Franklin's Tale,' in *Originals and Analogues of Some of Chaucer's Canterbury Tales*, ed. F.J. Furnivall et al., Chaucer Society Publications, 2nd ser., no. 20 (London: Oxford University Press, 1886), pp. 289–340. See also Anselm Aman, *Die Filiation der Frankeleynes Tale in Chaucers Canterbury Tales* (Erlangen: K.B. Hof-und Univ. Buchdruckerei von Junge & Sohn, 1912); J. Schick, 'Die ältesten Versionen von Chaucers Frankeleyns Tale,' in *Studia Indo-Iranaca: Ehrengabe für Wilhelm Geiger zur Vollendung des 75. Lebensjahres* (Leipzig: Otto Harrassowitz, 1931), pp. 89–107; and N. Mukerji, 'Chaucer's Franklin's and the Tale of Madanasena of Vetalapachisi,' *Folklore* [Calcutta] 9 (1968): 75–85. I am grateful to Kenneth Bleeth for sharing some material about the sources from his forthcoming Toronto bibliography of the Franklin's Tale.

11 Infante Juan Manuel, *El Conde Lucanor y Patronio: Libro de los Ejemplos*, ed. Julian Sanz (Valladolid: Miñón, 1965), p. 351 (Ejemplo 50). For discussion of this narrative and the Franklin's Tale, see Jesús L. Serrano Reyes, *Didactismo y moralismo en Geoffrey Chaucer y Don Juan Manuel: Un estudio comparativo textual* (Córboda: Universidad de Córboda, 1996), pp. 125–251.

12 Tzvetan Todorov, *Grammaire du Décaméron* (The Hague: Mouton, 1969), pp. 48, 57, points out that the lover's renunciation is not a cancellation but a species of desire.

13 Antti Amatus Aarne, *The Types of the Folk-Tale: A Classification and Bibliography*, ed. and trans. Stith Thompson, Folklore Fellows Communications, no. 74 (Helsinki: Suomalainen Teideakatemia, Academia Scientiarum Fennica, 1928), M223 (cf. N2.0.1, 'play for unnamed stakes'). Though Clouston entitles his collection of analogues 'The Damsel's Rash Promise,' this motif actually appears in only one of the texts he presents.

14 See the notes to *The Riverside Chaucer*, p. 901.

15 Nicholas J. Perella, 'The World of Boccaccio's *Filocolo*,' *PMLA* 76 (1961): 338.

16 Salvatore Battaglia, 'Schemi lirici nell'arte del Boccaccio,' *Archivium Romanicum* 19 (1935): 61–78; rpt. in Battaglia, *La coscienza letteraria del medioevo* (Naples: Liguori, 1965), pp. 625–44, traces the thematic sources of the *Questioni* to love lyric.

17 See the Parson's Tale X.790–5, 805–10, 830–5, and 1075–80 for 'the blisse of hevene'; and Parson's Tale X. 150–5 and X.490–5 for 'prosperitee.' The repeated references to bliss in the Merchant's Tale also provide an ironic commentary on the opening of the Franklin's Tale.

18 Eustache Deschamps's *Miroir de mariage* is typical of medieval marriage doctrine in proposing, 'Homs doit par dehors ordonner, / Femme doit dedenz gouverner' (221–2; cf. 231–40). Text in *Oeuvres complètes de Eustache Deschamps*, ed. Le Marquis de Queux de Saint-Hilaire, SATF, 11 vols. (Paris: Firmin Didot, 1878–1903), 9: 11.

19 Leonard Michael Koff, *Chaucer and the Art of Storytelling* (Berkeley and Los Angeles: University of California Press, 1988), p. 193.

20 The scene in the Friar's Tale in which the Summoner and the fiend pledge fidelity to each other is an ironic foreshadowing of the private, consensual agreement that Arveragus and Dorigen make between themselves: 'Everych in ootheres hand his trouthe leith, / For to be sworne bretheren til they deye' (III.1404–5). In the Shipman's Tale, the monk negotiates a night of sexual pleasure with the merchant's wife for one hundred francs; the narrator observes dryly, 'this acord parfourned was in dede' (VII.317). I am grateful to Erik Schwab for pointing out the structural similarities between the Shipman's and the Franklin's Tales.

21 Vittore Branca, *Boccaccio medievale e nuovi studi sul Decameron*, 5th edn (Florence: Sansoni, 1981), pp. 153–64.

22 Tarolfo follows Ovid's teaching, 'il quale dice l'uomo non lasciare per durezza della donna di non perseverare, però che per continuanza la molle acqua fora la dura pietra.' The image of penetration derives from *Ars amatoria* 1.475–6; cf. *Epistulae ex Ponto* 4.10.5.

23 The rhyming of 'mente' and 'entente' in Dorigen's refusal plays off ironically against the same rhyme in the Merchant's Tale (IV.2105–6) when May and Damian exchange their 'pryvee signes' to cuckold January.

24 For the symbolic meanings of the garden, see Millicent Joy Marcus, 'An Allegory of Two Gardens: The Tale of Madonna Dianora (*Decameron* X, 5),' *Forum Italicum* 14 (1980): 162–74.

25 Medieval ethics sets intent above manifest behavior and internal conditions over external circumstances. In Aristotle, there is no corresponding privileging of the internal over the external.

26 Richard Firth Green, *A Crisis of Truth: Literature and Law in Ricardian England* (Philadelphia: University of Pennsylvania Press, 1999), pp. 326–35.

27 Victoria E. Kirkham, 'The *Filocolo* of Giovanni Boccaccio with an English Translation of the Thirteen *Questioni d'amore*' (PhD diss., The Johns Hopkins University, 1971), p. 168.

28 See Carolyn Collette, 'Seeing and Believing in the *Franklin's Tale*,' *Chaucer Review* 26 (1991–92): 395–410, for the connection between medieval optics, faculty psychology, and the will as they bear on magic and illusion.

29 David Wallace, 'Chaucer and Boccaccio's Early Writings,' in *Chaucer and the Italian Trecento*, ed. Piero Boitani (Cambridge: Cambridge University Press, 1983), p. 154.

30 Lee Patterson, *Chaucer and the Subject of History* (Madison: University of Wisconsin Press, 1991), p. 196.
31 Aristotle (*Nicomachean Ethics* Bk. 8; 1155a3–1163b28) and Cicero (*De amicitia*) distinguish virtuous friendship from friendships based on utility and pleasure. Virtuous friendship can exist only when friends are equals – in the culture of antiquity, when they are freeborn males.

Index